THE 200-MPH
BILLBOARD

THE 200-MPH BILLBOARD

THE INSIDE STORY OF HOW BIG MONEY CHANGED NASCAR

MARK YOST

FOREWORD BY
BRIAN WILLIAMS
ANCHOR OF *NBC NIGHTLY NEWS*

MOTORBOOKS

First published in 2007 by Motorbooks, an imprint of MBI Publishing Company LLC, Galtier Plaza, Suite 200, 380 Jackson Street, St. Paul, MN 55101 USA

Motorbooks titles are also available at discounts in bulk quantity for industrial or sales-promotional use. For details write to Special Sales Manager at MBI Publishing Company, Galtier Plaza, Suite 200, 380 Jackson Street, St. Paul, MN 55101 USA.

To find out more about our books, join us online at www.motorbooks.com.

Yost, Mark.
The 200-mph Billboard : the inside story of how big money changed NASCAR / by Mark Yost.
      p. cm.
 ISBN-13: 978-0-7603-2812-5 (hardbound w/ jacket)
 ISBN-10: 0-7603-2812-9 (hardbound w/ jacket)
1. Stock car racing—United States—History. 2. Stock car racing—Economic aspects—United States. 3. NASCAR (Association)—History. I. Title.
GV1029.9.S74Y66 2007
796.72—dc22

                              2007007650

Editors: Lee Klancher and Leah Noel
Jacket Design: Tom Heffron
Designer: Jennifer Maass

Printed in the United States of America

DEDICATION

To Chris Economaki, who has taught the
world—and me—more about auto racing and
writing than anyone else.

And to Bobby Hamilton, who will forever be
known as one of the nice guys of NASCAR.
R.I.P, Hamster.

CONTENTS

FOREWORD

By Brian Williams

Whenever I'm introduced to someone claiming to be a NASCAR fan, my first question is, "What's your local track?" The answer is always telling. I guess I need to know a fan's motives: Is it in your blood? Are you among those of us who are easily intoxicated by exhaust fumes and the sound of an American-made, normally aspirated V-8 engine? Does the spectacle of the first, full-speed lap at Talladega or Bristol cause your chest to thump and bring tears to your eyes? Or did you read about the sport in *Time* magazine and watch the Daytona 500 from a glassed-in, luxury hospitality suite? The answer can tell me a lot about a fan.

I don't notice the billboards any more, or the laundry list of sponsors the drivers unabashedly mention during victory lane interviews. I notice the number on the door. Actually, well before I concentrate on any of those other things, I know who's driving. From a flash-frame glance at the car, I can tell you the make, the driver, the primary sponsor, the associate sponsors (those who buy only a mere mention of their product on, say, the trunk lid or rear quarter panel), how long that driver's been with that team, and how long the sponsor's been with the car. I can usually tell you who the crew chief is and a bit about his personal history. Real fans commit the starting field to memory; it's not a studied, by rote process . . . it's just like the way kids memorize Major League Baseball starting lineups or all the available accessories in the American Girl doll collection.

NASCAR's management and drivers are fond of repeating the sport's mantra: It's for the fans. The problem is—as with any big, burgeoning business—the fans are getting squeezed as the sport expands. Treasured regional tracks to which the sport can trace its storied lineage have been closed in favor of gleaming new facilities in new markets. Weeds grow through cracks in the asphalt where giants once roared just inches above. Some families have to save all year to see their favorite race—the annual tailgate gathering with friends has become a prohibitively expensive affair. Attending a premier NEXTEL Cup event can often mean hours in traffic, a parking spot miles away, ridiculous post-9/11 restrictions on coolers and parcels, and exorbitant prices on ticket packages that force fans to buy for three days worth of events when all they want to see is the main event on any given Sunday.

Fans all show up wearing the gear. It's virtually impossible to find a race fan in the stands who is not wearing at least one item of merchandise linking them to their favorite car in the field. They are sponsor-loyal (ask the folks at Tide what happened to their detergent sales after they started sponsoring a car), but also logo-neutral. They don't see it as wearing a leather jacket emblazoned with the Viagra logo so much as they see wearing the garment as a way of supporting Mark Martin, the longtime driver of the No. 6 Ford (of course, Martin now drives part-time in the No. 1 Chevrolet sponsored by the U.S. Army).

NASCAR's growing pains put the sport in the same position as the kid in high school who goes on to be a big success: Everyone at the twenty-fifth reunion pointedly watches to see if they've gotten too big for their britches in the intervening years. It's the old saying about "the one that brung you to the dance."

It's why I ask about local tracks. At its top levels, NASCAR is a huge, corporate-driven sport. As a family-owned and -controlled enterprise, it has no real comparison in American business. This nation's small stock car tracks—glowing islands of light, smoke, and noise that dot the countryside and roar to life on Friday and Saturday nights—are where fans encounter the sport in its purest form. The drivers are builders, mechanics, and plumbers by day, and on a good week they can steal away two nights in the garage to hammer out the dents and fix the ball joints after a rough heat race the week before.

Racing at the small-track level is hand-to-mouth—it survives on favors from friends, duct tape, and large amounts of luck. The fans in the stands often have a personal connection to the drivers. I've told my own children many times at our local track never to root too loudly against any given driver, because that might be his wife, mother, and kids sitting directly in front of us. Cars racing at small tracks have small sponsors (like Moresco Auto Body), and the fans have smaller amounts to spend. Hot dogs are cheaper, and Daytona seems light years away. But it's a step in the sport that no driver can afford to skip if they hope to compete and survive at the highest level. And the fans in the stands are the same ones the larger sport needs: after all, those are the people who brung NASCAR to the dance.

Brian Williams is Anchor & Managing Editor of NBC Nightly News.

ACKNOWLEDGMENTS

First off, I have to thank the folks at Motorbooks, especially Lee Klancher. This book was an idea that we had been kicking around for a few years that finally came to fruition. While it started off as just a neat project, we ended up delivering a book unlike any other that's ever been written about NASCAR. I also have to thank my project editor, Leah Noel, and Blake Johnson, who's not too bad at publicity for an open-wheel guy. And a special thanks to Zack Miller, for believing that Lee and I could deliver the book we promised.

Tom Cotter, another Motorbooks author, deserves a great deal of credit as well. In between finding lost Cobras and Hemis, he took the time to walk me through the history of the business of

NASCAR. He was able to do that because he was there, an integral player. The same goes for Ed Several, who, together with Cotter, revolutionized NASCAR sponsorship and developed the modern-day model. The sport has never been the same.

More importantly, Cotter introduced me to "Viggy," who started out as a part-time roommate, but who has since become my lifelong friend. Thanks for all your help in navigating the garage, getting through credentials, and introducing me to the true insiders in the sport. On a personal note, I'm so proud of what you've done with your life. I'm so glad my son, George, looks up to you. He could do a lot worse.

The people at the companies I've profiled are too numerous to mention, but know who they are. Allstate, Toyota, and Goodyear were especially helpful. A special thanks to Goodyear's Roger Rydell and his staff in Akron, who let me peek inside the company's corporate suite at the Daytona 500. They were also very candid about the challenges that every sponsor—even one as venerable as Goodyear—faces in maximizing its NASCAR sponsorship.

And thanks to Les Unger and Lee White at Toyota. Because of them, readers now know exactly how to begin and build a NASCAR sponsorship. While 2007 proved a rough start, I know that victory lane is not far in their future.

A special thanks to Ned Jarrett, Junior Johnson, and all of the other old timers. They take up just a few pages in this book, but NASCAR wouldn't be where it is today without them and so many others. Thanks, guys, for simply being who you are.

Keith Waltz and Humpy Wheeler of Lowe's Motor Speedway were a great help. Humpy is truly one of the great visionaries—and historians—of auto racing, and a first-class guy. It's easy to see

ACKNOWLEDGMENTS

why his daughter, Patti, has gone so far. She was a great guide through the ever-changing world of NASCAR television. And thanks to the guys at *National Speed Sport News*, especially Mike Kerchner, for opening up the racing publication's archives. It was a treasure trove of information for the early chapters of this book, especially the work of Chris Economaki, the journalist who has influenced me most. Chris, to whom this book is dedicated, saw the trends before NASCAR even knew what was happening. More importantly, he gave me an early education in writing and reporting that was the best foundation a young reporter could ask for. Thanks Chris, for all you gave me—and the world. I couldn't have written this book without you.

This isn't a NASCAR-sanctioned book, but I would be remiss if I didn't say a special thanks to Andrew Giangola, head of business communications for NASCAR in New York. Thanks for believing that I would deliver a product that was tough, but fair. You opened a lot of corporate doors for me, and gave me unbelievable access to the NASCAR B2B Council and the sponsors. This book truly wouldn't have happened without you. *Gratzi, paisano.*

Finally, as with every project, I have to thank my family. I couldn't have done any of this without the support of my loving wife, Boo Boo, and my son, George, both of whom are the light of my life. Thanks to both of you for being so understanding when Dad is hunkered down at the computer, on the phone, or on the road. I love you both, and can't imagine life without you.

INTRODUCTION

FIFTY YEARS OF RACING AT DAYTONA

Johnny Allen drove to his first Daytona 500 in 1959 and slept in his car. In subsequent years, he splurged on a three-dollar-a-night flea-bag motel on the Daytona beachfront.

In 2007, Jimmie Johnson, the defending NASCAR Nextel Cup champion, flew down to Daytona on a private jet and spent the week of the race on the 150-foot yacht that he owns with fellow driver Jeff Gordon. When he was at the track, Johnson spent his down time in his new 1.4 million-dollar motor coach, which features two forty-two-inch plasma screen TVs, a master suite with marble shower and gold fixtures, and a hyperbaric chamber that he uses to raise the oxygen level of his blood before races.

All the cars in the 1959 race were truly "stock." In the 1950s, many drivers literally drove their cars to the track, raced them, and drove them home (if they didn't wreck them). None of the cars looked alike. There were both coupes and convertibles.

In the 2007 Daytona 500, the only way you could tell the make of car was to look at the front bumper, where the words "Fusion" or "Camry" were printed. Except for the paint scheme, every car looked alike. Jimmie Johnson's car was a Chevrolet Monte Carlo in name only, a distant cousin of the ones being sold in showrooms. Johnson's car had spent hours in a wind tunnel, sculpted to make it as aerodynamic as possible. The headlights were just stickers.

In 1959, none of the practice, qualifying, or even the actual Daytona 500 race were televised. There were very few sponsors. Allen drove a '57 Chevy, finished eleventh, and earned $400.

In 2007, every minute of Daytona SpeedWeeks was broadcast somewhere—ESPN, Fox, SPEED, DirecTV. The lineup of sponsors was all encompassing, each paying about $20 million to be on the hood of one of the forty-three entries. Johnson, a former motocross and off-road truck racer from El Cajon, California, finished a disappointing thirty-ninth and won $298,886.

Allen didn't have a sponsor for the 1959 Daytona 500. In fact, most drivers didn't. "Sponsorship was race to race," Allen said. "You'd maybe get fifty dollars, which would pay your entry fee and gas money."

Pure Oil, one of the earliest NASCAR sponsors, understood the tough financial times these drivers faced. Before they left Daytona every February, drivers were allowed to pull up to the gas pumps and fill up the trucks they used to tow their race cars and the gas cans they used during the race with Pure Oil gasoline.

"That was a godsend," Allen said, "because most years I didn't have gas money to get home."

Many drivers came to races in the early days without a car or a sponsor. They would just show up with their helmet and look for a car owner who needed a driver. The deals were done with a handshake.

Jimmie Johnson's team is sponsored by Lowe's home improvement stores, number forty-two on the Fortune 500 list. The company pays a reported $25 million a year to have its name on the hood of Johnson's car for all thirty-six events of the NASCAR Nextel Cup season. The Mooresville, North Carolina, company also sponsors the Busch Series car driven by Kyle Busch.

Every minute of Jimmie Johnson's schedule during Daytona SpeedWeeks was accounted for in the BlackBerry of his public relations assistant and his business manager. Every deal he does is scrutinized by his attorney. Every contract is negotiated by his agent.

In addition to his driving duties, Johnson made personal appearances at local Lowe's stores during SpeedWeeks. He also signed autographs and shook hands with the bevy of corporate executives and employees that Lowe's entertains in its corporate hospitality suite at every race.

The most money Johnny Allen ever won was $7,500, for finishing second at the Atlanta 500 in 1960. Jimmie Johnson's single biggest payday was $1.5 million, for winning the 2006 Daytona 500. His bonus for winning the 2006 NASCAR Nextel Cup championship was $7.5 million.

Over his thirteen-year career, Johnny Allen won $62,963. Jimmie Johnson, who is in just his seventh year of Nextel Cup competition, has won more than $45 million. Chevrolet gave his wife, Chandra, a former model, a brand new Corvette at the NASCAR awards banquet in New York in December 2006.

"If a car dealer was your sponsor, they'd give you a car to drive for six months and a pickup truck for the team to use," Allen said.

How did NASCAR get from Johnny Allen to Jimmie Johnson? That is what this book is all about. Over the next three hundred pages, I will tell you the fascinating tale of how NASCAR grew from a small, regional, third-tier sport to the second-biggest sport in the United States and the number one motorsport in the world.

To compare and contrast yesterday and today, there's no better place than Daytona. Yes, Charlotte is the undisputed headquarters for NASCAR teams today. And the Daytona 500 is often a bore until the last twenty laps. But there's still no place like Daytona. This is where it all began.

That was the focus of the third annual NASCAR media bus tour of historic Daytona Beach, hosted by NASCAR historian Buzz McKim during 2007 SpeedWeeks. During the three-hour tour, we media types learned that the Daytona International Speedway cost just $3 million to build. It started out with 25,000 grandstand seats, but today has seating for more than 170,000. Another 70,000 pack the infield on race day.

But why the thirty-five-degree banking?

"That was the highest they could stack the dirt," McKim said.

There were other challenges. For instance, the builders weren't quite sure how to smoothly transition from the steep banks to the straightaways. They eventually used a mathematical formula of slope and angle that was first pioneered by the railroads, which had to negotiate steep grades and sharp angles across the Rocky Mountains. Once the Daytona track builders figured that out, laying blacktop at a thirty-five-degree angle was another challenge.

While the speedway has changed considerably since 1959, other NASCAR landmarks haven't. The Ebony Lounge, the proverbial smoke-filled room where NASCAR was formally organized in December 1947, is still located on the roof of the Streamline Hotel on the Daytona beachfront. Also still standing is the Boot Hill Saloon, where NASCAR PR man Bob Latford created the NASCAR points system on the back of a cocktail napkin. Just up the street is the gas station that NASCAR founder Bill France bought a few years after he moved to Daytona Beach from Washington, D.C., in 1934. In the shadow of a new high-rise condominium complex going up along the Intercoastal Waterway is the remnants of Smokey Yunick's historic race shop. When the condo complex is completed, the street will be renamed Smokey Yunick Way.

Providing color commentary for the historic Daytona tour were former drivers Johnny Allen, Marvin Panch, and car owner Junie Donlavey.

"I was born too early," Panch said with a tinge of regret in his voice.

He won the 1961 Daytona 500 driving a Pontiac for Yunick. He competed in 214 NASCAR races, won 14 poles, 17 races, and logged 97 top-five finishes. He also was voted one of the fifty greatest NASCAR drivers of all time in 1998. His career winnings? $262,966. That's $383 more than Tony Raines won for finishing 33rd in the 2007 Daytona 500.

More than prize money has changed since the early days of NASCAR. Today, the cars are expected to meet exact specifications, with little tolerance for error (just ask Toyota and the other teams that were penalized at Daytona in 2007). The following story from Panch about a race in 1959 illustrates how ad hoc the racing rules were back then.

"Bill France came to me and said that they were one car short for the convertible division," Panch said. "He said he'd give me a thousand dollars if I'd cut the roof off my car and race it as a convertible."

That was big money back then, so Panch was more than happy to oblige. But he earned his pay.

"When they dropped the green flag, I thought I was going to be sucked out of the car," he said with a chuckle. "About halfway through the race, the tonneau cover I'd fashioned came loose and started beating me on the head. I had to hold that down with one hand and drive with the other."

Many of the older drivers respect the talent of today's superstars, but they doubt they could have competed in the good old days.

"We didn't have spoilers, we didn't have wide tires," Panch said. "Today, these cars knock into each other and keep going. Back then, if you just tapped somebody, they were gone."

"These guys today are very talented," Allen said. "But I doubt they could handle the cars that we drove. After you wrestle with a car with no power steering for five hundred miles, you've had a hell of a workout."

And while many of the older drivers are envious of the money that can be earned driving in NASCAR today, they also see the headaches that come with the job.

"I wouldn't want to be a driver today," Allen said. "Too much pressure, with the press, the people."

He also noted that drivers have commitments beyond just driving a race car. "NASCAR, sponsors, your car owner, testing. They earn their money."

And for many drivers in the early days of NASCAR, driving wasn't a profession, but a hobby. "We worked hard and spent everything we earned," Allen said. "We raced for fun."

Indeed, back then, racing was mostly a weekend pastime. Today, it's big business. This is that story.

CHAPTER ONE

A GOOD OLD BOY GOES COURTING

How NASCAR Wooed Corporate America

My bonus for winning the championship this year is more than my entire budget my first year in racing.

—Rick Hendrick, December 2006

That quote from Rick Hendrick, who has been a NASCAR team owner for more than twenty years, tells you just how much the business of NASCAR has grown over the past two decades.

Most people know the story of how NASCAR has grown as a sport. Stock car racing traces its roots to post–World War II America, when Carolina moonshine runners got together to see who really was the fastest of the fast. In 1934, a Washington, D.C., gas station owner named Bill France moved south to Daytona Beach, and a decade later he decided to organize (and legitimize) what had been a mishmash of races and rules that made up early stock car racing. The first NASCAR drivers raced on the sand at Daytona Beach and on half-mile dirt tracks throughout the Southeast. A decade later came paved tracks and 2.5-mile super speedways where top speeds would one day eclipse 200 miles per hour.

Fast-forward to February 15, 1979, and the CBS broadcast of the first live, flag-to-flag coverage of the Daytona 500. A pounding winter snowstorm kept millions of viewers indoors in the Northeast, Richard Petty won his sixth Daytona 500, and the phenomenal ratings made television executives sit up and take notice of this then-little-known sport. NASCAR couldn't have scripted it any better.

The broadcast also made clear that the sport had a rough-and-tumble side. On the last lap, in front of the largest television audience NASCAR had ever seen, Cale Yarborough and Donnie Allison crashed into each other going down the back straight. Much of the postrace coverage—live on CBS and in newspapers across the country the next day—focused on the raucous fistfight that followed. At one point, all the cameras caught of the melee was Cale Yarborough's helmet swinging through the air, with an unseen Allison its obvious target. Unrefined and brutish? Yes. But Americans ate it up. At a time when professional sports were becoming more sanitized, polished, and corporate, the country began to fall in love with a sport that was filled with real people, driven by real emotions and a very real desire to win.

In 1981, an upstart cable network called ESPN came along and formed what would be the perfect sports broadcasting marriage. In a few years, the entire thirty-one-race NASCAR season was broadcast live, flag-to-flag. The groundbreaking coverage earned ESPN a shelf full of Emmys, and guaranteed producer and impresario David Hill a place in the broadcasting hall of fame. People across the nation, many of whom had never eaten a grit or heard of a place called Kannapolis, North Carolina, became mesmerized by a group of hard-charging good old boys who went flat out, nose-to-tail, door handle–to–door handle, week after week, and didn't seem to know the word "quit."

"Awesome Bill from Dawsonville," "the pass in the grass," and "Swervin' Irvan" became part of the American lexicon. Every week, more fans tuned in to watch these modern-day gladiators in their 3,500-pound steel chariots bump and bang on half-mile bullrings in North Wilkesboro and Martinsville. A week later, they would be mesmerized as forty-three cars ran in a tight pack for two hours around the 2.6-mile Talladega Superspeedway. Near the end of the race, the guy in second or third place would use this mysterious thing called "the draft" to make a daring last-lap pass and win more money in a weekend than his ancestors had earned in a lifetime.

These were the epic contests that captivated fans and marked the beginning of the phenomenal growth of NASCAR. Indeed, many argue that the 1980s were NASCAR's glory days. Guys named Bodine, Elliott, Irvan, Gant, Martin, Petty (Richard and Kyle), and Wallace battled it out, week after week, all hoping to beat a guy who everyone loved to hate named Earnhardt.

Over time, the sport slowly lost its southern twang. The Bodine brothers from Chemung, New York, became series regulars. So, too, did drivers from the Midwest-based American Speed Association. Ken Schrader, Mark Martin, Alan Kulwicki, and the Wallace brothers (Rusty, Mike, and Kenny) all cut their teeth on ASA short tracks in Michigan, Missouri, and Indiana and eventually made it to NASCAR's big time, the Winston Cup Series. In the late 1980s, NASCAR also attracted a brash young go-kart racer from California named Jeff Gordon. A decade later, he fostered the career of another promising West Coast talent, 2006 NASCAR Nextel Cup Champion Jimmie Johnson. As a result of this geographic diversification, more Nextel Cup drivers today are from California than the Carolinas.

As its driver and fan base expanded, so, too, did NASCAR. The sport, which had long been planted below the Mason-Dixon Line, began to race in places like Watkins Glen, New York; Loudon, New Hampshire; Sonoma, California; and Phoenix, Arizona. Today, NASCAR is as popular in Chicago as it is in Charlotte. Double-digit growth—in fans, ratings, and sponsorship— continued through the 1980s and 1990s. Today, NASCAR's estimated seventy-five million fans make it second only to the National Football League. And its fans are more diverse— geographically, racially, and economically—than ever before.

Yes, the remarkable ascendancy of the sport of NASCAR is well known. What many people don't know is that as the sport rose, so, too, did the business of NASCAR. That's what this book is all about.

Corporate America has been involved in NASCAR in one form or another from the very beginning. Stock cars have been running on Goodyear-branded tires since the day NASCAR was founded. The automakers and motor oil companies have been there, too. The STP corporate logo and its slogan, "The Racer's Edge," are as well known as the man the company has backed since 1972, the undisputed king of NASCAR, Richard Petty.

But in the early years, corporate sponsorship was nowhere near what it is today. Up through the 1960s, horsepower, written in big block letters on the hood of the car, was featured more prominently than a sponsor—if a driver even had a sponsor.

In the early days of the Daytona 500, the most likely sponsors were local motels, garages, or car dealerships. The name of the business would be hand-painted on the rear quarter panel of the car after a quick negotiation in the garage area or over a beer in the Boot Hill Saloon. These deals were sealed with a handshake, not the bevy of corporate attorneys, agents, and corporate CEOs who negotiate today's NASCAR sponsorships.

To augment their visibility at the track, these early sponsors might ask a driver to park his car out in front of their business during Daytona SpeedWeeks to generate traffic. In exchange, the driver would get garage space, a case of oil, tires, some gas, and maybe $50 cash.

This was as sophisticated as the business of NASCAR got up through the 1960s. The automakers even went away for a few years, agreeing to a self-imposed exile from auto racing, unconvinced that their involvement—and the rising cost of fielding a car—sold many cars at the dealership. If an executive—automotive or otherwise—were to make that argument today, they'd be laughed out of the boardroom.

The 1950s and 1960s were hardscrabble times for NASCAR drivers. These were the days before million-dollar payouts and $30 million corporate sponsorships. Racers often drove the family car to the track, because back then these truly were "stock" cars. Books from this era and film clips abound with photos of drivers pulling into the pits for gas and tires and rolling down the window of their street-legal passenger car to get a drink of water. Drivers would mortgage their house or farm on Wednesday, use the money to buy tires and parts, race all weekend, and, if they were lucky enough and good enough, win enough money to pay back the bank on Monday morning. When they lost, they often lost everything.

Richard Petty tells a story about his father, Lee Petty, flipping his 1946 Buick Roadmaster four times while running second in the first NASCAR strictly stock race, a 150-mile event at Charlotte Motor Speedway on June 19, 1949. Lee was fine; the problem was that the car was their ride home. It was the family sedan.

"I had to hitchhike home," Richard Petty said in an October 2006 interview. "The car was so tore up we had to send a flatbed down to get it the next day."

This was the world in which NASCAR drivers lived in those days. But all that started to change in the 1970s.

In 1971, the U.S. Congress passed legislation barring cigarette makers from advertising on television. Up until then, companies like Philip Morris and R. J. Reynolds had been spending tens of millions of dollars a year on radio, television, and print advertising. With television cut off, they looked for a new place to put their money.

R. J. Reynolds Tobacco Company was headquartered in Winston-Salem, North Carolina, the heart of stock car country. Within one hundred miles of the corporate headquarters were dozens of weekly racetracks, the half-mile bullrings where future NASCAR drivers cut their teeth. Four of NASCAR's major stops—Bristol, Tennessee; Charlotte, North Carolina; Martinsville, Virginia; and North Wilkesboro, North Carolina—were also nearby. RJR had been looking at advertising in stock car racing for some time. With the cigarette-advertising ban in place, it seemed like the perfect time to take the plunge. It was perhaps the greatest business decision ever made in the history of NASCAR.

In 1972, RJR put up $100,000 in prize money for NASCAR's

elite division, the Grand National Series, which from then on would be known as the Winston Cup Series. While $100,000 was a pittance for a major corporation like RJR, it was a fortune for NASCAR drivers. Indeed, the significance of this turn of events cannot be over emphasized in telling the story of the business of NASCAR. That's because RJR brought more than just money to NASCAR in 1972. Racetracks were rough places in those days. A lot of beer was drunk and fights often broke out. It was not the family-friendly place it is today with air-conditioned corporate suites and souvenir trailers decorated with corporate paint schemes selling $500 leather jackets. In short, what RJR did was clean up the sport.

It installed scoreboards in the infields and new seats in the grandstands. It modernized the bathrooms, many of which were glorified outhouses. RJR, forever brand conscious, also developed and paid for the uniform red and white paint scheme on the retaining walls of all Winston Cup tracks. And it sent out an army of publicity and marketing people to the racetrack every week, giving NASCAR a reach, sophistication, and consistency in its messaging and promotion like never before.

Most important, RJR brought its customers to the racetrack. This did two things for the business of NASCAR. First, it started the corporate hospitality business that flourishes today. Second, it also marked the beginning of the business-to-business deals—often referred to as B2B—that now define the business of NASCAR sponsorships.

Who were RJR's "customers"? From a retail sense, they were the people sitting in the grandstands. They were the lower- to middle-class Americans who in 1972 smoked like chimneys, drank Budweiser beer, and drove nothing but American-made cars and trucks. But RJR also brought its business customers to the races, the people who sold cigarettes to the people in the stands. RJR brought the grocery store owners, the convenience store managers, and the gas station operators. And they all had the same epiphany that RJR had when they looked up into the NASCAR grandstand.

"RJR came to the races and looked up in the stands and saw their customers," said Richard Petty. "They brought their business partners to the track and they looked up in the stands and said 'Those are my customers, too.'"

What this unleashed was a decade of corporate sponsorship flooding into NASCAR. By 1980, there was hardly a major corporation that didn't have some sort of involvement with NASCAR. Goodyear, Citicorp, Holly Farms, Budweiser, Coca-Cola. Corporate America had discovered NASCAR and loved it.

The state of the sport was summed up in a 1979 victory lane quote by NASCAR Champion Darrell Waltrip. A week before the live flag-to-flag coverage of the 1979 Daytona 500 on CBS, Waltrip won the season-opening race at Riverside, California. When he was interviewed in victory lane, he said, "I've got to thank God, Gatorade, and Goodyear for the way we ran today."

What started as a trickle of new business interest in NASCAR in the 1970s turned into a torrent in the 1980s. Sure, Coca-Cola had sponsored Bobby Allison in the mid-1970s and had long had a presence in NASCAR. So, too, did Mountain Dew, which sponsored Waltrip and Junior Johnson and created what many considered to be the first "corporate" NASCAR team, with big bucks, fancy uniforms, and an advertising and marketing budget to match. But in 1980, the vast majority of the sponsors were still beer, cigarette, and automotive companies.

That all changed over the next ten years, making the 1980s one of the most important decades in the business of NASCAR. It saw an influx of corporate sponsorship from Fortune 500 corporations like Procter & Gamble, Kraft, and General Foods. Yes, Budweiser, Miller, Skoal, and General Motors were still the predominant sponsors, but more mainstream, female-dominated brands began to creep into the sport. It was the dawn of the era of Folgers and Maxwell House coffee, Bullseye barbecue sauce, Tide laundry detergent, and Crisco. Even Underalls, a brand of women's undergarments, became a NASCAR sponsor.

Why the change? Corporate sponsors discovered two very important things about NASCAR in the 1980s. The fans were incredibly brand loyal, and nearly half of them were women. Tide is the textbook example that's often cited.

In the 1980s, Tide was one of the most upscale—and expensive—laundry detergents on the market. Furthermore, the NASCAR audience was not what it is today. It was still mostly lower middle class, the kinds of folks who made ends meet by buying bargain-brand laundry detergent. But when Tide became the primary sponsor on Rick Hendrick's car in 1989 with driver Darrell Waltrip, Procter & Gamble found that NASCAR fans purchased Tide loyally, despite its high cost. The reason? They appreciated the NASCAR sponsors and wanted to support them by buying their products.

Word of this discovery soon spread through the marketing and advertising offices of corporate America. What resulted was the greatest influx of sponsors in the history of NASCAR, many of them competing brands trying to wrest market share away from one another by cultivating the brand loyalty of the NASCAR audience. Coors and Stroh's sponsored cars to compete with Budweiser and Miller. Folgers dueled with Maxwell House for coffee loyalty. By the end of the decade, Budweiser, STP, Skoal, and General Motors weren't eclipsed by other beer, tobacco, and automotive sponsors. They'd been replaced by mainstream consumer brands such as Country Time Lemonade, Kool-Aid, DuPont, and Red Baron frozen pizza.

This diversification of NASCAR sponsorship continues to this day. Fast-food restaurants such as McDonald's and Hardee's were milestone NASCAR sponsors in the 1990s. As the home improvement business boomed, Home Depot, Lowe's, and Menards got involved. MBNA, the Wilmington, Delaware–based credit card company, tapped into NASCAR fan loyalty by producing a line of credit cards featuring fans' favorite NASCAR drivers. MBNA also sponsored the races at Dover Downs and the cars of NFL Hall of Fame coach Joe Gibbs.

With the dot-com boom of the 1990s came sponsors such as AOL, DirecTV, and the cellular phone companies. This sea change in NASCAR sponsorship was completed in 2003, when wireless service provider Nextel replaced RJR as the title sponsor and the top NASCAR series went from being called the Winston Cup to the Nextel Cup. Go to the racetrack today and instead of RJR giving away free packs of cigarettes, Nicorette is handing out chewing gum and has on-site health-care professionals to help people *stop* smoking. The retailers who sell all of these consumer products—Target, Best Buy, Circuit City—have also become NASCAR sponsors.

This is where we are today. When you look at the starting grid of a NASCAR race, you not only see some of the most competitive race car drivers in the world, but a literal who's who of not just the

Fortune 500, but the more exclusive Fortune 50. Nearly every major corporation in America—Allstate, Alltel, AMD, Bank of America, Bass Pro Shops, Best Western, Calloway, Caterpillar, Checkers, Cingular, Coca-Cola, Domino's, DuPont, Enterprise, FedEx, Georgia Pacific, Goodyear, Gulfstream, Home Depot, Ingersoll-Rand, Jack Daniels, Jim Beam, Kellogg's, Kodak, Little Debbie, M&M Mars, Office Depot, Sunoco, Unilever, UPS, and Visa—is involved with the sport in one way or another. You even see international brands marketing themselves in NASCAR. In 2006, Tissot, the Swiss watchmaker, became the official time-keeper of NASCAR.

Some of these corporations are primary sponsors, identifiable by their corporate logos, which are featured prominently on the hoods of the cars. They pay $25 million to procure that lucrative spot with a top team.

Some companies, like MBNA, the official credit card of NASCAR, are associate sponsors on race teams and sponsor cars in the cheaper—and less well known—Busch and Craftsman Truck Series. They pay $10 million or more to have a small logo on the rear quarter panel of the car every week. Some associate sponsors even negotiate deals that give them the entire paint scheme for a few races a year.

Other companies opt to be the "official [whatever] of NASCAR," leveraging their brand name and identity with the NASCAR audience. This is the NASCAR equivalent of the nam-ing rights bonanza in college football, which has resulted in January classics being turned into corporatized entities, such as the Outback Bowl, the Fiesta Bowl, and the like. A-plus is the "official convenience store of NASCAR," Dasani the "official water of NASCAR" and Tylenol "the official pain reliever of

NASCAR." These sponsors pay tens of millions of dollars to merely be associated with the sport.

Other companies are title sponsors of races or buy the naming rights to NASCAR racetracks. Lowe's, the home-improvement store that is the primary sponsor of 2006 NASCAR Nextel Cup Champion Jimmie Johnson, was the first company to buy naming rights at a NASCAR track. The company, based in nearby Mooresville, North Carolina, paid $35 million in 1999 to have what used to be known as the Charlotte Motor Speedway referred to as the Lowe's Motor Speedway in every press release, news story, and radio and television broadcast associated with the track's three big racing weekends every year.

The same year that Lowe's bought the naming rights in Charlotte, NASCAR took a page from the NFL playbook and consolidated television broadcast rights, signing its first national television contract with Fox and NBC for a cool $400 million a season for six years. In the 1980s, when NASCAR races were broadcast on a slew of cable networks—ESPN, TNT, TBS, and others—the broadcast rights to a single race cost just $200,000. Over a thirty-one-race season, that's a little more than $6 million. So you can see what a huge deal the $2.4 billion national television package was for NASCAR. More important, the TV package gave NASCAR the big-league legitimacy that it had long aspired to, both as a sport and as a business.

In December 2005, NASCAR essentially doubled its television rights revenue, signing an eight-year, $4.8 billion deal with Fox/SPEED Channel, ABC/ESPN, and TNT. It includes broadcast rights for NASCAR's premier Nextel Cup Series; the Busch Series, NASCAR's farm league; and the NASCAR Craftsman Truck Series. In 2007, DirecTV will offer five separate channels—allowing fans to watch an entire race through a single driver's windshield. And in 2007, Sirius Satellite Radio took over the broadcast rights from XM. Sirius launched its new NASCAR channel during the NASCAR banquet in New York in December 2006 and the inaugural broadcast of the *Tony Stewart Show*.

The phenomenal rise of the business of NASCAR is the story I will tell over the next three hundred pages. I'll tell you about the days when drivers felt blessed if they were given a free case of Pure Oil, a pair of sunglasses, or a set of tires; when they used ropes for seat belts instead of the highly engineered harness system that straps them into the car today; they didn't have reams of computer-generated data on tire wear, but often opened a trap door in the floorboard to see if the cord was starting to show.

After detailing the history of NASCAR sponsorship, I'll examine a handful of modern-day sponsors, asking each company three primary questions:

· Why NASCAR?

· How do you leverage your sponsorship?

· How do you know it is money well spent?

Some of the answers will surprise you. Some companies, such as DuPont, Lowe's, and FedEx, use their NASCAR sponsorship to build teamwork and spur excellence within their own corporate teams. Others use their sponsorship to bring important guests to the track—either employees who have done a tremendous job, or important business partners. Others simply want to be associated with the fastest-growing sport in America and the seventy-five million fans who follow it.

Interestingly, some sponsors will candidly tell you that they can't trace every dollar they spend on NASCAR or how much of a reward they reap—tangible or intangible. Others know the exact figure to the penny.

I'll also detail how television has contributed to the rise of NASCAR and how it's on the same meteoric path that the NFL took when it negotiated its first national television contract in 1962.

I mention the NFL a lot in this book because NASCAR is often compared to the NFL. There's no doubt that the NFL is the biggest and most successful sports league in the United States, possibly even the world. In fact, I wrote a book, *Tailgating, Sacks and Salary Caps: How the NFL Became the Most Successful Sports League in History*, making this very argument. This puts me in a good position to compare the two sports. And having looked at both, I have to say that there is one important area where NASCAR beats the NFL hands down: sponsorship.

NASCAR takes care of its sponsors better than any other major league sport in America. Primarily because NASCAR—the executives, the drivers, and the fans—realize that the sponsors are the lifeblood of the sport. They understand that the sponsors are the ones who pay the bills and allow the whole thing to happen.

"I put the sponsors right up there with the fans," Richard Petty said. "Without either of them, I wouldn't be able to do what I do."

NASCAR executives understand this all too well. In fact, in 2004, NASCAR created the B2B Council to foster positive relationships and collaborations among its sponsors. The group meets several times a year and talks about ways that NASCAR sponsors can work together—on the track and off—to better leverage their sponsorship dollars. It may involve a joint promotion at the racetrack, buying advertising time together, or simply letting each other know what their plans are for marketing and promotion. I will take you inside the B2B Council meeting at the 2007

Daytona 500 and show you exactly how this group works, and what they get out of it.

I'll also take you inside the Daytona 500, the Super Bowl of NASCAR. (Or, as one NASCAR executive likes to say, "the Super Bowl is the Daytona 500 of the NFL.")

Like the Super Bowl, the Daytona 500, which is the first race of the NASCAR season, is the corporate spectacle that most prominently features NASCAR's ever-growing list of corporate partners. I'll look at the starting grid not as a lineup of some of the best drivers in the world, but as a lineup of the most powerful and influential corporations in America.

I'll also take you inside the corporate suites that sit atop the towering grandstands, as well as the luxury motor coaches that sit in exclusive parking lots in the Daytona infield. And I'll give you an inside look at what an army of sales and marketing executives do in preparation for this one week in Florida every February, from advertising and promotions to corporate hospitality and the deals that get done in the corporate suites.

Finally, I'll look where NASCAR is going and the challenges that lie ahead.

Hang on. It'll be a fascinating and turbulent ride through the ever-growing business of NASCAR.

CHAPTER TWO

THE SUITE LIFE

Inside NASCAR Corporate Hospitality

On February 18, 2007, the Goodyear Tire and Rubber Company held a meeting for Wall Street analysts to explain its new consumer tire strategy and the new national advertising campaign it was launching. In attendance were the usual heavy hitters: Goodyear CEO Bob Keegan, CFO Richard Kramer, and Jon Rich, then president of the North American tire group. The new ad campaign was explained by Joey Viselli, director of Goodyear's consumer brands.

Following his presentation, Viselli opened up the floor for questions. Analysts asked about the new campaign and Goodyear's strategy for Europe, Latin America, and Asia. Afterward, analysts were served lunch and were able to mix and mingle with the Goodyear management team and other executives.

This meeting was not unusual. Goodyear and other Fortune 500 corporations hold regular analyst briefings every quarter. What was unique was that the briefing was held in Goodyear's luxury suite behind pit road at Daytona International Speedway on the morning of the Daytona 500. These analyst briefings are usually held at a five-star hotel in midtown Manhattan. In the evening, a few guests are invited to join the Goodyear management team amid the dim lighting and white tableclothes of venerable Manhattan dining spots, such as Cipriani or the "21" Club. They talk business and sip $500 bottles of wine and eat $300 cuts of Kobe beef. While the suites at Daytona aren't quite as plush, don't think for a minute that the conversations taking place here are any different than those in Manhattan. NASCAR is big business, and the companies that are sponsors are increasingly using their hospitality suites to woo customers and ink million-dollar deals. In many ways, the NASCAR suites have replaced the smoke-filled room and the golf course as the place where business gets done.

Goodyear brought the Wall Street analysts to the Daytona 500 because it wanted to emphasize to them just how important the NASCAR sponsorship is to the company and its future. If Goodyear is to succeed financially, one thing it must do is connect the dots between the tires that NASCAR teams use and the tires that consumers buy. And there's not a better place to explain all this than the Goodyear suite at Daytona.

Goodyear doesn't have just any suite; it has *the* suite. Two actually.

The Goodyear suites, which are about five hundred square feet and can comfortably hold about twenty-five guests, are on the third floor of the exclusive Daytona 500 Club, a three-story glass building that sits just behind pit road at the start/finish line. On the second floor is the Daytona 500 Club itself, where Brian France gave his State of NASCAR address earlier in the week. It was where honorary pace car driver Cal Ripken Jr., *American Idol* winner Kelly Clarkson, country duo Big & Rich, and race Grand Marshal Nicholas Cage mingled during the race. It's also where you'll find former drivers and their families, as well as NASCAR executives and their guests.

In addition to the star power pulsing through the room, the Daytona 500 Club is not a bad place to watch the race. It features several well-stocked bars and a carving table of fresh meats, side dishes, salad, and desserts. Cocktail tables are scattered around the room, as are plush couches and easy chairs. The front wall is smoked glass from floor to ceiling, cutting the glare and affording a great view of the track, from the exit of Turn Four, down the front straight, and halfway into Turn One. The pits are just one hundred feet away, so this is also a good place to see all the action there. On this day, Jeff Gordon, Tony Stewart, and Jimmie Johnson's pits were all within easy viewing. Right in front of the building is victory lane, so everyone who stayed until the end of the race got to see Kevin Harvick sprayed with champagne and pose for a thousand photos.

The Goodyear suites are on the third floor, with one suite toward Turn Four and the other toward Turn One. They are tastefully decorated, with a few cocktail tables and seating near the windows. From one suite, you can see the cars come down the back straight, go through Turns Three and Four, and speed just past the start/finish line. From the other, you can see from the start/finish line through Turns One and Two and part of the back straight. Next door to one Goodyear suite is the official NASCAR timing and scoring booth, giving you the added feeling that you are somewhere exclusive. Next to the other suite in 2007 was the Toyota suite, which was packed with its VIPs.

In addition to the Wall Street analysts, Goodyear hosted some of its tire dealers and partners. When they arrived on Sunday, there were fresh bagels, muffins, coffee, and juice. The bar, featuring complimentary beer, wine, and liquor, was open early, too. About midday, the hostesses—two to a suite—replaced the breakfast fare with chips and salsa. Copies of the *Daytona Beach News-Journal* and Daytona 500 race programs were laid out for guest to read. After the analyst briefing was over, display boards featuring the new Goodyear ads were set up. Just before the start of the race, the hostesses changed the food again, this time putting out Polish sausage and Philly cheesesteaks. There was also a dessert tray.

About fifteen minutes before the start of the race, Goodyear and its guests headed to the roof. Access was limited, but with the right wristband you could get up there. From the roof, guests were able to see the prerace show, which was unfolding just in front of them on the start/finish line. Featured performers were the 82nd Airborne glee club and Kelly Clarkson. Just as Big & Rich finished the National Anthem, U.S. Navy F-14s screamed overhead. And, of course, guests could see the Goodyear blimp hovering over the track, its LED display showing the tagline from the new ad campaign, "Get There." If anyone was thirsty, no need to go back downstairs. There was a bar with waitress service on the roof.

THE SUITE LIFE

Back in the suites, Eduardo Arguelles, head of PR for Goodyear in Latin America, was telling guests about the phenomenal success of the Busch Series race in Mexico City. Goodyear has leveraged its NASCAR sponsorship to create a ten-day extravaganza of tire sales, special promotions, dealer meetings, and press events around the Busch race in Mexico City. "Goodyear Day" is an officially sanctioned NASCAR event that features drivers from the Busch Series, as well as native drivers who compete in the NASCAR Corona Series in Mexico.

"It's our exclusive property," Arguelles said. "The only way the consumers can touch NASCAR is through us."

Like Daytona, Goodyear hosts a dinner for its Latin American dealers and preferred customers around the Mexico City Busch race. The company also brings five hundred of its best dealers and VIP guests to the race.

While all of this is impressive if you've never been to a corporate hospitality suite at a NASCAR race before, rest assured that Goodyear was not alone in the red carpet it rolled out for its VIP guests. There were forty-three starters for the Daytona 500, and you can bet that the sponsors for every one of them had some sort of corporate hospitality at the track. DuPont and Lowe's bring several hundred guests to each NASCAR race. Marathon Coach, which counts NASCAR driver Jeff Gordon and Supreme Court Justice Clarence Thomas among its clientele, brings about forty of its preferred customers to almost every NASCAR race. While company executives fete the guests with steak and lobster dinners and suite tickets, Marathon technicians service their RVs. All the while, Marathon executives are soft-selling their latest and greatest models. It's a good strategy. At the Phoenix race in November 2006, Marathon sold a half dozen new motor coaches, each with an average price tag of $1.5 million.

Many companies use a NASCAR race and corporate hospitality as the grand finale for their annual sales meetings or other corporate gatherings. By the time the analysts were feted at Daytona, Goodyear and many of its executives had been shuttling in and out of Florida for two weeks. On February 5, 2007, a week before the Bud Shootout, the official start of the NASCAR season, Goodyear announced that it had renewed its contract to be the exclusive tire supplier to NASCAR for the next five years. Goodyear made the announcement at its annual dealer conference in Orlando. Goodyear's Keegan and Rich, along with NASCAR President Mike Helton, made the announcement in front of two thousand Goodyear tire dealers.

"This extension of the more than fifty-year relationship of two American icons is one that we are extremely proud to announce," Kramer said. "Nothing says racing like NASCAR, and Goodyear has been recognized as the longest-running sponsor of the sport. We plan to have our Eagle tires in the winner's circle for another fifty years."

"Our longtime relationship with Goodyear is a testament to the consistent high-quality tire it supplies the race teams," Helton said. "Goodyear has been a vital partner, which has been essential to NASCAR's side-by-side competition."

That's more than just public relations hype. Goodyear has been supplying tires to NASCAR since the 1950s, making it the longest-running supplier to any major sport in the United States. Furthermore, the contract extension announced at the dealership conference began what would be two weeks of NASCAR corporate hospitality, culminating with the 2007 Daytona 500.

THE SUITE LIFE

On Friday, February 16, while the NASCAR Craftsman Truck Series was running its 250-mile race on the 2.5-mile high-banked oval, Goodyear executives and a handful of its most important dealers were in a dining room at Daytona USA, the track's on-site museum that sits outside of Turn Four. Surrounded by Dale Earnhardt's Daytona 500–winning car, Richard Petty's famous Superbird, and more driving suits than you could try on in a lifetime, the guests sipped cocktails and nibbled on hors d'oeuvres. In between, they heard a recap of Goodyear's Orlando dealer conference and the renewed NASCAR sponsorship. Then they got to hear from NASCAR drivers Buddy Baker and Ryan Newman.

One of the advantages of being a NASCAR sponsor is the access it gives a company to the drivers, team owners, and NASCAR executives. Sponsors often bring drivers to their annual sales meeting to fire up the workforce. Many of them are outstanding motivational speakers. Others use the drivers in advertising and promotions. On this night, Baker and Newman were there simply to get the tire dealers excited about the race, answer some questions, and sign autographs.

Following the Q&A with Baker and Newman and dinner, the Goodyear guests were shuttled back to their hotel. You see, NASCAR corporate hospitality is an all-expense-paid junket that would make congressmen and their K Street lobbyists blush. Guests are usually flown in a few days before the race, picked up at the airport, and taken to an upscale hotel that usually includes a concierge suite where they can gather for cocktails before the evening's activities. When these corporate guests check in, there's usually a goody bag waiting for them, filled with NASCAR souvenirs and corporate-branded knickknacks. Many open their closet to find NASCAR-branded apparel for them to wear. Throughout the weekend, they're given the VIP treatment: dinners, tickets to the corporate suite, a police escort to the track. The grand finale is the race itself. Guests get to tour the pits before the race, meet a driver or two, and then watch the race from the suites. These trips usually pay off for a company because over the course of an entire three-day weekend, the conversation eventually turns to business. And that's what these trips are all about.

In addition to the Goodyear dinner at Daytona USA on Friday night, guests were given tickets for the suite for the Orbitz 300 Busch Series race on Saturday, as well as Sunday's Daytona 500.

Sunoco, which signed a ten-year agreement in 2003 to be the official fuel of NASCAR, also hosted its annual dealer meeting in Orlando in the weeks leading up to the 2007 Daytona 500. Included in the presentations to its thirteen hundred dealers about the changing political climate, renewable fuels, and the latest retail trends was a presentation about Sunoco's NASCAR sponsorship. In addition to being the official fuel, Sunoco's A-plus convenience stores are the "official pit stop" of NASCAR.

"For us, NASCAR is all about brand positioning," said Chris Buitron, NASCAR brand manager for Sunoco. "It's about associating a high-quality, high-performance sport with Sunoco."

During the Daytona 500 weekend, Sunoco hosted one hundred fifty customers a day in its hospitality tent outside the Daytona front stretch, as well as forty to fifty VIPs in its corporate suite. At the Dover races every year, Philadelphia-based Sunoco brings thirteen hundred customers and employees to the race for the usual fare and VIP access.

"We really try and leverage the drivers," said Buitron, who had a driver in the Sunoco suite and hospitality tent every day during SpeedWeeks.

The company brought in Jimmie Johnson to its 2005 employees meeting. Rusty Wallace and Kyle Petty have made appearances at Dover in the past. In 2007, Sunoco is going to start working with new NASCAR driver J. J. Yeley.

During Daytona SpeedWeeks, Sunoco started running new NASCAR-themed television spots with drivers Kasey Kahne and Tony Stewart, as well as radio spots featuring Dale Earnhardt Jr. Sunoco has also partnered with the SPEED Channel for a weekly Pit Strategy of the Race segment, hosted by Chad Knaus, the crew chief for 2006 NASCAR champion Jimmie Johnson. Sunoco is also working closely with other NASCAR partners in some B2B deals. For instance, Sunoco offers a discounted fleet fuel card to select NASCAR sponsors, but it's somewhat limited in that Sunoco only has retail outlets in twenty-five states, mostly along the East Coast.

In addition to doing corporate hospitality at Daytona, Sprint Nextel, which replaced Winston as the series sponsor in 2004, debuted its new FanView product at Daytona. FanView is basically a small, hand-held device that bundles audio and video into a compact unit. Fans can rent one for $70 for the weekend, or buy one for $369. The television screen allows fans to watch the race broadcast, see up to seven in-car cameras, and pull up driver stats. On the audio side, fans can either listen to the race broadcast on MRN, or scan the frequencies for driver communications. It's extremely user-friendly. For instance, in the past to listen to radio communication you had to know exactly what frequency a team was on, such as 458.075. With FanView, when you punch in a driver's number you are given several options—stats, in-car camera, or radio communications. It's truly amazing and revolutionizing the way fans watch races at the track. *Time* magazine named FanView one of the best inventions of 2006.

Not everyone can watch the race from a corporate hospitality suite and shake hands with the drivers. But Nextel is changing how close fans can get to the drivers and the pits. It used to be that a pit or garage pass was golden. Only people who truly had a need to be there got one. That kept the fans at arm's length.

Now Nextel has created the Nextel Fan Zone in the Daytona infield. Just behind pit road, it's an open area that features concessions and live entertainment. Some of the racing shows, such as *NASCAR Live*, broadcast from studios and stages set up in the Nextel Fan Zone. The area also abuts a new garage area that has picture windows, so fans can look in and watch the crews working on the cars. The inspection area also bumps up against the Fan Zone. As cars go through inspection, fans can look on, similar to watching your car go through the car wash.

In addition to corporate hospitality, Daytona is also a place where sponsors make major announcements. UPS announced during SpeedWeeks that it had signed a new five-year agreement with NASCAR to continue as the official express delivery company through 2011. As part of the deal, UPS said it would continue providing its Trackside Services shipping service at all NASCAR Nextel Cup races as well as logistics, freight, and supply chain services. It's been a successful relationship. In Chapter Nine, you'll learn how UPS has leveraged is sponsorship to become the preferred shipping service for almost 99 percent of the more than one thousand NASCAR-related businesses, race teams, tracks, NASCAR business units, and other NASCAR sponsors and suppliers. That's a 55 percent increase in racing customers since UPS entered the sport in 2000.

"Over the past seven years, our relationship with NASCAR has made UPS synonymous with America's fastest growing sport," said Patrick Guilbert, UPS vice president of sponsorships. "UPS is celebrating its one hundredth birthday in 2007 and as we look to the future, we know this NASCAR partnership is contributing to the long-term growth of our company."

In addition to sponsoring NASCAR driver Dale Jarrett, UPS has six individual track sponsorships at Bristol Motor Speedway, California Speedway, Daytona International Speedway, Homestead-Miami Speedway, Richmond International Raceway, and Texas Motor Speedway. The most visible part of UPS's role in NASCAR has been its popular "Race the Truck" advertising series. The 2007 ads featured Dale Jarrett trying to assemble the perfect pit crew. He had several celebrity friends help him with the search. The new series of ads, like the Goodyear "Get There" ads, debuted during the Daytona 500.

Creative advertising has become such an integral part of sponsorship that NASCAR announced that its website, www.nascar.com, would show new sponsor advertisements *before* they aired on the Fox broadcast of the Daytona 500.

"We figured there is a lot of traffic on the morning of the race," said Andrew Giangola, director of business communications for NASCAR. "Our sponsors pushed for it. They see it as value-added."

During the 2007 Daytona 500, NASCAR sponsors Sprint Nextel, Allstate, Chevrolet, Coca-Cola, Gillette, Office Depot, Home Depot, Sunoco, Toyota, and UPS all debuted new commercials, which cost $500,000 for a thirty-second spot.

Office Depot announced its "Official Small Business of NASCAR" promotion during 2007 SpeedWeeks. The winner of the promotion had its company logo displayed on Carl Edwards' No. 99 Office Depot Ford Fusion during the Coca-Cola 600 at Lowe's

Motor Speedway in May. It will remain on the car through the final twenty-four races of the NASCAR Nextel Cup season.

Sirius Satellite Radio announced that it would have ten NASCAR-dedicated channels over the 2007 season. ESPN and Dish Network announced a multiyear, multimedia agreement that includes a *SportsCenter* weekly NASCAR report sponsored by Dish Network and six in-car cameras per season in the Busch Series. Gillette announced that Kasey Kahne was the newest addition to its Gillette Young Guns family of NASCAR drivers. Dale Earnhardt Jr. announced the launch of www.infieldparking.com, a new social networking website that he said "offers fans a cool new way to interact with drives and the opportunity to connect with other fans around the world." At the start of the 2007 season, nine drivers agreed to have infield parking web pages.

Why all the corporate news out of Daytona? Just look at the lineup for the Daytona 500. It's a who's who of the Fortune 500. Shell, the new sponsor of Kevin Harvick's Daytona 500–winning team, is third on the list. Bank of America is twelfth, Home Depot fourteenth, and Target is twenty-ninth. While many fans looked at the front row of David Gilliland and Ricky Rudd as the resurgence of Robert Yates Racing, corporate America saw it as a coup for Masterfoods International, the parent company of both sponsors M&Ms and Snickers.

And, of course, the big story at Daytona this year was Toyota, number eight on the Forbes Global 500 list. It wasn't the greatest weekend for the world's number two automaker. Of its two marquee drivers, Michael Waltrip was caught cheating and Dale Jarrett had to use his past champion's provisional to start forty-third. Jarrett posted the best finish among the four Toyota entries, finishing twenty-second. Pretty abysmal. But given where the Jarrett family started in racing, he's come a long way. So, too, has NASCAR.

CHAPTER THREE
BETTING THE FARM

The Early Days of NASCAR

A t the start of the 1959 season, Ned Jarrett, Dale's father, didn't have the premier sponsorship in the most popular auto racing series on the planet. He didn't even have a car.

He eventually found one. A Ford. In fact, Junior Johnson, who was already well known, had driven it many times and won. There was just one hitch: The car cost $2,000. That was more money than Ned Jarrett had in his checking account. So what did this sober, successful, Christian businessman do? He wrote the check anyway.

Jarrett waited until the bank closed on Friday, knowing full well that he didn't have enough money in his account to cover the check. His plan? He'd have to race—and win—two races over the weekend: a non-points event in Myrtle Beach on Saturday night and a Grand National race in Charlotte on Sunday. He'd also have to beat the check to the bank on Monday morning.

He won the Myrtle Beach race, but at terrific cost. It was common then for drivers to tape their steering wheels to give them a better grip. The steering wheel on Jarrett's Ford had been taped backward—with the edges exposed—and every time he turned the wheel, it tore up his hands. When he got out of the car at the end of the race, he needed a tourniquet to stop the bleeding. Despite being in great physical pain, he loaded up his race car and headed toward Charlotte for the race on Sunday.

He completed one hundred laps of the two hundred–lap event before the pain became just too intense. Unable to bear it anymore, he swung into the pits, only to find Junior Johnson standing nearby. Word of Jarrett's gamble—and his physical condition—had spread through the NASCAR garage. Johnson quickly jumped into the car and went on to win the race. Johnson said he did it because he knew of the predicament Jarrett was in, and he respected him for the gamble he took. The record books show that Ned Jarrett won the race, but he knows who really brought home the victory—and saved him from financial ruin.

"Even if you were enemies, you'd help out another driver if you could," Jarrett said of the early days of NASCAR.

Jarrett ran five races in that Ford in 1959. He won three times, and finished second and third. More important, Jarrett went on to become one of the greatest drivers in the early history of NASCAR. His nickname, appropriately, was "Gentleman Ned," because drivers knew that no matter how close and intense the competition, Jarrett would always race them clean.

When Ned Jarrett started racing in 1952, he didn't have nearly the financial and technical resources that his son Dale has today.

"The sport was not really well known," said the elder Jarrett, who grew up on his family's farm outside Newton, North Carolina, and was initially more interested in running the family sawmill than racing stock cars.

In the late 1940s, the Jarretts had to travel fifty miles to Charlotte or North Wilkesboro if they wanted to see a stock car race. Then in 1952, Hickory Motor Speedway was built. It would forever change the lives of the Jarrett family, as well as a slew of drivers, car owners, and crew chiefs from the Appalachian foothills of western North Carolina. Many of them would cut their teeth on the half-mile dirt oval and eventually make it to the big leagues of NASCAR. But for a lot of drivers of this era, Jarrett included, finding money to race was often tougher than winning.

Ned Jarrett entered his first race shortly after the new Hickory Motor Speedway opened, competing against a young Junior Johnson and many other future NASCAR stars. He finished tenth out of thirty cars, not bad for a novice driver. Still, stock car racing remained just a passing interest for the successful businessman.

"I didn't look at it as a career because there was no money in it," Jarrett said.

As the 1950s progressed, so did Jarrett's racing career. He competed in his first national NASCAR event in 1953, dropping out of the Southern 500 with an oil leak after just ten laps. He was the 1955 Hickory Motor Speedway champion and finished second in 1956 in the year-long points standings in NASCAR's Sportsman division, the equivalent of today's Busch Series. He went on to win the Sportsman national championship in 1957 and 1958. With these successes under his belt, Jarrett hoped that in 1959 a big-name car owner would come calling, begging him to move up to the elite Grand National division, the precursor to today's Nextel Cup. It didn't quite work out that way.

"I was the one who had to go knocking on doors to try and find a ride," Jarrett said.

In 1960, Jarrett won five races. A year later, he won the NASCAR Grand National championship, finishing in the top five twenty-two times over the forty-six-race season, and outside the top ten only twelve times. In 1964, with factory support from Ford, Jarrett won fifteen races, including his first super speedway victory at Atlanta, but he lost the Grand National championship to Richard Petty. The next year, he won thirteen races and another Grand National title. He finished in the top five an amazing forty-two times over the fifty-four-race season. He also won the 1965 Southern 500 by fourteen laps, the largest margin of victory in NASCAR history.

In 1966, Jarrett decided to call it quits, making him the only driver to retire as NASCAR champion. He faded from the NASCAR scene for more than a decade, devoting himself to his family businesses, but he obviously couldn't stay away. He became the promoter at Hickory Motor Speedway and then a broadcaster in 1978. He started out with MRN, the radio network that broadcasts the NASCAR races every week and is owned by International Speedway Corporation. Then in the 1980s he moved over to television, working for ESPN, CBS, and Fox Sports. He was in the CBS booth in 1993, calling the Daytona 500, when his son, Dale, won the race for the first time.

Over his career, Ned Jarrett won $289,146. His single biggest season was his last, 1965, when he won $77,966. Compare that to his son, Dale. To date, the younger Jarrett has won $45.5 million.

In 2006 alone, he won $4.5 million, down slightly from his single-season best of $4.7 million in 2005. This gives you a sense of how the business of NASCAR has changed. But the important point here is that Ned Jarrett's story is not unique.

Stories abound from the early days of NASCAR of drivers risking everything—farm, family, friends—to race. Dale Earnhardt, early in his career, often mortgaged everything he had to buy parts and equipment, win races, and claw his way up through the NASCAR ranks. Rick Mast, a modestly successful NASCAR Winston Cup driver in the 1980s and 1990s, reportedly sold his prized cow to buy his first race car. In short, sponsorship in the early days of NASCAR was not what it is today.

According to the official history of NASCAR, "one of the first items produced specifically for stock car racing was a racing tire manufactured and distributed by the Pure Oil Company in 1952. Prior to that time, street tires were all that were available for racing applications."

Atlanta businessman Raymond Parks was an early NASCAR sponsor. He owned several race cars and was one of the first to realize the advantages of advertising his businesses on these rolling billboards that were seen by thousands of people at racetracks throughout the Southeast every weekend. To get the biggest bang for his buck, Parks bought the best equipment, and hired only the best drivers and mechanics of the day. It paid off. Parks-backed cars won the very first NASCAR race and the first two NASCAR championships. But it quickly became evident to him that full-time NASCAR race teams needed to attract bigger sponsors with deeper pockets. He left NASCAR in 1951.

This boom-to-bust pattern of sponsorship and car owners was common in the early days of NASCAR. One day a sponsor would be there with buckets of money, and the next day they'd be gone.

Carl Kiekhaefer, who developed the Mercury outboard motor, saw NASCAR as a good way to promote his product. People who liked to watch NASCAR drivers go fast, he surmised, also liked to go fast themselves, whether it was on the road or on the water. His team dominated the sport in 1955 and 1956, winning the majority of the races and two championships. Then, just as quickly as he had appeared, he and his money were gone.

The first national NASCAR sponsor was Air Lift Corporation, which made inflatable bags that were fitted onto passenger-car suspensions to improve the ride and handling. NASCAR teams, always looking for any advantage, soon started putting them on their cars. Air Lift struck a deal with driver Bobby Griffin, an Oldsmobile dealer from Florence, South Carolina, to paint the Air Lift name on the side of his Olds 88. His No. 87 Air Lift–sponsored 1949 Oldsmobile now sits in the Darlington (South Carolina) Raceway Stock Car Museum.

Most of the early NASCAR sponsors usually had something to do with the automotive industry. More often than not, the sponsors were the automakers themselves. Hudson Motor Company gave the first factory backing to Marshall Teague after he won the 1951 NASCAR race on the sand at Daytona Beach. He and his teammate Herb Thomas were often seen on the southern dirt tracks with "Fabulous Hudson Hornet" emblazoned on the side of their cars. The Hornet was the most successful stock car on the NASCAR circuit from 1951 to 1954. But when Hudson merged with the Nash Motor Company in 1954, the company stopped sponsoring race teams.

In 1953, Oldsmobile, Lincoln, and Hudson introduced "severe usage" kits—mostly hubs, spindles, and other suspension parts—that were for passenger cars, but were quickly adopted by NASCAR teams. The automakers also started introducing high-performance options on production cars, thus making them eligible for use at the racetrack. The 1957 Buick Roadmaster had aluminum brake drums that dissipated heat better than steel brakes, thus making them popular with stock car drivers. Remember, in the 1950s, there was a reason they were called "stock" cars.

The 1950s saw a surge in factory support for stock car racing. Hudsons equipped with the Twin H head won twenty-two of thirty-seven NASCAR races in 1953. Two years later, Chevy and Ford both had modest factory programs. Carl Kiekhaefer's teams and Petty Enterprises both had unofficial factory backing from Chrysler during the 1955 and 1956 seasons.

But like many early NASCAR sponsors who had come and gone, the automakers went away in 1957. Some drivers and car owners complained that factory-backed teams were driving up the cost of racing, thus negating one of the primary appeals of NASCAR: affordability. The automakers also were unconvinced that sponsoring race teams sold cars in the showroom. So in 1957, the manufacturers agreed to stop helping NASCAR teams with parts and engineering support. Thankfully for the teams—and NASCAR—the ban was short-lived. In fact, it's widely believed that the manufacturers never really went away, but kept secretly working with the top teams of the day, giving them parts and engineering support. According to the official history of NASCAR, "Stories of race teams picking up cars from showrooms only days before races and converting them to race cars were commonplace."

Not all of the NASCAR sponsorships from the 1950s were sporadic and short-lived. The Union Oil Company, operating under the brand name Pure Oil, became the official gasoline of NASCAR in 1951. In later years, the company became Union 76, and nearly every NASCAR infield was adorned with the familiar orange "76" balls that were the trademark of the company's gas stations.

While the orange Union 76 balls were well known, even the most diehard NASCAR fans can't name Unocal's famous pitch-man, even though they've probably seen him hundreds of times. For thirty years, Bill Broderick was a fixture on the NASCAR Winston Cup circuit. He was the giant blonde-haired guy with the pompadour hairstyle that never moved. He was in every NASCAR victory lane in the 1970s, 1980s, and 1990s. He would help drivers change hats every twenty seconds so that a sea of photographers could take promotional photos for the various sponsors, who would then use the photos in advertisements in *National Speed Sport News*, *Winston Cup Scene*, and other racing publications. The NASCAR/Union Oil partnership lasted until 2003, making it the longest running sponsorship in racing history. Union 76 was replaced as the "official fuel of NASCAR" in 2004 by Sunoco.

As great and long lasting as the Union Oil sponsorship was, it was the exception, not the rule, in the early days of NASCAR. It was this uncertain world of here-today, gone-tomorrow sponsor-ship in which Ned Jarrett and others found themselves in the 1950s. It was also what made Jarrett write that check—and risk everything—in hopes of becoming a full-time driver on the NASCAR Grand National circuit.

Even sponsors that are fixtures in motorsports today were reluctant to get involved with NASCAR early on. After all, back then NASCAR was nothing more than an upstart, regional stock car series based in Daytona Beach. Many people didn't believe that

Big Bill France, no matter how smart, innovative, and forceful he was, would succeed at his stated goal of organizing, legitimizing, and standardizing American stock car racing.

Firestone was one of those sponsors that had been synonymous with auto racing, but it stayed away from NASCAR in the early days. Company founder Harvey Firestone had been supplying tires to the Indy 500 since 1909. Furthermore, he was a good friend of Henry Ford, whom many people don't know founded Ford Racing before he founded Ford Motor Company. Despite its rich racing history, Firestone didn't join NASCAR until the mid-1950s.

"Guys would come to them for tires, particularly [for] Darlington, because no one could figure out how to get around there and keep tires on the cars," said Humpy Wheeler, president of Lowe's Motor Speedway and one of the most knowledgeable auto racing historians around.

Wheeler tells a good story about Firestone and Smokey Yunick, one of the early engineering and mechanical pioneers of stock car racing.

"Smokey went up to Akron in the winter of 1955 and Firestone let him look through some old tires," Wheeler said. "He found some tires and brought them back and ended up winning the 1955 Southern 500 without changing tires."

The tires Yunick used weren't engineered specifically to run at Darlington, the way tires are today. In fact, they weren't even racing tires—or car tires, for that matter. They were sixteen-inch truck tires that he bought for a dollar a piece. But they were made of the right tire compound to withstand the abrasive surface at the South Carolina racetrack.

Again, NASCAR racing was completely different in the 1950s—both technically and financially—from the NASCAR we know today. NASCAR teams didn't have chassis specialists armed with reams of computer-generated data on tire compounds, air pressure, and the effect a one-degree change in temperature will have on tire wear and handling. These were the days when the height of technology was a trap door that driver Tim Flock installed in the floorboard of his car. He would open it while going down the straightaway, bend down, crane his neck, and check tire wear.

"When the white cord was showing, we had about one or two laps left before the tire would blow," Flock said.

But by the late 1950s, this started to change. Four years after Smokey Yunick won the Southern 500 at Darlington on a single set of Firestone tires, Goodyear came to Darlington and won the 1959 Southern 500 with New Yorker Jim Reed at the wheel.

"I think that's the seminal moment," Wheeler said. "At that point, there were no real sponsors in NASCAR. That sowed the seeds for the great factory wars of the 1960s."

Wheeler's absolutely right. Before 1960, sponsorship was paltry and inconsistent at best. All that started to change, albeit slowly, with the 1960 Daytona 500.

The automakers, which had walked away from stock car racing in 1957, returned in 1959 and began what many argue was the golden era of factory backing for stock car teams. It was when John Holman and Ralph Moody—working in their legendary North Carolina race engineering shop, Holman Moody—partnered exclusively with Ford to develop new racing technology for stock cars. At the same time, a young whiz kid named John DeLorean was busy transforming Pontiac into GM's performance brand. Pontiac driver Joe Weatherly took home the Grand National championship in 1962 and 1963, and Pontiac won more races in consecutive years—fifty-two—than any manufacturer in the history of the Grand National division.

In 1963, Chevy brought its 427-cubic-inch, high-lift engine to the track. While much of the mystique behind the new big block was just that, Ford reportedly spent $1 million trying to come up with an engine that would match it. In the meantime, the Ford Fastback Galaxy was one of the first passenger cars to be advertised as "a race car."

Mercury entered the stock car fray in 1963 with the Marauder, with Joe Weatherly and Rex White at the wheel. Fireball Roberts switched to Ford from Pontiac that same year and promptly won at Bristol. A year later, rookie Billy Wade swept four straight races driving a Mercury. Another car owner, Little Bud Moore (no relation to the Bud Moore of Motorcraft fame in the 1980s), switched to Mercury from Pontiac.

In 1964, Chrysler brought out the Hemi, marking the peak in the Detroit engine wars. Interestingly, the engine was developed in the early 1950s, but was shelved when the automakers enacted the racing ban in 1957.

In 1966, with more super speedways being built, aerodynamics started to become as important as horsepower. Chrysler unveiled its radically designed Dodge Charger. Ford and Mercury countered with the sleek-roofed, slope-nosed Ford Talladega and Mercury Cyclone. A February 23, 1966, article in *National Speed Sport News* offers some sense of just how intense—and evolutionary—the competition was between the Detroit marques. The article proclaimed, "If two weeks of practice are any precedent, this Sunday's Daytona 500 should go down in the history books as the race that dawned a new era for stock car racing."

The race included unprecedented levels of factory involvement, with both Chrysler and Ford backing half a dozen big-name
drivers. The 1966 race was the opening shot in an escalating war
between Ford and Chrysler that drove up the cost of winning in
NASCAR. The 1960s, a decade that many argue was the most
innovative and important in the history of stock car racing, came
to a close with the debut of Chrysler's winged Dodge Charger
Daytona and Richard Petty's Plymouth Superbird.

The automakers' intense interest in stock car racing in the
1960s had an impact well beyond ever-increasing horsepower and
sleeker rooflines. The most obvious impact was the huge increase
in the amount of money the automakers were willing to spend on
stock car racing. In 1957, the spigot of sponsorship dollars from
Detroit had been almost completely shut off. By the end of the
1960s, it was gushing with parts and engineering expertise.

Ironically, the influx of factory dollars made sponsorship less
important to teams in the 1960s. After all, if they had the big-
bucks backing of Ford, GM, and Chrysler, they didn't need to sell
advertising on the hood to pay their bills. But there was another,
more important, long-term consequence of the intense factory
support from Detroit. It actually made NASCAR more appealing
to corporate sponsors. That's because Detroit's involvement gave
the sport a legitimacy that it hadn't had before. The message corporate America deciphered was this: If NASCAR was important
enough to garner the interest of Detroit, which at that time was
the epicenter of the automotive universe, then perhaps the rest of
corporate America should take an interest as well.

It also helped that the automotive press was starting to pay
more attention to corporate sponsors. In 1959, the lineup for the
Daytona 500 that ran in most newspapers and automotive magazines

listed just the car owner and the manufacturer. Sponsors were noticeably absent from racing stories as well.

"Curtis Turner, at the wheel of one of the Holman Moody prepared 1959 four-place Ford Thunderbirds scooted around the track at 143.12 mph, and promptly predicted that the T-Birds would be the cars to beat in the NASCAR race here Feb. 20 and 22," reported *National Speed Sport News*.

This started to change slightly in the early 1960s, especially at big races like the Daytona 500 and the Southern 500. Sponsors, many of them local, would buy the car for a week, but that was it. For instance, a February 10, 1960, front-page photo in *National Speed Sport News* shows one of the Daytona entries. On the passenger side front quarter panel you can clearly read "Ralph's Motors, Home of Cream Puffs, Daytona Beach—Columbus, Ga.," written in fancy script.

Below it is another photo with the headline "Top Economist." The caption reads: "M.F. Thomas, left, of Corona Del Mar, California, holds his trophies, but his chief interest is the check, which Bill France, Pres. of NASCAR, is holding. Thomas, driving a 125-horsepower Rambler American 6-cylinder, took top honors in the 1960 Pure Oil Economy Trials at the Daytona International Speedway last week. Thomas drove his Rambler 51.281 miles on one gallon of gas—nearly seven miles farther than his nearest opponent."

Del Webb's Sun City resort in Arizona was another sponsor featured in the 1960 Daytona 500. A photo in the February 3, 1960, *National Speed Sport News* is headlined, "Sun City Entry." The caption reads: "Arizona's entry in the stock car races at Daytona Beach is being piloted by Mel Larson of Phoenix and carries the name of Arizona's newest community, Sun City, a retirement village built by a firm headed by Del E. Webb, nationally known building contractor, and with Dan Topping, owner of the New York Yankees. Driver Larson is pictured at the wheel with his car and crew in front of the entrance to Sun City." Painted on the driver's side front quarter panel of the car is "Arizona," on the rear quarter panel is "Del Webb's SUN CITY."

Sponsor stenciling and logos are also clearly visible in photos from the 1960 Daytona 500. In a photo showing Tommy Irwin's No. 36 Thunderbird being pulled out of Lake Lloyd in the Daytona infield, Pure Oil and Champion Spark Plugs stickers are clearly visible. In another photo, "Courtesy Ford" can be seen in big letters on the left rear quarter panel of Marvin Panch's 1960 Ford. On the right rear quarter panel of Roy Tyner's 1960 Chevrolet is an ad for Tuxedo Plumbing Company. While these are all examples of the beginnings of NASCAR sponsorships, it's important to note that the engine specs—"320 HP"—are written across the hoods of these cars in big, bold letters that dwarf those of the sponsor names and decals.

Sponsors also started to get mentioned in NASCAR notebook items and sidebars. Chris Economaki, then the editor of *National Speed Sport News*, was one of the first automotive journalists to understand the importance of sponsors starting to take an interest in stock car racing. His columns often took special note of the performance sponsors, those who didn't just race to advertise, but who supplied vital equipment to race teams.

"One of the ironic happenings during the Daytona SpeedWeeks, racing at the new 2.5-mile speedway, was the modified win by Bubba Farr of Augusta, Georgia, on Lodge Spark Plugs," Economaki wrote in his February 24, 1960, Gas-O-Lines column. "The Champion and Auto-Lite companies were campaigning vigorously for drivers, and the race was green flagged with forty drivers on Champions, twenty-six on Auto-Lites, and one each on AC and Lodge—and of course it was Farr's Lodge-equipped car that took the first money, but no accessory prize as far as spark plugs are concerned."

But almost as soon as sponsors started to take notice of NASCAR, a controversy erupted that could have derailed the whole enterprise. The United States Auto Club (USAC), which had long sanctioned races of all kinds, issued a position paper stating that it considered sponsorship from automotive parts makers and suppliers to be detrimental to the sport. They dubbed these sponsorship deals as "payola."

To fully grasp this, you have to remember that this was in the era when record companies and radio stations were embroiled in their own payola scandal. Back then, record companies often bribed radio stations to give their artists airtime. It was a big deal. So much so that Congress held hearings on radio station payola. The result of this was a 1960 FCC ban of payola in broadcasting.

While USAC stated that free distribution of items used by all competitors (spark plugs and oil) was fine, exclusive-use contracts to single drivers or teams were detrimental to the sport. The ban was strictly enforced, and in 1979 it led to a split in the sport. In 1979, unhappy at being treated almost as second-class citizens by USAC, car owners, led by Dan Gurney, formed Championship Auto Racing Teams (CART). The financial terms were so much better for the owners that CART soon became the dominant open-wheel motor sport in the United States.

The USAC ban didn't have much impact on NASCAR; it was widely derided. Sports editor Benny Kahn (for whom the Daytona press box is named) called USAC's suggestions "libelous" in a column in the March 30, 1960, *Daytona Beach News-Journal*:

> There are many reasons why it is incorrect, yea almost libelous, to call such contracts "payola." There is no subterfuge about these contracts. They are made in writing, paid by check openly, and are untainted. They violate no law or any ethical code . . .
>
> For either USAC or NASCAR to scold members and promoters for "exclusive contracts" and to seemingly espouse open and equitable competition is underestimating the public's intelligence. They both operate in racing as "closed shops." They both require of prospective members and promoters that they sign "exclusive contracts." USAC members can't participate in any other competition except USAC's. Ditto NASCAR. The punishment for violation is fines, suspension, or banishment.
>
> The March mask USAC put on doesn't hide the truth.

Fortunately, this controversy quickly blew over and sponsors weren't scared away from NASCAR. The March 23, 1960, *National Speed Sport News* reported that Gabriel Shock Absorbers had put up $525 in prize money for the upcoming NASCAR race at Martinsville. Total prize money for the event was nearly $14,000, with the winner taking home about $3,200. A few months later, Dow Chemical announced a new racing sponsorship program that would pay drivers for using its Dowgard coolant. While much of the Dowgard money was dedicated to the Indy 500, the company posted prize money at nine NASCAR races, including the 1961 Daytona 500.

Thus was the state of sponsorship of NASCAR through the 1960s, which included few national backers—mostly automotive related—with a smattering of mom-and-pop sponsorships in local markets. But through the decade, the sponsorships—and exposure they received—began to grow.

Mom-and-pop hotels bought sponsorships and were rewarded with not only space on the cars, but also complimentary blurbs in the racing press. Companies like Fram Filters and Hanes Underwear also sponsored cars, and advertisements with NASCAR stars appeared alongside more coverage of the publicity stunts staged. At Daytona in 1967, Hanes Underwear gave the drivers free flame-retardant long underwear and offered the winner a $1,000 bonus if he opened his race suit to show off the Hanes printing underneath in victory lane. Economaki wrote about race winner Mario Andretti saying, "Mario had the skivvies on, but forgot to unzip, blowing the grand."

By the end of the decade, big-dollar, season-long sponsorships were starting to materialize.

In January 1969, Firestone announced that it would post a record $750,000 in prize money for NASCAR. The money was not just for its premier Grand National Division, which would get $649,000, but the remaining $101,000 would go to the Pacific Coast Late Model, Late Model Sportsman, Modified, and Grand Touring circuits.

"This will provide added incentive for all competitors," said NASCAR President Bill France. "Now every competitor will have a chance at some of the money available from tire manufacturers." Economaki's February 26, 1969, Editor's Notebook encapsulated nicely just how much progress the business of NASCAR had made during the 1960s:

> The metamorphosis that racing has undergone and is undergoing was vividly brought to light in the events leading up to the eleventh annual Daytona 500. The VIP list for the race included the president of the Ford Motor Company, Bunky Knudsen; General Motors Vice President John DeLorean, who is the new head of the Chevrolet division; three Chrysler vice presidents, R. B. McCurry, Phil Buckminster, and B. H. Bouwkamp; Governor Wallace of Alabama and his vice presidential running mate, General Curtis LeMay; ex-Florida Governor Haydon Burns and Representative Mendel Rivers of South Carolina; Bob Anderson, former Chrysler Plymouth head and now president of North American Rockwell; and Fred Hartley, president of the Union Oil Company of California.

But a year later, NASCAR was on the verge of going bust again. The automakers, breathless from the frantic pace of the manufacturer wars of the 1960s, were again questioning just how much they were getting out of the millions they were spending on stock car racing. Auto racing publications covering the 1970 Daytona 500 were filled with stories of the reported cutback. Ford teams were hit the hardest. The Dearborn, Michigan, automaker cut back its factory sponsorship to just three teams—the Wood Brothers, Junior Johnson, and Holman Moody. They each received a parts and engine allowance of $60,000, but just running the super speedway races alone cost a team about $200,000 in 1970, teams said. This was a marked decline from the days when all of Ford's NASCAR engines were built at Holman Moody and given to Ford teams.

"We'll have to go out and find sponsors, and we'll have to obtain more help from various promoters if we hope to continue running on a similar basis," one source said in a February 18, 1970, *National Speed Sport News* article. "The sponsorship deals will be hard to come by. It takes a whole lot of money to operate a Grand National team."

"We will still be racing," said another source, "but I'm not sure how long we can stand it."

Bill France, founder and president of NASCAR, thought it was a good thing.

"If it is true that Ford will no longer directly subsidize its teams, I would say it is a step in the right direction," France told *National Speed Sport News*. "I have always maintained that parts and supplies should be produced in quantity by the automakers and made available to anyone who wants to buy them at reasonable costs."

Economaki said the cutback was about more than money.

"One wonders how much the Ford action is based on disenchantment and how much on sound business practice," he asked in his February 18, 1970, Editor's Notebook. "One of the big reasons for a motor company falling out of love with racing is the necessity for special cars that are unlike those sold—the long-nosed Ford Talladega and the winged Dodge Daytonas being cases in point. These are out-and-out racers, and the knowledgeable public (including the kids) know this. Last year Mark Donohue's Z-28 Camaro was—in the minds of those attending Trans-Am races—closer to a showroom Z-28 than Cale Yarborough's No. 21 was to anything one could find at a Mercury dealership. The sooner the stock gets back into stock car racing, the better things will be."

A few weeks after the 1970 Daytona 500, only half of the Ford factory teams showed up for the race at Rockingham. Defending NASCAR Grand National Champion David Pearson and Donnie Allison both missed the race.

"I can't afford to run Rockingham and spend our own money," said Banjo Matthews, crew chief on Allison's car. "I am in the market for anyone who wants to put his name on the side of my cars since Ford has decided to cut expenditures."

Unsponsored Ford teams were reportedly asking for $2,000 in appearance money from Rockingham. Speedway officials told *National Speed Sport News* that the purse was only $85,430, with $18,215 to the winner, making it financially impossible for them to pay appearance money.

With Detroit getting out of racing—again—would anyone else step in?

CHAPTER FOUR
FROM RAGS TO RICHES

Junior Johnson Turns Tobacco into Gold

April 8, 1970, was quite possibly the darkest day in Junior Johnson's life. One of the most successful drivers and owners in the history of NASCAR stood solemnly in his Brushy Hollow, North Carolina, race shop, contemplating a future he would have never imagined. The man who "discovered" drafting during practice for the 1960 Daytona 500 and went on to win the race in a Chevrolet despite a ten-mile-per-hour top speed disadvantage to the dominant Fords and Pontiacs; the man author Tom Wolfe had called "the last American hero;" and the former moonshine runner whose raw driving skill had bested every federal,

73

state, and local lawman in Wilkes County, North Carolina, had just announced that he was closing his shop and folding his race team due to a lack of financing. The announcement shocked the racing world. How could this be?

"It's just too expensive," Johnson said in his soft Carolina drawl. "We just don't have the funds."

The financial pinch for Johnson came as a result of the non-compete agreement between Ford, Chevy, and Dodge. The big three were the lifeblood of parts and engineering support for NASCAR race teams, and they had agreed to another multilateral withdrawal from stock car racing. While major corporate sponsorship money was rare and extraordinarily cheap in 1970, NASCAR had become a full-time, professional racing circuit that was very much driven by money. With the automakers gone, money was tight.

"When the manufacturers got out, NASCAR suffered a reeling blow," said Charlotte Motor Speedway President Humpy Wheeler. "It left the competitors with a bunch of soon-to-be-tired equipment, no money, and really caused the whole thing to reel hard for a couple of years."

Johnson was hit as hard as anyone, and made no bones about the challenge he faced.

"I wasn't racing for glory," Johnson said. "I was racing for money, and I don't mind admitting it. I wasn't going to spend money out of my pocket. I never had to depend on what I won racing and I wasn't going to start now."

Johnson knew of what he spoke. He grew up dirt poor in the hardscrabble Brushy Mountains of post–World War II western North Carolina. By 1960, he was earning $100,000 a year as one of NASCAR's most successful drivers. It was a career that almost never came to be.

"One day my brother L. P. suggested I drive one of his cars in a fill-in race at North Wilkesboro Speedway," Johnson said. "I figured racing would be more exciting than plowing, so I stopped at the house to pick up my shoes and finished second in the first money race I'd ever been in."

But on April 8, 1970, there was no money. The automakers had gone away and what corporate sponsorship there was wasn't enough to make up the difference. Unless a major sponsor came calling with about $75,000, Johnson was going back to chicken farming.

"I told my driver, Lee Roy Yarbrough, that if he found a ride to go ahead and take it," Johnson said.

Despite these dire warnings, Johnson did show up at his home track, North Wilkesboro Speedway, a week later for the four hundred–lap NASCAR race.

"'Quitting' was the wrong word," Johnson told reporters. "When you say that, it means you quit altogether. We were still looking for a sponsor, and the biggest reason I decided to run at Wilkesboro was to put an end to the story that I was quitting for good."

In fact, Johnson didn't quit. He continued to run his race team out of his own pocket.

At the same time that Johnson and every other NASCAR team was struggling to find money, the R. J. Reynolds Tobacco Company was facing a financial dilemma of a different sort. The federal government had passed a ban on tobacco advertising on television and the Winston-Salem, North Carolina, cigarette maker didn't know what to do with all the money it had been spending with the networks.

"R. J. Reynolds had been spending millions of dollars a year on television advertising," said seven-time NASCAR champion

Richard Petty. "When the TV ban came in, they had all this money to spend and nowhere to spend it."

Johnson had been trying to get R. J. Reynolds interested in stock car racing for years. He was as good a businessman as he was a driver. He understood that the fans who filled the NASCAR grandstand every week were RJR's core customers.

"That's middle America up there," Petty said.

Very few people understood that in 1970. But it was something that the whole world would soon discover. And it would forever change the business and economics of NASCAR. With the financial help, and advertising and marketing acumen of corporate America, NASCAR would grow over the next three decades from a small, regional sport barely heard of north of the Mason-Dixon Line or west of the Mississippi to a worldwide multimedia, multibillion-dollar operation that today is second only to the National Football League. And if there's anyone to thank for that success, it's Junior Johnson.

In the wake of the television-advertising ban, RJR went to Johnson and said that it was finally interested in sponsoring his race team. But in what was perhaps the most unselfish—and fortuitous—act in the history of NASCAR, Johnson, desperate to find sponsorship money for his race team, said no to the biggest sponsorship check that was ever offered to a car owner.

"Junior didn't need millions; he just needed enough to sponsor one car," Petty said. "In 1970, a good team could run on two hundred thousand dollars a year. Many teams ran on much less."

So instead of taking the money for his own team, Johnson told RJR executive Ralph Seagraves that he needed to think bigger than just Johnson's one-car team. He needed to think about sponsoring the entire series. And in 1971, RJR could do it for a fraction of what it had been spending on national television advertising.

"Junior's argument was, 'Why have just one car when you can have them all?' " Petty said.

It would turn out to be the most momentous business decision in the history of NASCAR.

"The advertising of tobacco products on radio and TV this year was worth two hundred thirty million to the networks," Chris Economaki wrote in his November 18, 1970, Editor's Notebook. "Federal law dictates that all such commercials end come December 31 this year. This means that these tobacco companies must find other ways to exploit their products. If racing knows how to treat the tobacco companies, there's no reason why a goodly portion of this money cannot be bled into our sport."

That's exactly what happened. In December 1970, the R. J. Reynolds Tobacco Company announced that it was going to sponsor the top tier of stock car racing, then known as the NASCAR Grand National Series, through a season-long point fund that would pay drivers $100,000. In exchange, the series would become the Winston Cup. NASCAR would never be the same.

What's important to note here is that the $100,000 was just for the single-season point fund. Over the next decade, RJR would spend tens of millions more to sponsor individual races; renovate run-down racetracks; launch regional and national marketing and advertising campaigns; and pay ever-increasing purses, contingency funds, and bonuses to drivers, car owners, and racetracks. The impact was huge and immediate and started a ripple effect that continued for the next decade.

A week after RJR announced that it was funding the $100,000 Winston Cup point fund, it said it would pay more than one and a half times that much for just one race. The company would be the title sponsor of the five hundred-mile event at Talladega, Alabama, which for the next thirty years would be known as the Winston 500. The sponsorship, at $150,000, made it the richest stock car race in the world.

"The Winston 500 completes our sponsorship package for 1971 stock car racing and gets us deeply involved in this popular sport," RJR said in a press release. "We are very excited about starting our association with NASCAR and intend to work closely with them in making 1971 the best year ever for the sport of stock car racing."

That was an understatement. NASCAR Chairman Bill France put things in perspective by noting that with Winston's $100,000 point fund, 1971 would be the richest season in the history of NASCAR, with prize money for the season expected to exceed $350,000. Less than a decade later, it would be ten times that much.

"Our agreement with Winston calls for heavy advertising and promotional support on a nationwide scale, which will aid not only NASCAR racing, but all of stock car racing," France had said.

And it couldn't have come at a better time, especially with Detroit souring on NASCAR. In November 1970, Ford had announced that it was ending its multimillion-dollar auto racing programs. That was a significant blow. In 1967, Ford's racing budget, a portion of which went to NASCAR teams, peaked at $12 million. By 1970, it had dwindled to just $2 million.

"For some years, Ford Motor Company devoted considerable money, manpower, and energy to the support and sponsorship of various auto racing activities in North America," Matthew S. McLaughlin, Ford's vice president for sales, said in a statement at the time. "We believed these efforts worthwhile as an aid to the promotion of both the sport and our products. However, we believe racing activities have served their purpose and propose now to concentrate our promotional efforts on direct merchandising and sale of our products through franchised dealers. Accordingly, effective immediately, we are withdrawing from all forms of motorsports competition except for a limited divisional and dealer support of drag and off-road racing."

"Everybody was going broke," Humpy Wheeler said. "Factory equipment was wearing out. It was really tough."

NASCAR had made significant strides financially since the days when Ned Jarrett wrote that $2,000 overdraft. The Grand National Division, NASCAR's top tier, paid out $1.8 million in 1969 and $2.5 million in 1970. In late 1970, before the announcement of the RJR sponsorship, the Grand National Division was expected to pay out more than $3 million in winnings and bonus money over a fifty-four-race season that including one 600-mile race, eleven 500-mile races, and four 400-mile races.

While the RJR money was welcome, what was more important was the legitimacy that major corporate backing gave NASCAR. It was no longer just some redneck sport populated by country bumpkins who ran mostly on half-mile ovals in small southern burgs that no one had ever heard of. It had the backing of one of the richest and most profitable corporations in the world. And that gave NASCAR a legitimacy it had never had before.

In a December 16, 1970, column, Economaki again put in context just what the RJR sponsorship meant. He noted that NASCAR had once been an unregulated, dangerous, unpredictable sport relegated to the dusty red clay tracks of the Southeast. Thanks to Bill France, the sport had grown in stature, safety, and financial rewards.

"Those knights of the roaring road who jousted during NASCAR's gestation period are for the most part retired now," Economaki wrote. "But the new breed of colorful jocks has its share of dissidents who are often quick to put the rap on Big Bill and his methods. We wonder if last week's announcement that tobacco giant R. J. Reynolds would get behind NASCAR racing with a one hundred thousand dollar cash contribution and promotional backing, heretofore unheard of in the sport, made them reconsider. If it didn't, then the second shot in the double-barreled week of announcements, that the Winston 500 at the Alabama International Motor Speedway in Talladega, for a minimum purse of one hundred sixty-five thousand dollars—at a track that has yet to celebrate its second birthday—should start the thought processes churning. The records show that the boys who run at Indy had to race thirty-two years before that 500 paid better than the 165 big ones. Don't bet Reynolds came running. Months of proposing, selling, negotiating, urging, and compromise were necessary before the deal was finally struck. Where does the money go? To the participants. Who was the salesman? Big Bill. And his commission? Satisfaction in making stock car racing and NASCAR—in that order—ever bigger and ever better."

More important than the money and legitimacy that RJR brought to NASCAR, the company also brought its customers. This is important. Most people think that the business-to-business partnerships so prevalent today among NASCAR sponsors didn't start until the 1980s. In fact, they began with the Winston sponsorship in 1971.

"RJR's entry into NASCAR was seminal because of the fact that they wanted to bring their customers in to entertain them," Humpy Wheeler said.

And who were RJR's customers? Grocery stores, convenience stores, gas stations. They, in turn, brought their customers to the races. Meat and poultry producers, soft drink companies, snack and frozen food makers, and beer companies.

"Each new group that came to a NASCAR race had the same epiphany that RJR did in 1971," Wheeler said. "They looked up in the grandstand and said, 'Those are my customers.'"

Shortly after RJR announced its sponsorship, other companies announced that they, too, had decided to back NASCAR teams and races. Miller Beer signed up to sponsor the race at Ontario Motor Speedway in California, boosting the prize money to more than $200,000. Schaeffer Beer agreed to sponsor the Pocono 500. STP, which was a year away from forming perhaps the greatest partnership in the history of NASCAR with Petty Enterprises, sponsored driver Fred Lorenzen for the 1971 season at $5,000 per race, with a $120,000 ceiling over twenty races.

Over the next two decades, many of the companies that are today marquee NASCAR sponsors came on board. Coca-Cola sponsored driver Bobby Allison. Hardee's, the South Carolina–based fast food chain, sponsored driver Cale Yarborough in the 1970s and Ward Burton in the 1990s. Tide sponsored Darrell Waltrip and Ricky Rudd in the 1980s and 1990s. TranSouth Financial, the largest mortgage lender in the Southeast, sponsored the spring race at Darlington. All of this resulted—and quite possibly never would have happened—had it not been for the RJR sponsorship in 1971.

"The customers that RJR brought in were the chains," Wheeler said. "The grocery stores, the convenience stores, the drug stores. When those people came to a race, they went back and talked about it. And they brought their customers."

"No one had ever done that before," Wheeler said. "Nobody had really pushed the business side of NASCAR. That was huge."

"The sponsors took NASCAR nationwide before NASCAR went nationwide," said Richard Petty, who signed with STP for the 1972 season for $250,000, then the largest sponsorship in the history of NASCAR. "They sold these products—including their racing connection—all over the country. So when NASCAR eventually expanded out of the Southeast in the 1980s and 1990s and went to Kansas, New Hampshire, Chicago, and California, the sponsors had pre-sold the sport for us. They did a lot of the work before we even got there."

But none of this would have happened if Junior Johnson hadn't selflessly refused the RJR sponsorship money and compelled the tobacco company to think bigger and enter talks with NASCAR about sponsoring the entire series. That one decision led to a decade of financial growth that built the foundations for the business and sports behemoth that is NASCAR today.

In addition to its $100,000 point fund contribution, R. J. Reynolds also cleaned up the racetracks. In 1971, NASCAR tracks were nasty places. Some of them were dirt tracks, with mud and other debris constantly spitting into the stands off the back wheels of the cars. The concessions were no better than those stale hot dogs and flat Cokes found at Friday night high school football games. The bathrooms often consisted of stainless-steel troughs and dirty stalls with no doors and filthy toilets that didn't flush. The racetrack wasn't somewhere you took your wife and kids. These were places where bikers and other undesirables consumed cases of cheap beer. Fights often broke out. When a driver did something that the fans didn't like, a stream of beer cans, whisky bottles, and anything else the drunken fans could get their hands on would fly over the fence and onto the track, with little regard for the safety of the drivers. Winston changed all that.

"They cleaned up the speedways and made them look better," Humpy Wheeler said.

In fact, it was Winston that came up with the red-and-white paint scheme—the same one featured on the company's cigarette packaging—for the retaining walls. It made every NASCAR track look clean and uniform. Winston also started stenciling its name on the walls—and selling blank space on those walls to other sponsors. The tobacco company replaced high-school-quality scoreboards with those used at professional stadiums. It helped track owners and promoters improve the purse by either buying advertising space itself, or selling it to other sponsors like Coca-Cola and Union 76.

In short, RJR cleaned up NASCAR and helped the track owners generate more revenue. That not only brought more sponsors into the sport, but also upped the ante for the newly named Winston Cup Series, as well as NASCAR's smaller support series.

Before the start of the 1971 season, Bill France and Permatex President Pete Benoit announced that the company would essentially double the national point fund prize money for drivers in NASCAR's Late Model Sportsman and Modified divisions by matching the amount of money posted by all the weekly tracks. Permatex, like Winston, also said it would lend promotional support to any NASCAR track that ran a Permatex event during the season. Red Farmer, who took home $5,000 of the $25,000 point fund for being the 1970 Late Model Sportsman champion, said he was "thrilled" about the development.

"The Permatex Company has long been a friend to the weekly competitors who make NASCAR the fine organization it is," said France. "This new program, one of the most substantial in the history of the two divisions, will be a great boon to our competitors."

Sponsorship and point-fund deals even trickled down to the smaller weekly racing series. In March 1971, the Genesee Brewing Company of Rochester, New York, announced that it was establishing a $10,000 point fund for New York state Modified stock car competitors. The top driver on the Genesee Beer Championship Trail, a string of stock car tracks in Upstate New York, would take home $5,000 at the end of the season, a phenomenal amount for that level of racing at the time.

It didn't take long for all this sponsorship money to start impacting the drivers. In March 1971, Richard Petty pushed his 1971 NASCAR prize money total to $101,005. It was the earliest point in the season that any NASCAR driver has ever reached the $100,000 mark. The previous record had been held by Lee Roy Yarbrough, whose victory in the Firecracker 400 in July 1968 put him over the $100,000 mark.

At the end of the 1971 season, NASCAR announced that total prize money for the upcoming season would be more than $3 million, with $500,000 coming from the point fund alone, making it the largest year-end point fund in auto racing history. The bulk of that $500,000 came from Goodyear, which announced that it would start a $365,000 contingency fund award program. More than $70,000 went to the first five finishers in the thirty-two races and $18,250 was added to the Winston Cup point fund and divided among the first ten drivers in the final point standings at the end of the season. The Goodyear contribution swelled the 1972 Winston Cup point fund to $551,650. Goodyear also said it would give racing tires to the fastest ten qualifiers at all Winston Cup races.

The value of the RJR sponsorship—and the effect it had on other sponsors—was not lost on NASCAR. In one of his first acts as president of NASCAR, a position he took over from his father in January 1972, Bill France Jr. issued a White Paper outlining NASCAR's new policy on television and advertising.

Chris Economaki commented at the time on the policy, saying "The racing organization's new regulations eliminate the possibility of a conflict between the R. J. Reynolds Company, whose Winston cigarette brand sponsors NASCAR's senior series of late-model stock car races, and a competitive cigarette brand name appearing on a competing car in a televised race," in *National Speed Sport News*. "The gist of the statement, aimed at car owners and drivers, in essence puts NASCAR in the position of taking precautionary action to avoid possible embarrassment to the U.S. government and its TV restrictions currently in effect. The new policy restricts owners of cars in televised races from displaying on their cars advertising and/or decals promoting products that are currently subject to the congressional ban on TV advertising of cigarettes and the industry ban on hard liquor advertising."

And in February 1972, during Daytona SpeedWeeks, NASCAR hosted its first Promoters' Workshop, today an annual event that draws thousands of track owners, car owners, and sponsors to discuss business opportunities and strategies. The first Promoters' Workshop was sponsored by K&K Insurance, an early NASCAR backer, and hosted by two-time Grand National Champion Ned Jarrett. The agenda included seminars entitled "Why Auto Racing Businessmen Need Each Other," hosted by Bob Blundred, executive secretary of the International Association of Amusement

Parks; and "Relations with the Sports Press—Selling the Sport," hosted by Fred Marik, president of Professionals in Motion.

And so it went through the 1970s. New sponsors continued to discover the advertising and marketing potential of NASCAR, and those who already had simply poured more money into the sport, often at the expense of other racing series.

In January 1974, Royal-Crown Cola announced that it was leaving the Sports Car Club of America's Can-Am series and its sponsorship of one of the Porsche teams to spend its money in NASCAR with Ford car owner Bud Moore. Lack of televised SCCA series events was one of the reasons given. NASCAR had a contract with ABC for several races, some of which were shown live. The same week, RJR announced that it was upping its point fund sponsorship by another $20,000 to $140,000 for the twenty-nine-race Winston Cup season.

Despite the huge influx of money from a variety of corporate sponsors, it was still tough for many NASCAR teams to make ends meet. Richard Howard, a partner with Junior Johnson, told Chris Economaki that the team actually lost money.

"Howard tipped that the cost of running thirty-one races in 1972 came to $218,000," Economaki wrote in his Editor's Notebook column. "Income, in round numbers, totaled $440,000 broken down this way: Winning and point money $300,000; Coca-Cola sponsorship $80,000; and $60,000 in appearance money from tracks. The driver's share, fifty percent of winnings, only came to $150,000, leaving a net profit for the owner of $72,000. But 1973 was a different story. The cost of running twenty-nine races (during which eight wrecks took place) came to $258,000, with income of $337,000 split as follows: Prize money $162,000; Kar Kare sponsorship $80,000; appearance money from tracks

$80,000; and $15,000 from Valvoline. Deduct the driver's $81,000 share and you discover Mr. Howard had to reach into his pocket for $2,000 to even up after the season ended. It's big business, no question."

With the influx of corporate sponsorship, the television networks started to take a serious look at the Daytona 500, and NASCAR leveraged that. According to the 1974 Daytona 500 entry form, television rights generated $300,000, distributed through the standard NASCAR formula of 55 percent to the track, 25 percent to the drivers, and 20 percent to a pool for track operators who did not have televised events. As a result, each of the forty drivers had $1,800 tacked onto his winnings thanks to television.

Ironically, while Junior Johnson had done much to help stock car racing get to where it was, his financial problems had not ended. At the end of the 1974 season, his sponsor, Carling Beer, said it would not be back for another season.

"We're faced with a situation where we lose two dollars per barrel of beer sold in the Southeast," said Al Brooke, director of racing for Toronto-based Carling. "The more sales we generated, the more money we lost. We had hoped to turn this situation around, but after sitting down and analyzing the cost factor, we saw no way to do it."

Carling made a smashing entrance into stock car racing when it purchased Johnson's equipment and hired him to field the team and Cale Yarborough as driver. Carling invested an estimated $350,000 into the team.

"I'd say the sponsorship was the best in the Grand National Division," said Johnson, whose team won ten races and was runner up in the season-long points race, grossing $232,000 in winnings.

The problem for Carling was that it was a national brand—NASCAR was not.

"The Carling decision to withdraw from sponsorship of race cars could have easily been predicted when one realizes that the Canadian brewer sells its beer in this country under three names: Tuborg in the West, Stag in the Midwest, and Carling elsewhere," wrote Chris Economaki. "Whatever television exposure Cale Yarborough and Junior Johnson generated for the Carling brand, it was wasted in two-thirds of the country. This reflects a poorly conceived program going in, and when a program is not effective for a sponsor, out he goes in a hurry."

Royal Crown also left the Bud Moore team at the end of 1974, citing skyrocketing sugar prices as the reason.

"Who ever would have thought the cost of sugar would affect a stock car racing program?" Economaki asked.

Rising sugar prices didn't keep Coca-Cola from signing with Bobby Allison for the 1975 season.

While the business of big-time stock car racing continued to be plagued by the cyclical ups and downs that face any multimillion-dollar business, NASCAR's biggest problem remained how to spend all the money that was pouring in through sponsorships.

"Biggest problem for NASCAR is how to distribute three hundred fifty thousand dollars in additional promotions money from the tracks to the drivers," Economaki wrote in a December 1974 column.

Indeed, the NASCAR purse alone—without contingency money—was nearly $3 million in 1975. A new television deal with CBS for just five races paid NASCAR more than $650,000, making it the largest television contract in the history of auto racing at that time. And R. J. Reynolds continued to lend all its advertising and marketing might to NASCAR. The Winston sales staff had NASCAR promotions down to a science. In the week leading up to a race, it would set up displays, posters, co-op deals, and schedule appearances for the many Winston show cars and drivers. Where would these events happen? At the same grocery and convenience stores that were becoming increasingly interested in NASCAR because other products they sold—soda, candy, prepared foods—were NASCAR sponsors. By most estimates, RJR's paid display advertising in major media and other special promotions easily added an estimated $200,000 of benefits to NASCAR.

In 1976, the prize money increased to more than $3 million, and Darrell Waltrip and Gatorade made their first appearance together. In many ways, 1976 was a watershed year in sponsorship.

"With the Daytona 500 coming up next month, attention is focused on the success NASCAR and its Grand National gentry has had in the area of sponsorship," Chris Economaki wrote in his January 7, 1976, column. "Just about every major sponsor has returned. They include STP with Petty; Purolator with Pearson; Holly Farms with Yarborough; Nitro 9 and Hylton; K&K Insurance with Marcis; Truxmore with Dick Brooks; King's Row and Benny Parsons; plus Coca-Cola with a switch to David Hobbs from Bobby Allison. Bobby A. picks up one of five new Winston Cup car sponsors, CAM2, with an assist from First National City Travelers Checks. Other new paint jobs in NASCAR this year include Gatorade with Darrell Waltrip; the return of Pepsi-Cola with Lennie Pond; Armor-All with rookie Buddy Baker after their successful debut in the Times 500. What's more we hear an airline, a motel chain, and still another beverage are considering backing NASCAR cars this season."

In addition to direct sponsorship money, RJR and others kept pumping more money into the point fund, increasing the total purse for 1976 to more than $4 million. The point fund alone nearly doubled from $856,211 in 1975 to $1.3 million in 1976. The increase was for the new "Winner's Circle Awards Program," still around in today's Nextel Cup Series.

Before 1976, promoters often paid appearance money to make sure that the big stars—Richard Petty, Junior Johnson, Cale Yarborough—appeared at every race. Instead of making it ad hoc, track-by-track, NASCAR decided to formalize appearance money in 1976. The Winner's Circle money went to eight car owners in 1976; seven who had won at least one race in 1975 and the first non-winner to win a race in 1976. The list of winners included the STP Dodge (Richard Petty), K&K Insurance Dodge (Dave Marcis), King's Row Chevrolet (Benny Parsons), Gatorade Chevrolet (Darrell Waltrip), Holly Farms Chevrolet (Cale Yarborough), Norris Ford (Buddy Baker), and CAM2 Mercury (Bobby Allison).

"This added awards program to our already existing point funds will mean that racing teams and track operators can plan their activities on an annual basis," NASCAR President Bill France Jr. said. "The teams who have earned a spot in the program are assured of eighty thousand dollars each, and the track operators are assured of having these top teams as entrants in their 1976 Winston Cup events."

Teams on the Winner's Circle program were paid $3,000 per race for each of twenty events on tracks of one mile or more in length, and $2,000 for each of the ten events on shorter tracks. This explains why if a rookie driver finishes fifth and a veteran driver finishes fifteenth, the veteran driver makes more money. Their winnings are boosted by their participation in the Winner's

Circle program and other contingency monies that go only to the top teams. There were cries that this created a division of haves and have-nots within the sport, but the protests were never strong enough to make it go away. In fact, over the years the Winner's Circle program expanded, making it more equitable.

And so it went. In 1977, the NASCAR point fund increased to $4.5 million. By comparison, the IMSA Camel GT point fund paid just $90,000.

All of this money and the publicity paid off for NASCAR. In 1976, NASCAR drew 1,431,292 fans to the racetracks. It was the first time in the history of auto racing that NASCAR was the number one sport worldwide, beating Formula One's attendance of 1,190,500 fans. Furthermore, sponsorship and the subsequent attendance it drew became so prominent in NASCAR that each was in the lead paragraph of the Daytona 500 story in *National Speed Sport News* for the first time.

> Cale Yarborough won his second Daytona 500 on a day that attracted a record 135,000 people to the Daytona International Speedway and ran his week's earning to a tidy $93,600. Yarborough slipped his Holly Farms Chevelle to victory in the $414,500 race, beating Benny Parsons' First National City Travelers Checks' Laguna by 1.39 seconds to collect a record $63,700.

By the end of the 1977 season, Yarborough set a new single-season NASCAR earnings record of $400,576, and won his second-straight Winston Cup championship. Richard Petty earned $318,425 for the year, followed by Benny Parsons with $268,806, Darrell

Waltrip with $254,243, David Pearson with $175,561, and Buddy Baker with $118,081.

In January 1978 it was announced that NASCAR had beaten Formula One again in attendance—1.48 million to 1.42 million. And a record purse of $453,400 was on tap for the Daytona 500, besting the previous year's record of $407,800. During Daytona SpeedWeeks 1978, drivers raced for $766,000 in prize money.

NASCAR also made its first visit to New York City in January 1978. It held a press conference at the Plaza Hotel and its annual banquet at the Waldorf-Astoria Hotel. Very few in the local media covered the events, but it was a milestone nonetheless for NASCAR. In addition to the top nine drivers, all of their corporate sponsors showed up to bathe in the Gotham lights: R. J. Reynolds, First National City Travelers Checks, Stokely VanCamp, STP, Norris Industries, and Hawaiian Tropic. The banquet was held in Midtown, but very much had a Wall Street flavor, reflecting how corporate America had embraced NASCAR. And NASCAR recognized this. During the New York banquet, Citicorp's First National City Travelers Checks was given the Myers Brothers award by the National Motorsports Press Association. The award is given each year to the entity that made the greatest contribution to racing. It was the first time a major corporation had been given the award.

The tracks were starting to benefit from the increase in corporate sponsorship, as well. Charlotte Motor Speedway showed a profit of $253,403 in 1977, an increase of more than $100,000 from $143,890 the year before. In its annual report to shareholders, it reported gross revenues of $2.8 million in 1977, up from $2.3 million in 1976. Revenue from the World 600 and NAPA National 500 Winston Cup were $1.4 million and $1.2 million, respectively.

Much of that increase in revenue can be attributed to corporate sponsorship. In a 1978 interview, Bill France Sr. tipped that Pepsi-Cola buys $5,000 worth of tickets to the Daytona races each year and ticket purchases by American businesses amount to "at least fifty percent of our whole gate." That prompted Chris Economaki to observe that "the only two U.S. racing groups organized for profit and run as a business rather than a club are NASCAR and NHRA. Nuf sed."

And in 1978, the entry list for the Daytona 500 that ran in most major newspapers included a column indicating the sponsor for each driver for the first time. Television revenue was up again, as well, to $450,000. Even NASCAR crew members, who were paid little and were not well known outside of the garage area, started to benefit from all the corporate sponsorship. Ingersoll-Rand announced that it would pay $1,000 to the winning pit crew at ten NASCAR races and give $200 worth of tools to the team that moved up the most positions during a race. If NASCAR needed any more convincing that it had arrived, it came in September 1979, when President Jimmy Carter invited a group of stock car racers to the White House.

"Major league stock car racing is just thirty years old," sports columnist Bob Myers wrote in the *Charlotte Observer*. "The sport has never been quite able to outrun its image. Unfortunately and falsely, all too many people still associate stock car racing with moonshine running, fights, wild women, and a generally low class of participant and spectator.

"Granted, that's the way it once was. But that act has long been cleaned up. Time and money, the involvement of corporate giants, the improvement of super speedways, and the necessity for good public image and relations have given the sport status and prestige."

The article continued, noting the following:

Racing has become such big business that drivers, some of whom have become millionaires, team managers, and car owners have become exceedingly conscious of their image. The sanctioning body strives to settle disputes inhouse before they rage publicly and has adopted more stringent measures in dealing with violators. Stock car racing is not pure by any means, but compared with other professional sports, most of the noise is confined to the track.

If escalating attendance in NASCAR's Winston Cup division means anything, the sport has greater appeal to the broad middle class. But the upper crusts, the silk stockings and white collar set, which once snubbed the sport, is being converted. More posh and comfortable facilities and the involvement of big-buck corporations have brought the higher social status to the sport.

The nation's No. 1 stock car racing fan having the racing people to the White House for a party is simply another prestigious step in the sport's rise to respectability and its bid to escape the original image.

"I believe the future is bright," Jack O. Watson, director of special events and specialty advertising products for R. J. Reynolds, said in a January 1979 interview. "I believe corporate sponsors will increase their interest in and commitment to motorsports sponsorships. Advertisers are having increased difficulty in using traditional media, because those wanting to advertise are still beating the doors down. In magazines alone, advertisers spent twenty-one percent more in 1977 than they did in 1976. The result is advertising clutter; the situation where more and more ads and commercials are fighting for the consumers loyalty and attention. The upshot of this is that advertisers will be increasing their search for alternative ways to deliver their messages, and racing sponsorships offer such an uncluttered environment."

Darrell Waltrip's victory lane interview after winning the 1979 season-opening race at Riverside Raceway spoke volumes about how far the sport had come. "I've got to thank God, Gatorade, and Goodyear for the way we ran today."

As the 1970s came to a close, it was clear that it had been an astounding decade of growth for the business of NASCAR, thanks mostly to the RJR sponsorship that began in 1971. The 1980 season was projected to have an all-time record purse of $6 million. The Winner's Circle program had grown astronomically since its inception just a few seasons before. Teams participating in the lucrative program would each receive $114,950 during the 1980 Winston Cup season, a $23,250 increase for each team from the previous year.

"When R. J. Reynolds Tobacco Company stepped in, it was a God-sent thing," Richard Petty said. "Winston's participation has brought out more fans by making the competition more intense and attendance grows each year."

"The Winston folks coming into racing has done more for our sport than any other single thing since I have been in racing," Cale Yarborough said.

Indeed, 1980 marked RJR's tenth year of NASCAR sponsorship. While the tobacco company made it clear that it was in the business of selling Winston cigarettes, not in sanctioning races, the partnership worked remarkably well and went beyond anything that anyone had imagined in 1971. In the decade of Reynolds' involvement in NASCAR, stock car racing had become the richest motorsport in the United States and for the last four of those years the worldwide leader in attendance.

In 1970, the year before Winston entered the picture, Ford Motor Company withdrew and Chrysler Corporation announced it would support only two teams in 1971. The car owners and drivers went in search of sponsors to replace revenues no longer forthcoming from Detroit. Junior Johnson, the legendary driver who retired in 1966 to become one of the sports most successful car owners, struck up a fortuitous conversation with an R. J. Reynolds executive in his sponsor hunt.

"I'm very happy I didn't get them as a sponsor," Johnson said. "They have done more for the sport by sponsoring the complete series, plus a couple of races each year."

Although the sponsorship went beyond just money, it is a good yardstick to measure NASCAR's progress since teaming up with RJR. In 1970, NASCAR's prize money for forty-eight Grand National events was $2.5 million. By 1979, it was more than double that at $5.6 million for seventeen fewer races. The Winner's Circle, launched in 1976 and paying teams $114,950 in 1979, assured promoters that big-name drivers would appear at every event on the NASCAR schedule. The Winston Cup point fund had grown to $210,000, with an added $30,000 bonus at season's end.

Until early 1976, Petty Engineering, the Wood Brothers, and Junior Johnson were the "big three" of stock car racing, running big-bucks programs thanks to sponsorship from STP, Purolator, and Busch Beer. As a result, they had won about 70 percent of the races in the 1970s. But that all started to change. National Engineering, Gatorade, Appliance Wheels, Norris Industries, Truxmore, Stratagraph, Hawaiian Tropic, CRC Chemicals, and other sponsors signed on with equally lucrative team sponsorships. As the decade progressed, the list of NASCAR sponsors grew.

In 1980, Melling Tool Company stepped in to sponsor the M. C. Anderson cars driven by Benny Parsons. Champion Spark Plug picked up the rookie of the year program from First National City Travelers Checks. The Sears Craftsman and Union 76 pit crew competitions both increased their payouts for 1980. The drivers' share of the television money for the 1979 Daytona 500 was larger than any single event purse in 1970.

Busch Beer started a pole position award at every race in 1978 and added the Busch Clash, the richest per-mile event in racing history, in 1979. Charlotte Motor Speedway hadn't offered less than $10,000 for a pole position since 1975. NAPA, CRC Chemicals, and Winston cigarettes each sponsored two races a year. Other race sponsors included Holly Farms, Champion Spark Plug, Coca-Cola, Busch Beer, Gabriel Shock Absorbers, Sun-Drop, Northwestern Bank, and the *Los Angeles Times*. Sears DieHard batteries, Champion Spark Plug, Purolator, STP filters, Union 76 oil and gasoline, Goodyear Tire and Rubber Company, Ingersoll-Rand, and many other companies provided technical assistance along with their products.

As R. J. Reynolds had learned, other companies found the Winston Cup series to be a good place to market their products. The end result was that everyone was a big winner. And it was really just beginning.

CHAPTER FIVE

THE SPONSORSHIP SHEPHERDS

Four Hundred Cases of Coffee and a Side of Viggy

S tanding in the parking lot of the Wegmans grocery store in
Corning, New York, in August 1991, most people would have
been hard pressed to understand that they were looking at the pinnacle of NASCAR sponsorship marketing. It was the beginning of
what would be the tremendous boom in business-to-business
partnerships that dominate—and drive—NASCAR sponsorships
today. It was, for the business of NASCAR, the dawn of a new age.

Set up outside the grocery store was John Vignona, or "Viggy,"
a twenty-nine-year-old former coffee truck driver from Lake
Ronkonkoma, New York. Next to him was the Maxwell House

Racing Simulator, the newest and most advanced tool in NASCAR marketing.

Show cars—old race cars that had been retired and were now being used for promotions—had been around for a long time. Winston created the first show cars in the 1970s. The company parked them outside grocery stores, gas stations, and convenience stores during race week to lure race fans into the stores. By the mid-1980s, nearly every team and sponsor had a show car, decked out in its racing colors, which a fleet of drivers hauled around the country thirty weeks a year. Fans were excited just to be able to stand next to one and have their picture taken. I still have a photo somewhere of me at the 1988 Daytona 500, standing next to Bill Elliott's show car in the strip mall that sits across the street from Daytona International Speedway.

But General Foods, parent company of Maxwell House, Country Time, and Kool-Aid, had taken the whole show car promotion business to a new level. More than a mere show car, the Maxwell House Racing Simulator was an interactive marketing tool. Fans didn't merely stand next to it and have their picture taken, but actually got to sit in a car that had once raced around the high banks of Talladega and rubbed fenders at Martinsville. They also got to drive it. Not literally, but figuratively. It was a video game on wheels. It was a precursor to those NASCAR-themed racing games that people pump quarters into for hours on end at the arcade.

Fitted into the windshield of the Maxwell House Racing Simulator was a thirty-five-inch LCD monitor. Under the hood was not horsepower, but gigabytes. And people lined up around the block to see it and drive it.

"It was amazing," said Vignona, who today drives the motor coach for 2006 NASCAR Nextel Cup Champion Jimmie Johnson. "I would set up [the simulator] at nine o'clock in the morning and the line wouldn't stop until I closed down at eight or nine o'clock at night."

But more important than what was going on outside the store was what was going on inside. Displayed prominently were hundreds of cases of Maxwell House coffee. During the weeks leading up to the NASCAR Winston Cup race at Watkins Glen International, the store ran promotions for die-cast cars, team jackets, and other NASCAR racing collectibles. Everyone who sat in the simulator got an autographed picture of Maxwell House driver Sterling Marlin. The person with the highest score on the simulator could win race tickets or other merchandise.

In short, the Maxwell House Racing Simulator was the smartest, savviest marketing tool that had ever been developed for a NASCAR sponsor. More important, it showed corporations how they could leverage their NASCAR sponsorship and tap into the NASCAR fan base, one of the most loyal consumer segments in all of sports.

The whole marketing plan was the idea of two guys: Ed Several of General Foods and Tom Cotter, the NASCAR public relations executive who managed the account. Vignona, who handled the Maxwell House Racing Simulator, was Cotter's brother-in-law. How the three came together is as unlikely as any story in the history of American business.

Just as interesting—and indicative of how NASCAR was starting to slowly diversify beyond its traditional base—is the fact that none of the three guys involved in this landmark NASCAR promotional effort came from the South. All were New Yorkers. That may not sound so amazing today, but in the late 1980s, NASCAR was very much a southern sport dominated by southern folks.

Tom Cotter was born in 1954 in Holbrook, New York, on Long Island. His German grandfather was a car collector.

"He not only had a Mercedes-Benz, but a 1934 Ford truck," Cotter said. "He liked imported cars, which for him meant American cars. That's where I got my love of automobiles."

Cotter went to his first auto race at Islip Speedway with his Cub Scout troop when he was nine. He saw modifieds and late-model stock cars and fell in love with racing. When he was a teenager, he bought a 1940 Ford convertible for forty dollars.

"I fell in love with that car because Lumpy Rutherford on *Leave It to Beaver* drove one," Cotter said. He also bought a 1939 Woody and today has one of the most impressive Woody collections in the country.

When he graduated from high school, Cotter went to Suffolk County Community College and studied criminal justice, hoping to become a police officer or FBI agent. But a lot of people had that idea in the early 1960s.

"When I took the New York state troopers exam, there were sixty-four thousand applicants for fifty positions," Cotter said.

When a career in law enforcement didn't pan out, he went back to his first love: cars. He opened an auto repair shop in Blue Point, New York, specializing in sports cars. But even that didn't make Cotter happy.

"It was not cutting it for me," he said. "I was working six days a week; working on Christmas and Easter."

Unsure of what to do with himself, he and his wife, Pat, took the summer off and drove across Canada and the United States. Pat Vignona was the daughter of second-generation Italian immigrants on Long Island. Her grandfather laid sheetrock and was strong enough to carry two huge slabs under each arm. Her father installed hardwood floors and carpeting. When Cotter was dating Pat, he would sometimes see her younger brother, a laid-back surf bum named John who loved reggae music and hanging out at the beach all day.

When Cotter returned to Long Island, a friend was opening a Jennifer Convertibles furniture store in Manhattan. Today, Jennifer Convertibles is a nationwide chain; then, it had only three stores.

Cotter worked in the furniture business for the next five years and was on the verge of opening his own store. But he was unsure. A friend told him he was too old to change careers, but Cotter did anyway. It was 1979 and he decided he needed to get back into the car business.

That was tough in the late 1970s. The economy was in the tank; Detroit was starting to show the decay that would eventually rot the American car business to its core. Chrysler was on the verge of filing for bankruptcy protection and asking President Reagan for a federal bailout. Cotter wrote to every car company in America and didn't get a single response. He finally settled for a job at Sayville Ford on Long Island.

Joe Henry, the sales manager, told him, "Tom, there's a natural order of things in the world. Everything revolves in a circle. If you put a lot of effort into doing something, you will be rewarded, even if it comes from another direction."

"That gave me some hope," Cotter said.

He started writing about auto racing and cars for *Newsday*, the daily paper on Long Island. He also met Steve Potter, an automotive journalist who wrote for *AutoWeek* and *National Speed Sport*

News, the Ridgewood, New Jersey–based auto racing weekly owned and operated by legendary sports broadcaster Chris Economaki.

"I was doing everything I could," Cotter recalled.

Finally, Joe Henry's prediction came true. Cotter got a call from Dick Bauer, who owned a small public relations agency in Montvale, New Jersey. He had read some of Cotter's articles in *National Speed Sport News* and was looking for a deputy to help him at the agency.

"I was making thirty-two thousand dollars a year at the dealership, had a company car, and it took me fifteen minutes to get to work," Cotter said. "Going to work for Bauer, I'd make sixteen thousand dollars a year and it would take me two hours to get to work each way."

Cotter took the job and never looked back.

"I owe so much to Dick Bauer," Cotter said. "He looked inside my soul and saw that there was this kinetic energy waiting to make something happen."

Cotter was put in charge of the Ingersoll-Rand account, a NASCAR sponsor.

"I had no interest in NASCAR," Cotter said. "I was a sports car guy. But I saw NASCAR as a stepping stone. I thought that if I could learn the ropes in NASCAR, maybe one day I'd be good enough to go to work for IMSA [the premier sports-car racing series at the time]."

"I really fell in love with the industry," Cotter said. "I loved the business deals, the journalists, the manufacturers. Everything about NASCAR started to click."

Cotter's first NASCAR race was at Pocono International Raceway in July 1983. The agency hosted a barbeque and its guests were an up-and-coming team from Georgia headed up by the Elliott brothers—mechanics Ernie and Dan, and driver Bill.

"They were a team without a lot of money, but a lot of promise," Cotter recalled.

By the end of the season, Bill Elliott had won his first race in a square-body Ford Thunderbird. Bobby Allison won the championship.

"I saw all this and I had been in racing for only four or five months," Cotter said.

He handled Ingersoll-Rand for two years. The company's big event was the annual Pit Crew Championship, which honored the unsung heroes in the pits. Then in 1984 the company got out of racing, and with no other work, Cotter was relegated to editing a technical manual for Continental Rubber Company.

"I missed the pits, the races," he said.

But Joe Henry's words of wisdom kept coming true for Cotter. Dover Downs and Charlotte Motor Speedway called. Both had jobs open in their track PR department.

"I went to Charlotte, met with Humpy Wheeler and Ed Clark, the head of PR, and got the job."

Charlotte in 1985 was "fertile ground," Cotter said. "That was where I got to plant my feet in the industry. It was an amazing environment."

A lot of people were intimidated by the speedway's president, Humpy Wheeler, in those days. But Cotter flourished under him and the guidance of Ed Clark.

"To this day, [Wheeler is] one of my best friends," Cotter said. "He's an amazing human being."

Wheeler is also the P. T. Barnum of NASCAR promoters. He stages outlandish prerace shows that make the circus look like Sunday School. The speedway has featured skydivers and daredevils. In 1987, when the country was in a panic about jobs going overseas, he considered shooting a Honda Accord out of a cannon. In 1991, he staged a scene from the Gulf War. As a part of the show, a cardboard replica of the U.S.S. *New Jersey* rose up over the Turn Three wall and fired a salvo at Saddam's troops.

"The people who are intimidated by him are the ones who question their own talent and ability," Cotter said. "He's critical, he's enthusiastic, he's motivational. The four years I spent there built Tom Cotter from a furniture salesman to a racing PR person."

From 1985 to 1989, Cotter became one of the best-known PR guys in the business. After Dale Earnhardt completed the famous "pass in the grass" to win the controversial 1987 Winston all-star race, Cotter and his staff struggled to come up with a way to promote next year's race.

"It was the last lap, three cars had a chance to win," Cotter recalled. "Earnhardt in the Wrangler car, Geoff Bodine in the Levi Garrett car, and Bill Elliott in the Coors car. Earnhardt was forced down into the grass, kept control of his car, and shot into the lead. It was incredible. There were fights in the pits, fights in the grandstands."

The next January, Wheeler came to Cotter and said, "So, what's your plan to promote the Winston?"

That was a tall order, because there was no points battle. The Winston was a stand-alone, all-star event.

"We knew we had to conjure up those images again," Cotter said.

So he and his staff put grass seed in envelopes along with an invoice from the Acme Grass Seed Company addressed to Dale Earnhardt and sent them out to the media. They also took hunks of grass, some shattered automotive parts, and a beer can, put them in a box and sent them to racing journalists with a note that simply said: "Remember the Winston?"

In short, those four years at the Charlotte Motor Speedway were the greatest education Cotter could have received in racing public relations.

"Charlotte was *the* place for stock car racing in the late 1980s," Cotter said. "It was way bigger than Daytona. But it was still regional, secular. NASCAR was still an obscure, little-known sport."

But Cotter continued to grow as a publicist. His press releases and stunts became legendary throughout the business. For instance, one year he printed a press release backward, so that journalists had to hold it up to a mirror to read it.

"We were breaking ground in the PR world," Cotter said. "It just felt good to make things happen in an unorthodox manner. That was the kind of freedom that Humpy gave us."

About two and a half years into his tenure at Charlotte Motor Speedway, Wheeler called Cotter into his office for his annual review and asked him what he wanted to be doing in five or ten years.

"Like every boss, he wanted me to say, 'I want your job.' But I said I wanted to own the best PR agency in the business."

Cotter saw a lot of weakness in the industry. Part of it was due to the fact that NASCAR was still so regional and insular. Both the sport and the business were still developing. Many public relations and marketing agencies merely went through the motions, putting out the obligatory press release that got tossed into the recycling bin thirty seconds after it was opened. They made their drivers available when they finished in the top five, but did nothing to garner press when they were running in the back of the pack.

Cotter met with Max Muhlman, himself a legend in the business. He had been Ford impresario Carroll Shelby's first press agent.

"How do I do this?" Cotter asked. "Quit the speedway and wait for business to come my way?"

"The moment will come when a cornerstone piece of business will come your way," Muhlman said. "Just trust me on that."

Not long after that, Cotter got a call from Ed Several, a young hot-shot brand manager at General Foods who oversaw the Country Time Lemonade account. He wanted to talk to Cotter about leaving the speedway and opening up his own public relations agency. Cotter did just that, starting Cotter Communications. Little did the two men know that they would make NASCAR business history together.

There are remarkable similarities in Ed Several and Tom Cotter's biographies. Several grew up in suburban Mount Kisco, New York, just north of the Bronx. Like Cotter, he caught the racing bug on a small local short track, the Danbury Race Arena. In fact, he raced go-karts with two future NASCAR stars: Randy LaJoie and Jerry Nadeau.

After his brief go-kart racing career, Several graduated first in his class with a degree in marketing from Northeastern University. In 1987, after just two years as a brand manager at General Foods, Several suggested that the company look at NASCAR to promote Country Time Lemonade.

"At the time, it was a pretty outlandish suggestion in mainstream corporate America," Several said.

Two things worked in his favor. One was competition.

Some mainstream consumer brands had dabbled in NASCAR. Coca-Cola had long been a sponsor, along with Mountain Dew,

Gatorade, and a few others. But the first significant breakthrough for sponsors outside the traditional NASCAR categories of beer, tobacco, and automotive products came in 1985. That's when Folgers coffee, a rival brand to General Foods' Maxwell House, became a NASCAR sponsor. That first year, Folgers partnered in an ill-fated effort with new car owner Larry McClure and driver Joe Ruttman. A year later, things improved significantly when Folgers signed on with multicar team owner Rick Hendrick, a successful Charlotte car dealer, and up-and-coming NASCAR superstar driver Tim Richmond.

The Hendrick operation was much more successful, on and off the track. And Richmond's Hollywood good looks charmed the ladies and got Folgers more attention than it would have otherwise received. But here's what got corporate America's attention: Going into the 1986 season, Folgers was the third or fourth best-selling coffee in the country, well behind longtime industry leader Maxwell House. By the end of the 1986 season, Folgers was number one.

"Very few people know about the success of that sponsorship," Hendrick said in a December 2006 interview. "It was really the start—the trickle, really—of mainstream brands discovering the power of a NASCAR sponsorship and coming into the sport."

The deal that Folgers struck with Hendrick was based on the relatively new concept that a NASCAR sponsorship could be used to do more than just advertise a brand; it could sell product to a growing and incredibly loyal fan base. About the same time Ed Several became interested in getting Country Time Lemonade into NASCAR, Folgers told Hendrick that it would back his car if he could guarantee that the sponsorship would sell two hundred thousand cases of coffee.

"I laughed," Hendrick said. "I knew the power of a NASCAR sponsorship. Yes, it was a fraction of what it is today, but I knew we could sell two hundred thousand cases easy. I said, 'Where do I sign?' "

The sponsorship was a phenomenal success in terms of selling Folgers coffee. Folgers stayed with Hendrick through 1989, albeit with a different driver in the car almost every year. Former NASCAR Champion Benny Parsons, who died from lung cancer in January 2007, and up-and-coming driver Ken Schrader both took turns behind the wheel. In 1990, Folgers partnered with car owner Jack Roush and driver Mark Martin and missed winning the Winston Cup championship by just twenty-six points. After that, the sponsorship faded.

The success of the Folgers sponsorship was somewhat overshadowed by the sordid demise of Richmond, who died in 1989 from AIDS, then a little-known disease. News of his illness quickly spread and sent shock waves through the otherwise staid NASCAR garage. Regardless of the scandal, by any measure the Folgers sponsorship was a success. It vaulted the brand to the number one spot in its category, and its structure, based on the sales and promotion of the product, marked a new and important chapter in the evolution of NASCAR sponsorships. But it was Tom Cotter and Ed Several who would take the business model to a new level.

In 1987, the only mainstream NASCAR sponsors were Folgers and Kodak. A year later, Procter & Gamble, the other big U.S. conglomerate that discovered NASCAR racing in the late 1980s, came in with Crisco. A year later, P&G used its Tide brand to sponsor three-time NASCAR champion Darrell Waltrip.

But in 1987, NASCAR was mostly virgin territory—and a hard sell. Fortunately, Jeff Yapp, a senior marketing executive at

General Foods, had recently shot a Country Time commercial with a child actor whose father happened to be Raymond Beadle, a NASCAR team owner.

"Jeff Yapp really helped me convince the other folks at General Foods that NASCAR was a viable marketing tool," Several said. "He had talked to Beadle while they were shooting the commercial and he was very interested in looking at NASCAR."

Several knew that once he got the go-ahead, he could do great things with the sponsorship.

"It was truly a two-pronged approach," Several said. "One focus was to drive case sales at the retail level. The other was to raise brand awareness for Country Time among the broker sales force."

Back in the mid-1980s, there were hundreds of grocery store brokers. There was one for every market in the country and they sold a variety of brands and products.

"Country Time was part of a larger portfolio that included Kool-Aid and Crystal Light," Several said. "Country Time was the number three brand in that portfolio mix, so we saw racing as an opportunity to get brokers excited about the product and to gain more attention among that sales force."

The first full year of sponsorship was 1988, with new team owners Chuck Rider and Lowrance Harry and driver Michael Waltrip, Darrell's younger brother by nearly twenty years. But the Country Time car actually debuted at the last race of the 1987 season at Atlanta Motor Speedway. It was the first race car to feature the redesigned Pontiac Grand Prix bodywork that would also debut in 1988.

Several and the Country Time team hit the ground running. They were the first to do many of the sponsorship tie-ins and promotions that were new then, but commonplace today. For instance, they held corporate sales meetings at the Bahari Racing shop in Mooresville, North Carolina, outside Charlotte, using the excitement of NASCAR to motivate and drive the Country Time sales force.

Country Time was also one of the first to do cross promotions with some of its business partners. For instance, during the 1988 season, the company ran a sales contest among its brokers. The grocery broker that sold the most Country Time Lemonade during the season would get its name on the rear quarter panel of the car. As the Country Time Lemonade Pontiac pulled onto the track in Atlanta for the last race of the season, Dugan Doss, a grocery brokerage in Indianapolis, had its name splashed across the rear quarter panels of the car. At other races, Country Time gave the quarter panel to important business partners like Kroger, which sold a lot of Country Time and also sponsored the Kroger 200 Busch Series race at Indianapolis Raceway Park.

Country Time also used the track for corporate hospitality. The company would bring grocery store managers and brokers to the racetrack and entertain them in the corporate suite. This is commonplace today, but it was revolutionary in 1988. By 1991, Country Time was bringing two hundred fifty customers to the Daytona 500. It was a unique opportunity to relax, watch the races, and build business partnerships.

"We offered everything from go-kart races to golf outings," Several said. "But we also found time to make presentations on our new product lines and schedule meetings with our sales force."

In many ways, it was a cutting-edge sponsorship.

"We were taking it an extra step by doing innovative things to promote the brand," Several said. "In addition to having sales meetings at the race shop, we'd have tire changing competitions among our sales people. We were truly using the NASCAR sponsorship as a sales and motivational tool throughout the organization. We were really leveraging all the assets."

In 1989, Several brought in another General Foods brand, Maxwell House, which was still stinging from losing the number one spot in its category to NASCAR sponsor Folgers. Several—and now Cotter—pushed the envelope by developing a paint scheme that had half the car painted Country Time yellow and the other half painted Maxwell House blue. Even though Several didn't manage the Maxwell House account, his success with the Country Time brand had earned him a well-deserved reputation as the NASCAR sponsorship guru inside General Foods.

"Country Time had a built-in infrastructure for executing racing," Several said. "We had already done it for a year and had some expertise. So it made sense for us to bring Maxwell House onboard, even though it was managed by another brand team within General Foods."

It was also in 1989 that the Country Time Racing Simulator debuted. While NASCAR video games abound in arcades and along the midway at NASCAR races today, the Country Time Racing Simulator was the first.

"Again, we wanted to push the boundaries on the sponsorship," Several said. "Everyone had a show car, but we had one that the fans could actually climb into and drive."

The simulator was the brainchild of Dick Stahler of Pinnacle Marketing, another longtime auto racing PR person. He's the one who helped Country Time work out the logistics and find the technology to equip the car. Interestingly, the simulator was built by a new race team based in Ashville, North Carolina. TriStar Motorsports was a partnership between entrepreneur George

Bradshaw, crew chief Dave Fuge, and engine builder Mark Smith. In 1991, the Country Time sponsorship moved to TriStar and driver Bobby Hamilton, who went on to win rookie of the year. (Sadly, Hamilton died in January 2007 after a long battle with cancer. This book is dedicated to him.)

Again, the simulator was not just a toy. Maybe the fans saw it that way, but Several and Cotter saw it as a sophisticated marketing tool to help them achieve their ultimate goal: sell more cases of Country Time and Maxwell House. In order to get the simulator in the parking lot during race week, a store manager had to commit to buy a certain number of cases, display them, promote them within the store, and take out local advertising.

"At its core, it was a tool for sales and marketing," Several said. "But in many ways, it was so much more. It literally drove traffic to the stores. It created a lot of excitement versus just a plain show car, which was static."

Several and Cotter also understood that the people who transported and oversaw the simulator were as important as the machine itself.

"They were literally the ambassadors for the brand," Several said. "Of all the potential touch points a consumer could have with our brand, they were the most important. If the consumer had a bad experience with them, then it didn't matter what kind of promotion you were doing in the store or how clever your advertising campaign was."

While retailers and distributors had to meet certain requirements to get the simulator, Country Time was generous in spreading it around.

"We worked with all the retailers, so that everyone got a number of show car days," Several said. "Because of the depth and breadth of our program, we were able to make sure everyone got a chance to have the simulator at multiple locations."

And because each customer and market had different needs, Cotter and Several created what they called the Country Time Tool Box, a first-of-its-kind NASCAR sponsorship innovation.

"We wanted to be able to tailor our program for the customer," Several said. "So we had a menu that they could choose from. Promotions, simulator, corporate hospitality, in-house sales contests. It ran the gamut."

In 1990 the program grew again. Maxwell House split from Country Time and had its own, full-time sponsorship. Kool-Aid, another General Foods brand, also came onboard, sponsoring Michael Waltrip on the Busch circuit. With the phenomenal success of the program, it became more and more elaborate. For instance, famed NASCAR artist Sam Bass, whose gallery sits just outside Turn One at Lowe's (formerly Charlotte) Motor Speedway, did the paint scheme for the Kool-Aid car.

"We turned to him because he really captured the Kool-Aid brand," Several said. "The paint scheme featured a pitcher splashing Kool-Aid across the hood."

Like the Country Time and Maxwell House sponsorships, General Foods was increasingly innovative in promoting the Kool-Aid brand. The Kool-Aid character showed up in the pits, there were Kool-Aid die-cast cars, and a Wacky Warehouse promotion encouraged kids to save up points from Kool-Aid labels to buy NASCAR merchandise.

It was also in the Kool-Aid car that Michael Waltrip survived one of the most horrific accidents in Busch Series history. It was at the spring race in Bristol in 1990. Coming out of Turn Two, his car was shunted to the right and he slammed head on into the indentation in the wall that marked the crossover gate. The car exploded, disintegrating into a thousand pieces. Sitting in the press box that day, it was the quietest I have ever heard a track. Everyone assumed Waltrip was dead, killed instantly.

Suddenly, the sheet metal, which was strewn all over the track, started to move. The hood pushed up. Waltrip, who had literally been thrown from the car when it disintegrated around him, stood up, unharmed. There was a collective gasp from the crowd as they saw him rise from the rubble, and then thunderous applause. There were tears flowing in the grandstands and in the press box. Michael Waltrip had literally cheated death.

"The angels were there for him," his older brother Darrell said on ESPN, tears streaming down his face. Today, the car sits in the Talladega Motorsports Hall of Fame. While it will forever be remembered for that horrific accident at Bristol, it should be remembered as being part of one of the most innovative—and groundbreaking—sponsorships in the history of NASCAR.

With the success of the Country Time sponsorship, the spigot of national brands began to flow. It hasn't stopped. Moreover, these new sponsors have found increasingly creative and innovative ways to promote their sponsorships. While the images of NASCAR drivers on consumer products such as cereal, soda, and cell phones are commonplace today, it all started in the mid-1980s, first with Folgers, but most successfully with Country Time and Maxwell House.

Procter & Gamble's Tide brand often gets credit for starting the influx of mainstream sponsors into NASCAR. It certainly played a key role. Tide came onboard in 1989 with car owner Rick Hendrick and three-time NASCAR champion Darrell Waltrip. Moreover, it was a Tide brand loyalty survey that confirmed the sales and marketing power of NASCAR for many mainstream corporate sponsors.

In 1989, Procter & Gamble found out that even though Tide was the most expensive laundry detergent, NASCAR fans, regardless of their income, were incredibly brand loyal. When news of this study made its way into corporate marketing and sales offices at Fortune 500 companies around the country, the sponsorships soon followed. And much of the credit has to go to Tom Cotter and Ed Several.

"I don't know if we wrote the book, but we activated it," Several said. "We looked to activate it at every point with innovative ideas. The simulator, the tool box, our Collector Series labels featuring different drivers. In many ways, it was the first real merger between corporate America and NASCAR that unlocked all that NASCAR has to offer."

Both Cotter and Several went on to future and phenomenal success. Ed Several moved up the chain in what became Kraft Foods. He eventually became vice president of sports marketing for Kraft, overseeing everything from minor league baseball to the Super Bowl. He then went to Spaulding, the equipment manufacturer, and became vice president of marketing services.

"A lot of the things I learned in NASCAR, I was able to apply at Spaulding," he said.

As an exhibitor at the annual PGA trade show with Spaulding, Several met Reed Expositions, which handles the promotions and logistics for a variety of trade shows throughout the country. Today, he's a senior vice president of marketing, overseeing the PGA Show; the Eastern Sports Show, the country's largest consumer outdoor show; and other events.

Tom Cotter took his experience and expertise from Country Time and built one of the most respected NASCAR public relations agencies in the business, Cotter Communications. He also worked with former Burson-Marsteller advertising executive Bob Boyles to create the first ever sponsor-spokesman training programs for drivers. The program taught drivers how to answer—and sometimes dodge—tough questions, and how to mention the sponsor without having it sound rehearsed or forced.

Cotter also developed a reputation within NASCAR as being the go-to guy for new sponsors who wanted to come into the sport. Among those companies he brought into NASCAR were Sears, Western Auto, Gwaltney, and John Deere.

One of Deere's first corporate hospitality events was a disaster. It was the 1997 opening of the Texas Motor Speedway, which was only partially completed. It rained, turning unpaved parking lots into seas of mud. Traffic control was so abysmal that fans abandoned their cars on the side of the road and walked to the speedway. Many were still outside when the green flag dropped. Some of the food that was served in the hospitality NASCAR suites was uncooked. All of this only exacerbated the John Deere chairman's general dissatisfaction with NASCAR and the company's sponsorship.

"I'm not predisposed to racing," he told Cotter. "I'm predisposed to golf because we sell turf products."

"This company had just spent three million dollars on a Busch sponsorship and everything that could go wrong, did go wrong," Cotter said.

Despite all that, by the end of the race the sales manager had a commitment from a former Caterpillar customer to convert to John Deere.

"This just made my year," he told Cotter after the race. "This one deal paid for the whole racing sponsorship."

John Deere wasn't the only sponsor to discover the power of NASCAR. In 1991, Western Auto and driver Darrell Waltrip used the model that Cotter and Several had developed at General Foods and took it to a new level. The team created what they called a Performance Team Vendor Program, and it was truly unique and innovative.

Western Auto was the primary sponsor on the car. Its logo and colors appeared prominently on the hood of the car and the front of Waltrip's uniform. But "associate sponsors" ultimately paid for the sponsorship.

The associate sponsors were the key to the Performance Team Vendor Program. Western Auto sold space not on the car, but in retail stores, to sponsors. Here's how it worked: If you were part of the associate sponsorship program, you paid Western Auto for preferred shelf space in the store. You also became a preferred supplier, meaning that if someone came into a Western Auto store and asked for an oil filter for a 1991 Chevy, but didn't specify a brand, they automatically got a filter from a Performance Team Vendor Program sponsor.

AC Delco was Western Auto's biggest partner on Waltrip's car in the early 1990s. In fact, the car was identified as the "No. 17 Western Auto/AC Delco Chevrolet." Other sponsors who got preferred space in the store, on the car, and on the side of Waltrip's hauler were Fram and Havoline.

"There were platinum, gold, and bronze sponsorship packages," said Van Colley, Waltrip's longtime business partner. "If you paid X amount, it got you prominent display at the end of an aisle in Western Auto stores. Western Auto also put your name on its bags. Some of the bigger sponsors had access to Darrell for corporate events, and all were mentioned in television commercials."

In fact, some NASCAR sponsors that were also Western Auto customers used Western Auto television commercials to promote their drivers and products. For instance, driver Davey Allison talked up the benefits of Havoline Oil, his sponsor, whose products were for sale at Western Auto stores. So, too, did Hut Stricklin, who was sponsored by Raybestos brakes.

"It was another way to skin the cat," Colley said. "It was a pioneering way to fund an expensive program. And it was contrary to what most other sponsors were doing, which was just coming in and writing a check for the whole car."

These innovative deals have become increasingly important as the price of a NASCAR sponsorship has gone up. When Waltrip and Western Auto began the Performance Team Vendor Program in 1991, a full-time sponsorship cost about $2 million. In just a few years, it had more than doubled to about $5 million. And Waltrip wasn't making any money off the deal.

"He would take the money he got from Western Auto, appearance money, and put it all back into the team," Colley said. "He never took a paycheck."

By 1997, the cost of a NASCAR sponsorship was too high—for Waltrip and Western Auto. A year later, Dale Earnhardt Jr. signed with Budweiser for a reported $10 million.

"That raised the price of poker," Colley said.

Since then, the price of NASCAR sponsorships has continued to skyrocket. Lowe's pays a reported $25 million to be on the hood of NASCAR Nextel Cup Champion Jimmie Johnson's car. Even average teams are getting upwards of $20 million.

"As recently as three or four years ago, the base was ten to twelve million dollars," Colley said. "Today it's fifteen to eighteen million dollars."

Good or bad, this is all the result of the phenomenal sponsorship growth that began in the mid-1980s. In the 1970s, sponsorships were dominated by beer, auto parts, and cigarettes, and the price was much lower. "Fifty thousand dollars would get your name on the best car in the field," Cotter said.

In the 1980s, the average sponsorship was six figures. Lake Speed, an average driver who saw modest success in NASCAR, got $800,000 from sponsor Bullseye barbeque sauce. In the 1990s, sponsorships eclipsed the million-dollar mark.

"It cost five million dollars to be on the hood of a top car," Cotter said. "It was the business-to-business generation. It was Caterpillar and John Deere and companies that did business with those companies. The decade really saw consumers become secondary to the sponsorship equation, because consumers couldn't go out and buy anything from Caterpillar."

In short, the advent of sophisticated B2B sponsorships like those at General Foods and Western Auto were by far the greatest business development for NASCAR in the 1980s. They got corporate America interested in NASCAR like never before. With increased corporate interest came a boon in television advertising and revenue. This in turn pushed NASCAR to expand beyond its traditional southern roots. These two trends—television and regional growth—are detailed in the next two chapters.

CHAPTER SIX

MAMA, I'M GONNA BE ON TV

The Small Screen Revolution

N o look at the phenomenal growth of NASCAR sponsorship would be complete without a discussion of the impact of television. At the end of 2005, NASCAR announced an eight-year, $4.8 billion television contract with Fox/SPEED Channel, ABC/ESPN, and TNT starting with the 2007 season. This deal put NASCAR in the same financial stratosphere as Major League Baseball, the NBA, and its chief rival, the NFL. Like much of NASCAR's financial evolution, it took a long time to get there.

"In the early 1980s, the top drivers in NASCAR were still eating bologna sandwiches, sitting on a Goodyear tire on the back of their trailer," said Patti Wheeler. "Television changed all that."

She should know. Patti Wheeler was an eyewitness to the phenomenal growth of NASCAR and television. The daughter of Charlotte Motor Speedway President Humpy Wheeler, she grew up in the sport. When she was a teenager in the 1970s and NBC and ABC were broadcasting one or two races a year, she was already working for the networks.

"NASCAR was not covered outside of a few local papers," she said. "So these very intelligent TV guys would come down from New York and they really didn't know anything about NASCAR. It wasn't their fault; no one else outside of the Southeast knew very much about it either."

Wheeler became their muse. She explained what "push" was, why teams took out a "round of wedge" during pit stops halfway through a race, and this mysterious thing called "the draft." She also directed them toward the most colorful personalities in the sport. She introduced them to "the King," a tall lanky guy with a bushy moustache, toothy grin, and straw cowboy hat who was the Terry Bradshaw, Reggie Jackson, and Dr. J of NASCAR. She also introduced them to an unstoppable guy from Kannapolis, North Carolina, who some called "Ironhead," but the whole world would eventually know simply as "Dale."

Wheeler is a good guide through the history of NASCAR and television. She lived it.

In 1982 she went to work for World Sports Enterprises, an independent production company that was part of TBS. In addition to directing race coverage, she also produced a weekly half-hour racing program. Through the late 1980s, she was the producer for a variety of networks—TBS, ESPN, USA—covering a variety of motorsports—NASCAR, CART, NHRA.

"You name a series and a network, and we did something with them," Wheeler said.

In 1991, she went over to The Nashville Network (TNN) to become director of motorsports and executive producer and line producer for the network's NASCAR broadcasts. Three years later she moved back to Charlotte and became president of World Sports, then the largest motorsports production company in the world. When Fox/NBC bid for the universal rights to NASCAR television, she formed Wheeler Television and began producing race coverage for Fox. She also did special productions, such as Dale Earnhardt's funeral. Most recently, she was named executive producer of NASCAR Images, the sport's photo and film archives.

NASCAR's relationship with television up through the early 1980s had been hit and miss at best. The number of races shown and the price for broadcast rights had both gone up, but it was nowhere near where it is today. Like many people and projects in the world of NASCAR, television got off to a rather inauspicious start.

The record books will tell you that famed NASCAR driver Marvin Panch won the compact car races at Daytona in February 1960. What most won't tell you is how he did it.

There were two races that day. After the first race, Panch and his crew decided to install a new rear end in his car. But that was not what held him up for the start of the second race.

"I was tied up by the TV people after the first race," Panch told *National Speed Sport News*. "[Race officials] had promised me they'd hold up the second race but they didn't."

Panch missed the start of the second race, delayed by a television interview. By the time he got his car back onto the track, the lead pack was already headed down the back straight. But luck was with him that day. A huge wreck took out the front runners, and Panch missed it because he was in the back of the field.

"It looked doubtful that I could come from so far behind," he said in a postrace interview. "But they handed it to me. I was lucky I started out last. I'd probably have been in that front pack and got tangled up with them in the mess."

While many mark 1979 as the first year the Daytona 500 was broadcast live, that's not exactly true. TelePrompTer, then the largest cable network in the United States, used twelve cameras, slow-motion instant replay, and trackside interviews to produce a live broadcast of the 1971 Daytona 500. It wasn't shown on television, but broadcast into movie theaters around the country.

"For the first time in live coverage of a motorsports event, TelePrompTer will be able to show four separate pictures simultaneously on the larger theater and auditorium screens across the country where the greatest of all stock car races will be shown," the press release said.

Three years later, the 1974 Daytona 500 generated $300,000 in television rights money. In 1975, CBS signed a deal with NASCAR to broadcast five races at a cost of $650,000, the largest television rights money to date for a motorsports event. The two also agreed to broadcast the World 600 from Charlotte and the Winston 500 from Talladega, but on a tape-delay.

"Not only is added televising of NASCAR races a boon for the sport itself, but it will be highly attractive to sponsors of racing teams at a time when exposure for them is most needed," NASCAR President Bill France Sr. said at the time. The rights fee was not disclosed, but France said the exposure for the sport and for sponsors far overshadowed any added revenue.

In 1975, NASCAR also signed a three-year deal with ABC to broadcast the Daytona 500. This contract marked the first baby steps toward broadcasting NASCAR races live. ABC showed the start of the race live, but then switched over to coverage of the Olympics from Innsbruck, Austria. The network then returned to Daytona later in the afternoon for live coverage of the race finish.

A year later, 19.5 million Americans watched the race on ABC, earning the broadcast a 12.9 Nielsen rating, or 35 percent of the total TV audience. That was still small in comparison to the Super Bowl or the World Series, but for NASCAR those were huge numbers. In early 1978, legendary NBC sports producer Don Ohlmeyer announced that the network was interested in more than just NASCAR's premier Winston Cup Series. The network would start broadcasting select NASCAR Modified and Sportsman events, as well as USAC midget and sprint car races.

"Our basic philosophy is that interest in auto racing extends beyond the Grand National cars in NASCAR and the champ cars in USAC," Ohlmeyer said. "What we hope to have is a well-rounded racing schedule, and we are including one national championship and one stock car race in USAC."

Later that year, CBS inked the five-year deal to broadcast the Daytona 500, including the first live wire-to-wire coverage. The pact was reportedly worth more than $1 million per race, and it would set the stage for the historic 1979 broadcast that concluded with Donnie Allison and Cale Yarborough duking it out on the backstretch and Richard Petty capturing his sixth Daytona 500 win. That broadcast, many argue, is what set NASCAR on the path to the billion-dollar television contract it has today.

"The true significance of Monday's announcement seems to be that television has included auto racing in the current sports rating wars, which have seen major viewing events like the Olympics, the Kentucky Derby, and the World Series switching networks at ever-increasing prices," Chris Economaki wrote in his Editor's Notebook column of the *National Speed Sport News*. "With such price increases, most experts feel, comes a corresponding increase in the significance and prestige of the televised event as the networks struggle for larger and larger audiences."

The money couldn't have come at a better time as NASCAR teams, despite increased purses and sponsorships, were still struggling to make ends meet. Benny Parsons told Economaki in 1978 that it cost $500,000 to run a one-driver, three-car Winston Cup Grand National team over the thirty-race season, but that his 1977 winnings totaled only $312,000.

Bill France Sr., speaking of the importance of sponsorship and television said, "A football lasts a whole season. Connecting rods, crankshafts, and valves don't."

This is the television world that Patti Wheeler walked into in the early 1980s. What many people didn't know then was that NASCAR's television future lay with cable, not the broadcast networks.

"Cable in the early 1980s was not well distributed and they had no money," Wheeler said.

NASCAR had tried to start a syndicated network to broadcast its races on tape delay on cable. NASCAR took its radio network, MRN, and created MRN TV. It failed financially, but only "because it was before its time," Wheeler said.

By the mid-1980s, cable started to get better market penetration, especially in urban areas. A few cable networks even started to turn a profit. But NASCAR was still a conundrum to many network executives. They didn't understand the appeal, and NASCAR races weren't well suited for television's rigid format. Races lasted anywhere from four to five hours, which was a huge commitment for a television network in the 1980s. And if it rained, there were no tapes of old races you could run.

The one thing that NASCAR had going for it in the 1980s was that it was cheap in comparison to the major stick-and-ball sports. The rights to individual NASCAR races were selling for $200,000 or less. That was a paltry sum compared to what other sports were getting.

Then a little-known cable network from Bristol, Connecticut, ESPN, came calling and forever changed NASCAR. ESPN wasn't in the greatest financial shape and its distribution was still paltry compared to the broadcast stations, but it was looking for Sunday afternoon programming that would compete with the NFL, which was dominating the time slot. This, combined with the relative low cost of a NASCAR broadcast, created one of the greatest marriages in the history of sports broadcasting.

ESPN broadcast its first NASCAR race in 1981. Three years later, the upstart cable network was televising sixty-three auto races a year, including a dozen NASCAR Winston Cup Series events. In 1987, the network was given the Myers Brothers Award for outstanding contribution to the sport. After accepting the award, the network announced that it would carry fifteen Winston Cup races, live, flag-to-flag, in 1988.

As the NASCAR-television marriage progressed through the decade, there was one minor hiccup. Dr. Alan Blum, editor of the *New York State Journal of Medicine,* gave voice to what many people saw, but were afraid to say. R. J. Reynold's sponsorship of NASCAR was nothing more than a lawyerly way around the 1971 tobacco-advertising ban. In 1985, he called for the federal government to throw NASCAR off of television because its Winston Cup Series was in direct violation of the 1971 statute. He asked the federal government to review what he called the "flaunting by television networks and their cigarette advertisers" of the law.

Dr. Blum was right. The NASCAR races, with prominent sponsorship from R. J. Reynolds and its Winston brand, were in violation of the cigarette advertising ban. Fortunately for NASCAR, his cries of foul fell on deaf ears. No one ever really investigated his claims and the issue died a quick death. The financial juggernaut that was NASCAR and television continued to roll.

In 1991, Wheeler became director of motorsports at TNN in Nashville. While NASCAR had matured significantly over the past decade in terms of its television business model, tracks were still selling individual broadcast rights to races. With few exceptions, those rights were sold for just a few hundred dollars. NASCAR was still relatively cheap by industry standards.

In 1990, the NFL sold its television rights package for $925 million. By contrast, by the end of the decade the cable and broadcast networks were still only paying about $1 million per race for NASCAR. Then in 1999, NASCAR announced that it was consolidating the rights to broadcast all its races. For the 2000 season, Fox Sports, F/X, NBC, and TNT agreed to pay $2.4 billion for a new six-year package, covering the Winston Cup and Busch Series. It was a convoluted deal. Fox and F/X would televise races one through sixteen of the 2001, 2003, and 2005 seasons and races two through seventeen of the 2002, 2004, and 2006 seasons. Fox would air the Daytona 500 in the odd-numbered years. All Busch Series races during that part of the season would also be on Fox/FX. NBC and TNT would televise the final seventeen races of the even-numbered years as well as the Daytona 500 and the last eighteen races of the odd-numbered years, as well as all Busch Series races held in that time of the year. ESPN retained the rights to the Craftsman Truck Series through 2002 under a separate contract. Beginning in 2003, the SPEED Channel became the exclusive broadcast home for the trucks. While it was not the perfect, single-network consolidated deal that many had said NASCAR needed, it put NASCAR on a footing with Major League Baseball, the NBA, and the NFL.

There was a minor hitch in the deal, which was blown out of proportion by some media reports. In 2001, SpeedVision was owned by a consortium of cable companies. Fox bought the network and changed the name to SPEED Channel (now just SPEED). NASCAR started a program called *NASCAR TV on SPEED*. Some speculated that this was a fallback position, that Fox had agreed to create a twenty-four-hour NASCAR-only channel as part of the television rights deals. That's not exactly how it happened.

"NASCAR did not believe a twenty-four/seven channel would be as effective and fan friendly as *NASCAR TV on SPEED*," said NASCAR spokesman Andrew Giangola.

Whether intentional or not, SPEED has essentially morphed into the NASCAR channel over the past few years. Its lineup includes a slew of NASCAR content, including prerace and postrace analysis shows, weekly call-in shows, and rebroadcasts of historic races. It also broadcasts the NASCAR Craftsman Truck Series races. In 2007, ESPN also started a nightly half-hour NASCAR show, in addition to its race coverage.

NASCAR and Fox also formed NASCAR Images, a film archive and production company, when they signed the 2000 broadcast deal. Today, NASCAR is the sole owner of NASCAR Images. The net result of all this is that NASCAR is now in the same league with the other major sports in terms of television broadcast rights.

The NASCAR broadcasts also made incredible technological strides during the 1980s and 1990s. Originally, the broadcasts just featured the cars going around in the track, with maybe two cameras, and the commentators in the booth. Over the decades, ESPN increasingly adapted new technology to the broadcasts. One of the most unique was the "foot cam." The network installed a small camera in the floorboard of Ricky Rudd's Tide Chevrolet at Sears Point, the two-mile road course outside San Francisco. Considered one of the best road racers among NASCAR drivers, the camera showed Rudd's footwork as he negotiated the twisty turns.

Another favorite—especially when Dale Earnhardt was driving—was the bumper cam. It showed fans just how close drivers came to one another going into the tight corners at Martinsville or moving up to maximize the draft at Talladega.

Like Roone Arledge, the legendary ABC producer who revolutionized televised football coverage, ESPN adapted every new technology that it could to the track. It earned ESPN a slew of Emmy Awards, and firmly established the network as a smart, sophisticated broadcaster of sporting events.

Fox took it up another notch in 2000 when it bought the NASCAR television rights. Perhaps the most innovative thing the network did was have veteran NASCAR crew chief Jeff Hammond standing by with a cutaway car. As technology issues came up during the race— spring settings, tire wear, camber, and caster—Hammond would explain to the television audience just what was happening on the track. It was revolutionary for NASCAR television broadcasts.

But in terms of our discussion, the true revolution was the consolidated television contract, which put NASCAR on equal footing with the NFL, NBA, and other major league sports.

"It put them in the big leagues," Wheeler said. "Having me and my counterparts at ESPN and TBS bid on the races individually wasn't 'big league.' By consolidating the broadcast rights, NASCAR used all its leverage and it paid off."

What NASCAR was doing was taking a page out of the financial playbook of the NFL. Professional football had struggled up through the late 1950s. It wasn't until the 1958 NFL championship game between the New York Giants and the Baltimore Colts that America discovered the NFL. Up until then, in the minds of most American sports fans, the NFL was a weak third league to Major League Baseball and college football, which many considered a purer form of the game.

That all started to change in the early 1960s, when legendary NFL Commissioner Pete Rozelle and New York Giants owners Jack and Wellington Mara convinced the other NFL owners that it was in their long-term financial interest to consolidate broadcast rights and share revenues equally. In short, it created a revenue structure that guaranteed that a team from Green Bay, the sixty-eighth television market with about 430,000 households, could compete with the Giants, who reside in New York, the number one television market with about 7.4 million television households.

In the first national television contract in 1962, CBS paid $4.6 million a year to broadcast NFL games. In 1964, that figure jumped to an astonishing $28.2 million for two years, or $14.1 million a year. Since then, the NFL television rights package has grown astronomically. In 1974, the NFL earned $63 million for its national broadcast rights. Five years later, the figure jumped to

$164 million. In 1982 it was $427 million, in 1987 it jumped to $468 million, and in 1990 it rose to $925 million.

This is the path NASCAR hopes to follow with its new consolidated broadcast rights package. As it delivers bigger audiences, it can demand increasingly more money for the rights to reach that audience. The upward pressure on NASCAR broadcast rights is further aided by the well-known brand loyalty of NASCAR audiences and the fact that many Fortune 500 companies aren't just NASCAR advertisers, but sponsors.

While all this makes perfect business sense, what ultimately sells a sports broadcast is good competition, which ultimately makes for good television. This may be NASCAR's Achilles' heel. Wheeler and others are quick to point out that it was the authenticity of NASCAR—the fierce battles and rivalries, the real personalities—that first captured a national television audience in the mid-1980s.

"It was phenomenal drama that we may never see again," Wheeler said.

She points to extraordinary races like the 1986 Richmond race where Dale Earnhardt and Rusty Wallace took each other out and Kyle Petty, who had been in third place much of the day, won.

"Hollywood scriptwriters couldn't have come up with this stuff," she said. "When you really look back at the 1980s—watch 1980s races—the names, the characters, and the stories are just phenomenal. Talk about the ultimate male soap opera."

She also cites some other important trends from the 1980s that boosted the popularity of NASCAR and the cost of broadcast rights. She gives a lot of credit to David Hall, the president of TNN, who decided to start a bidding war with ESPN and TBS for the rights to NASCAR races in 1991.

"He did more than up the ante," Wheeler said. "He started bringing country music stars to the racetrack, and producing other shows that melded the two key interests of TNN's core audience—country music and NASCAR. It was more than just putting races on the air."

She also notes that what got both television networks and sponsors interested in NASCAR in the mid-1980s was the revelation that nearly 50 percent of the NASCAR audience was female.

"It has never been below forty percent, even way back then," she said. "Because women drive cars, too. We don't play football, but we drive cars."

She cites the examples of Tim Richmond and Folgers coffee and Ricky Rudd and Tide and the incredible increase in sales that corresponded with those sponsorships in the mid-1980s.

"The key difference was that they weren't automotive products," Wheeler said. "They were women's products, and that's what got everyone's attention in New York. Men do not buy laundry detergent."

She also credits David Hill, the producer at Fox who took the NASCAR broadcast to new heights in terms of production and quality when Fox acquired the broadcast rights in 2000.

"I think what David Hill did with their talent, graphics, and production quality is phenomenal," Wheeler said. "It not only took the quality and content of the broadcast to a new level, but the genuine joy and love of the sport that they have is evident. Many of the things we'd tried and dabbled with in the 1990s, they made work. They put the resources in it to make it work."

But ultimately what makes NASCAR so appealing is not the technical quality of the broadcast or the colorful commentary of the broadcasters, but the very real personalities that sold NASCAR to a nationwide TV audience in the 1980s and keeps them tuning in today.

"The key challenge that NASCAR faces is not turning off the fans," Wheeler said. "They have to keep the whole corporatization of the sport under control. Fans don't tune in to see a billboard, they tune in to see a character and a great story."

It was those great stories and personalities that grew the NASCAR television audience exponentially through the 1980s and 1990s. Today, NASCAR is second only to the NFL in terms of regular season ratings. From 1994 to 2003, the number of NASCAR households and viewers increased by more than 140 percent.

The average number of viewers that tuned in to network broadcasts of NASCAR races during the 2003 season was 8.6 million, up 15 percent from the 7.5 million who tuned in during the 1994 season. In 2003, over two-thirds of the NASCAR Winston Cup Series season aired on network television. The average network rating for the 2003 NASCAR Winston Cup Series season was 5.4, unchanged from the average network rating of 5.4 in 1994.

Over on cable television, the average number of viewers during the 2003 season was 5.6 million, up 92 percent from 2.9 million in 1994. The average cable rating in 2003 was 4.3, up 34 percent over the 3.2 average in 1994.

The rating for the rain-delayed 2003 Daytona 500 was 9.8 on Fox, up 2 percent from the 9.6 rating for the 1994 Daytona 500 on CBS. An average of 16.8 million viewers tuned in to the 2003 Daytona 500, up 24 percent from the average of 13.6 million viewers in 1994.

NASCAR's junior series are also doing well on television. All of the twenty-eight NASCAR Busch Series events were aired on cable television during the 2004 season. In 2003, there were thirty-four events, only nine of which aired on network television. In 1994, the NASCAR Craftsman Truck Series did not exist. The first year of the series was 1995. In 2003, all twenty-five events of the series aired live on SPEED Channel.

NASCAR hit a speed bump in 2006 when ratings declined by 6.4 percent from 2005. Attendance at the track was also down. I discuss this at length in the Epilogue, but the short answer is that it's too early to tell if the 2006 ratings dip is part of a broader trend.

Of course, as NASCAR television coverage grew through the 1980s and 1990s, NASCAR sponsorships and purses continued to increase, as well. Newer drivers continued to benefit from NASCAR's Winner's Circle program. Terry Labonte's win at the Southern 500 in 1980 earned him a winning paycheck of $27,325. But because it qualified him for the Winner's Circle program, it also meant $32,600 in bonus money for the remainder of the 1980 season and $104,700 in 1981.

As the decade progressed, the purses and bonuses continued to grow. At the start of the 1981 season, Darrell Waltrip collected $71,500 just for winning the Busch Clash, the relatively new all-star race at Daytona. By season's end, he had his first Winston Cup championship and set a new single-season money record of $764,842. Waltrip's season-long total, with sponsorship from Mountain Dew, shattered the former mark of $591,599 set by Al Unser in 1978 when he won the Indy 500. In press interviews during the first NASCAR banquet held in New York, Waltrip revealed that he spent $300,000 of his own money the previous season to buy out his contract with DiGard Racing and move over to Junior Johnson's stable. Thanks to his 1981 winnings, he was able to pay it all back after the October Charlotte race. He said the loan was a "gamble," but added jokingly that if he would have known how the 1981 season would turn out, he would have borrowed "twice as much."

NASCAR paid out $726,920 in season-end bonuses in 1981, with Waltrip taking home $124,292. He won $693,342 during the season and $10,000 as driver of the year. In total, NASCAR paid out $7.2 million in 1981.

DiGard didn't fare so bad, either. In February 1982, Bobby Allison took home $120,630 for winning the Daytona 500 and he earned another $50,000 for winning the Busch Clash. Down the road, his victory qualified him for the Winner's Circle, and he took home $135,000 in 1982 and $140,000 in 1983.

NASCAR was another winner on the financial front. In December 1984, International Speedway Corporation reported a record net profit for the year of more than $2.6 million. Gross receipts increased to $20.2 million, up from $17.1 million the previous year. Net income was up $776,000 to $2.6 million, or 68 cents a share, from 48 cents a year ago.

In 1986, Geoff Bodine, driving Rick Hendrick's Levi Garrett/Exxon Chevrolet, took home $192,715 for his Daytona 500 victory. Dale Earnhardt, who finished fourteenth, earned $61,655 in the 500.

Chris Economaki, writing in his February 19, 1986, Editor's Notebook, wrote: "SpeedWeeks 1986 will go down as hard to beat— from a business standpoint. Sunday's 500 wasn't one of the best races, but the crowd—the biggest in Florida sports history—loved the exciting finish. There were more companies, more top executives, more marketing chiefs, more advertising agency account execs, more product PR men, and more out-and-out hustlers in

MAMA, I'M GONNA BE ON TV

town than ever before. Some guy tried to sell me a watch while I
was having a cup of coffee at a HoJos! Meetings between team
members and corporate reps were an ongoing process. Whereas a
company, a few years back, tried to align itself with a team that
could field a car capable of winning, now they hope they can find
one that can make the field! Racing has come a long way, baby."

The end of the 1986 season marked another money record.
But it also marked a milestone in terms of contingency spon-
sors. At the year-end banquet, champion Dale Earnhardt picked
up post-season awards checks of $750,779, including one from
RJR for $55,779, which included point fund awards from
Winston cigarettes and NASCAR's Winston Cup tracks.
Earnhardt also won $100,000 through the Unocal 76 Winners
Contingency Point Fund; $25,000 for winning the True Value
Hard Charger Award; $25,000 for winning the Stewart-Warner
Track Force Award; $20,000 through the Gatorade Circle of
Champions program; $10,000 from Goodyear Tires; $10,000
from Goodyear Belts; $10,000 from Champion Spark Plugs; and
$5,000 from the STP Corporation.

All told, in 1986, more than $2 million in postseason awards
were presented to the top twenty drivers and car owners: $205,000
from Unocal to the top-four drivers, $50,000 from True Value,
$40,000 from STP, $30,000 from Busch Beer, $20,000 from
Gatorade, $10,000 from Champion Spark Plugs, and $20,000
from Goodyear. Ingersoll-Rand gave away $60,000 to the winners
of its Ingersoll-Rand Pit Crew Championship, $40,000 of which
went to Gary Nelson, crew chief for Geoff Bodine. Earnhardt
picked up an additional $25,000 through the Stewart-Warner
Track Force Award for completing the most competitive miles
over the season. Bud Moore, crew chief for Ricky Rudd's

Motorcraft Ford, received $20,000 as TRW Mechanic of the Year, while Randy Dorton, engine builder for Bodine and Tim Richmond, won $10,000 through the Michigan Engine Bearings Engine Builder of the Year.

In February 1987, Bullseye barbecue sauce offered a $100,000 bonus to driver Ron Bouchard if he won the Daytona 500. When he didn't, the company said it would pay a $50,000 bonus for a victory in the Motorcraft 500 at Atlanta, the Coca-Cola 600 at Charlotte, the Miller High Life 400 at Michigan, the Firecracker 400 at Daytona, the Talladega 500 at Talladega, and the Delaware 500 at Dover Downs. The $400,000 deal ($100,000 for the Daytona 500 and $50,000 for the subsequent six races) would have paid one-third to the driver, one-third to the car owner, and one-third to the crew.

In March 1989, Alan Kulwicki, one of the transplants from the Midwest-based American Speed Association, eclipsed the $1 million mark in winnings with his second-place finish at Rockingham. It only took him 88 races to do it. By comparison, it took Darrell Waltrip 158 starts to earn his first million, Bill Elliott 117, and Rusty Wallace 96.

Wallace was the 1989 Winston Cup champion and took home the richest point fund check in racing history—$1,042,360. Wallace's season-long winnings totaled more than $6 million. NASCAR's first champion, Red Byron, won just $5,800 in 1949. Wallace has television to thank for helping him collect that paycheck.

Wallace also was the first NASCAR champion from outside the Southeast since New York's Bill Rexford, who won the title in 1950.

"Those close to the sport note an increasing interest in personnel crew chiefs, engine builders, and drivers from the

Midwest and North," Economaki wrote in his Editor's Notebook from the 1989 Winston Cup banquet. "The standout performances of Wallace and fellow Missourian Ken Schrader; along with Mark Martin (Arkansas) and Butch Miller (Michigan), who was recently named to replace southerner Rick Mast in the Travis Carter Racing operation; and upstate New Yorker Steve Hmeil as Martin's team head; plus Midwesterners Rick Wetzel and Mark Isler winning the top two positions in the Engine Builder of the Year contest signals that the southern monopoly in Winston Cup racing may come to an end. Those who know racing say the brightest newcomer on the stock car scene yet to make a Winston Cup start is Rich Bickle of Wisconsin. . . ."

Columnist Benny Phillips summed up the accomplishments of the decade in a year-end piece in *National Speed Sport News* entitled, "NASCAR Racing Grew Into Adulthood in the 1980s." He wrote:

> The 1980s mark the end of a major era in NASCAR racing expansion, new stars, new tracks, and new sponsors.
>
> Late in the decade, television, led by CBS and ESPN, began carrying every race live, flag-to-flag.
>
> NASCAR, now playing to sellout crowds everywhere, took the show into new markets like San Francisco and Phoenix, and also added legendary Watkins Glen to its schedule.
>
> The 1980s have also seen the cost of racing jump from eight hundred thousand dollars or so up to well over two million dollars a year. This

has led to the demise of many independents in the sport.

Guys like Stan Barrett, the Hollywood stuntman who would sometimes show up at a NASCAR race, and Jocko Maggiacomo, the Upstate New York driver, not only didn't have the money to run an entire twenty-nine-race season, they didn't even have enough to show up for a race weekend. The last of the independents was Dave Marcis, the great driver from Wisconsin. The only reason he was able to still compete was the fact that he was one of the Goodyear test drivers. Driving for Goodyear, not his own independent team, was what paid the bills.

These independents were increasingly replaced by multicar teams, which many saw as the corporatization of NASCAR. It was no longer a sport where a good driver could bring the family sedan to the track and hope to compete. You had to have a multimillion-dollar budget to support your one hundred thousand square foot race shop that housed sophisticated engine and car building equipment that was operated by engine builders, chassis specialists, and aerodynamic engineers.

Rick Hendrick was one of the first of this generation of multicar team owners. In the mid-1980s, he had a three-car team with Geoff Bodine, Ricky Rudd, and Terry Labonte. That was the beginning of the end for the independents. Soon would come other multicar teams owned by Jack Roush, Roger Penske, and Joe Gibbs. The last of the successful single-car teams was Richard Childress, who campaigned well into the 1990s fielding cars for Dale Earnhardt.

The rising cost of NASCAR also made it difficult for new drivers to get into the sport. And while NASCAR has a sophisticated diversity program today that has yielded moderate results, women are rare in the garage area. Patty Moise ran a limited schedule in the Busch Series in the 1980s and competed in the Daytona 500. In January 1988, Janet Guthrie, the only woman to drive in the Indianapolis 500 and the Daytona 500, called NASCAR a "closed shop."

"Winston Cup racing is the only top-level sport in the country that meets the standards of an Aryan nation," she said. "It's white and it's male."

"The only thing men have that women do not have—and it's not what you think—is money," she said during an address at the Charlotte Motor Speedway's annual media tour. "If you think the reason for the absence of some in racing is an absence of talent, you should probably re-examine your thinking."

Guthrie's pleas were not taken seriously. It would be nearly two decades before a serious woman driver—Danica Patrick—would flirt with NASCAR. Of more grave concern was the rising corporate presence in NASCAR, and how it was changing the sport. Personally, I've always seen progress and technology as a double-edged sword. Yes, you lose some of the past, but what you gain is often better. I think NASCAR is on the cusp of this today. As the 2007 season begins, NASCAR has lost some of those fans who rooted for the Earnhardts and Wallaces of the 1980s. These were the guys who weren't quite as polished as Jimmie Johnson and didn't mind trading a little paint on the track. But whatever fans NASCAR lost from the old days have been replaced by the new fans who either don't remember those days or don't care. They like what they see and are pushing NASCAR's popularity.

Gary London, my colleague at *National Speed Sport News* and one of the greatest columnists in all of motorsports, represents the other camp. He wrote the following in his July 31, 1991, Racing Journal column:

> Sponsorship, schmonsorship. That's what I say.
>
> So many things in racing have changed in recent years. The biggest is the commercialism involved in the sport. Television has a lot to do with it. The trouble is a lot of people are treating it like it is more important than the racing itself. There are actually individuals who think people go to or watch races on TV just to be sold something.
>
> I'm alarmed at how so many drivers have prostituted themselves because they think they have to blurt out their sponsors' names every time someone asks them the time. A good example is Mark Martin, who has Folgerized us to death every time a mike is shoved in his face. I guess it didn't do any good as Folgers is getting out of racing. Remember how many zillion times Geoff Bodine blurted out 'Levi Garrett' when he drove for that team? Where's Levi Garrett today? Bodine does the same sickening act for Budweiser and the word is that Anheuser-Busch wants another driver in Junior Johnson's No. 11.
>
> There are many drivers who never feel inclined to give their sponsor those embarrassing plugs, yet manage to keep them. I get letters from people who say please don't offend any of these sponsors since they are needed. Absurd.

"These conglomerates and other smaller companies are not in racing for charitable purposes; it's a tax deduction. Sure, with all the television exposure, they are getting plenty of airtime. This is done for their own self-serving interests. Yet for some strange reason, somebody in racing got the idea that you must follow these people around with a roll of toilet paper (please make it the official toilet paper of NASCAR while you're at it). I see no other sport or activity where this prevails.

If Folgers is allowed to use television to further its IRS return, then I might have to change this column to the *Valley Stream Little League/Valley Stream Volunteer Fire Department/American Cancer Society/North Shore Animal League/Racing Journal*. How would you like that?

For the most part, people were just fine with the torrent of sponsorship that poured into NASCAR in the 1980s and 1990s. This sponsorship is what created the NASCAR we have today. And sponsorship continues to grow.

In 2007, NASCAR and DirecTV will provide a new service called Hot Pass that will cover the races from the team's perspective. The brainchild of Fox Sports President David Hill, DirecTV will have a state-of-the-art, high-definition production truck at each race to broadcast five dedicated driver channels that will each have their own broadcast team.

"We have been working with NASCAR for a couple of years now," said Eric Shanks, vice president of advanced products and new media for DirecTV. "And we have noticed that while there is a race going on, there are fans who really follow a driver, or a car, or maybe a team and they do it all race long. So, there are as many as forty races within the race that fans are following."

In addition to the live national broadcasts of the races, DirecTV will offer driver point-of-view cameras looking out the front windshield with telemetry readings. There will also be overhead cameras, pit box cameras, and corner cameras.

And in 2007, Sirius will replace XM as the new home of NASCAR. In addition to the race broadcast, Sirius will have ten "team talk" channels that will carry driver-to-crew communications.

Clearly NASCAR has come a long way from the days when the Daytona 500 was broadcast live into a movie theater. Along the way, it has also expanded geographically.

CHAPTER SEVEN

WHEN NASCAR COMES TO TOWN

How Much Is That Track in the Midwest?

K ansas City Mayor Carol Marinovich had been called a lot of names during her political career, but this was the first time anyone had compared her to Adolf Hitler. What could motivate such vitriolic name calling of the otherwise well-liked city leader, the first woman to ever hold that position? She wanted to bring a NASCAR track to town in 1997.

Two predominant trends drove NASCAR's explosive growth in the 1980s. One was the diversification of national sponsors, away from traditional beer and tobacco companies and toward more mainstream consumer brands like Tide and Country Time.

The other was television. Thanks to flag-to-flag coverage of the Daytona 500 and other big races, as well as the almost-perfect marriage of ESPN and NASCAR, the sport expanded well beyond its traditional southern roots during the 1980s.

In the 1990s, these trends continued. Increasingly diverse sponsors came into the sport. The ESPN audience grew exponentially, creating competition for the broadcast rights from other cable stations like TBS, TNN, and USA. Then a third growth element was added.

To meet increasing demand for its product around the country, NASCAR started going to racetracks beyond its traditional southern base. It started with pre-existing tracks, like Watkins Glen, New York, and Sonoma, California. With the success of those races, International Speedway Corporation (ISC) and Speedway Motorsports Inc. (SMI), the two predominant and publicly traded NASCAR track owners, began to build new racetracks in new markets and acquire existing ones. By the end of the decade, just a handful of independent tracks remained. SMI built new tracks in Texas and Las Vegas, while ISC built new venues in Chicago, Kansas City, California, and Miami. In short, during the 1980s, television and a growing number of diversified national sponsors brought NASCAR into homes across America. In the 1990s, NASCAR literally moved into new markets across the country.

Racetracks are important to the growth of the business of NASCAR for a number of reasons. It was during the 1990s track expansion and buying spree that Speedway Motorsports Inc. sold the first naming right for racetracks—to the Lowe's home improvement chain in Charlotte and to Silicon Valley high-tech firm Infineon for what used to be Sears Point International

Raceway. But that's where the trend stopped. No other track has sold naming rights.

Tracks also are important because of what fans have come to expect in terms of comfort and amenities. As I've noted, when R. J. Reynolds came into NASCAR in 1971, it started by cleaning up the sport. Back then, putting doors on the bathroom stalls was considered progress. Today's NASCAR fans and sponsors expect much more. Comfortable seating. Good sight lines. Luxury amenities such as suites with gourmet food and a place to park their $1 million motor homes.

All of the new tracks built in the 1990s—Texas, Las Vegas, Chicago, Kansas—incorporated these new standards. Kansas Speedway is a good example of the kinds of new tracks that are being built, as well as the political battles that NASCAR and its partners often have to fight. For most of the 1990s, these were battles that NASCAR eventually won, but that has not been the case recently. For more than a decade, NASCAR tried to get a track built in the New York metropolitan area. It finally gave up in late 2006. As this book went to press, NASCAR abandonded its bid to build a track in Washington, across Puget Sound from Seattle. But we're getting ahead of ourselves again.

"At first, I didn't know what a speedway was," Marinovich said. "But all it took was one trip to convince me of the possibilities a new NASCAR track brings to a community. I went to the opening of the California Speedway in 1997 and said, 'Let's go for it.' "

Like a lot of municipalities, Kansas City, Kansas—known as KCK to distinguish it from neighboring Kansas City, Missouri, which is known as KC MO—was interested in a NASCAR track as an economic revitalization tool. KCK had long been the ugly step-brother of its bigger, more successful Missouri namesake. KCK was considered the wrong side of the tracks. As one local resident said, "A lot of episodes of *Cops* are shot over there."

Despite the fact that KCK needed an economic booster shot, getting the track built would not be a slam dunk. But two things worked in Mayor Marinovich's favor.

The potential economic impact from the speedway—estimated at $170 million a year—was more money than KCK had seen in decades. Furthermore, it would be new money to the local economy, with the majority of fans coming from outside the metropolitan area to spend money on race tickets, souvenirs, hotels, dining, and the like.

Interestingly, the mayor wasn't initially convinced that the racetrack would be as big a financial boon as the projections predicted. But she thought it might be a spark to ignite economic development of the long-stagnant area, and to her that made the whole project worthwhile.

She was also helped by the fact that the two governments on the west side of the river—KCK and Wyandotte County—had been unified.

"We had only one local government involved," she said. "That made it immensely easier, especially when it came to some of the tough economic decisions, like tax-increment financing. Instead of two bodies—city and county—these measures only had to pass one."

The fact that there was just one government entity also made it easier for International Speedway Corporation, the single largest owner of NASCAR tracks, which brought the proposal to Mayor Marinovich and her staff.

Initially, ISC was looking at a number of sites around Kansas City. Gardner, Kansas, about twenty-five miles south of the city, was in the running until the whole thing fell apart at an ugly public meeting where local residents who would be relocated by the track became almost violent in their opposition. The meeting turned into a developer's nightmare, with residents crying and shaking their fists at the local politicians who were supporting the track. With Gardner out, the bidding came down to just two sites: Kansas City, Kansas, and Kansas City, Missouri.

"From KCK's perspective, we were interested in it because we wanted to use the track to spur development along that corridor," Marinovich said.

The proposed site was about twenty-five miles west of downtown KCK. It was an older, urban community that had no major retail chains or hotels, and just a handful of locally owned mom-and-pop restaurants.

"People had to leave the community to shop, go out to eat, go to the movies," Marinovich said. "Development had sort of passed it by. The sense of community was pretty low."

The long-term goal, the mayor said, was to use the track to spur development in the area, as well as expand and diversify the tax base. Yes, the NASCAR track would bring in a huge influx of cash and business for two weekends a year, but the mayor hoped the track would be the catalyst for a broader economic revival of the area. Even if it proved to be the huge economic juggernaut that proponents claimed, that catalyst would come at a steep price. The initial cost projections for the track were $200 million, but that figure quickly grew to $250 million. But unlike other major sports stadium and arena projects—something discussed at length in a few pages—NASCAR wasn't asking for the city and state to pick up two-thirds of the cost. NASCAR typically asks for about 20 percent of the cost from taxpayers, usually in the form of tax abatements or low-interest state financing.

"There was an eighty million dollar gap at one point between what the city was willing to contribute and what ISC was willing to contribute," Marinovich said. "We got it down to three million."

But this debate, like many economic development projects, was about a lot more than economics. Like the politicians in Gardner who had nearly been tarred, feathered, and run out of town on a rail, Mayor Marinovich, the county board, and board staff still faced some tough public meetings.

"We knew it was going to be very contentious," she said. "We were going to force one hundred sixty families to relocate. It was a very emotional setting."

Going into the meeting, she wasn't sure if she would even make a motion to vote on the track. She wanted to hear what the residents had to say.

"I wasn't quite sure yet what was in the best interest of the public I served."

The meeting lasted five hours and was as wrought with emotion as anyone had expected. A lot of senior citizens—direct descendants of the people who had originally homesteaded the property—showed up, angry that they were going to be forced to move so that the government could build something that they saw as nothing more than an overgrown entertainment complex that would cause traffic jams twice a year and forever change the neighborhood they loved and cherished.

"It quickly became obvious to me that no new information was being provided during the meeting," Marinovich said. "I quickly saw how emotional the people were becoming and thought all another public meeting would do would be to heighten those emotions and it would be a lose-lose for everyone."

She made a motion to the newly created Unified Board of Commissioners. Before the vote, she said that she would vote only in the case of a tie, but that if she were the first to vote she would vote "yes."

"I thought as mayor I needed to put my neck out first."

The measure passed ten to zero.

This may seem odd given the vehement opposition from residents. But this truly is a case of politicians doing what they thought was right for the community. Indeed, Marinovich and the rest of the county board were vilified by former residents for months in letters to the editor and in newspaper stories leading up to the opening of the track. But the government leaders had become so frustrated that any efforts to revitalize KCK had so far failed, that they saw the NASCAR proposal as their one and only hope. In short, it was a big gamble for them, for NASCAR, and for the city.

Although the track had just cleared an important procedural hurdle, it was far from a done deal. Over the next few months, local government would fight over what type of financing to use, how long to finance it, and how much the state would contribute. Again, Marinovich was lucky in that Kansas Governor Bill Graves was an early and strong supporter of the new NASCAR track. And throughout the negotiations and debates, Mayor Marinovich kept pressing her key goal that this was about more than just the racetrack; it was about long-term economic development for the city.

"Before the Kansas Speedway project came along, we didn't know if our city was dying or dead," she said. "There was nothing out there. But I knew development would come once the speedway was built.

"The racetrack's economic benefits will be immense, not only for Wyandotte County and metropolitan Kansas City, but for the entire state of Kansas," Governor Graves said when he signed the bill that would help finance the track. "My hat is off to Mayor Marinovich and the Unified Government for their leadership in helping bring major league auto racing to Kansas. Their enthusiasm and support for this effort are what enables us to be where we are today."

Where the city and county were was on the hook for 20 percent of the construction cost. Again, the deal was nowhere near as egregious—and over-exaggerated in its economic impact—as the average NFL stadium financing project, but it was still a big chunk of change. Under terms of the agreement, the taxpayers would pick up about $50 million of the estimated $250 million cost. And unlike other local sports stadium initiatives, such as the Truman Sports Complex, the package did not require financing through general obligation bonds.

The project's final financial breakdown looked like this: ISC committed $90 million in cash. An additional $107 million was financed through two bond issues, to be paid for through speedway revenues over thirty years. Interest would accrue, putting the total repayment of the bonds at $178 million. The balance came from $33 million in state highway funds to provide needed road improvements and $22 million in state and local incentives. So in essence, the taxpayers were on the hook for about $55 million.

The local chamber of commerce estimated the speedway's annual economic benefit to be about $170 million a year—or, as it said, "the equivalent of a Super Bowl in Kansas City every year." A Coopers & Lybrand study said the speedway would generate about $40 million in economic activity per year just in Wyandotte

County. That's about $1.2 billion over the thirty-year life of the bonds. The study also estimated the adjusted total output created for the state of Kansas at about $120 million a year. And unlike an NFL stadium, which draws the majority of its fans from the immediate metro area, only 30 percent of race attendees were expected to be from the Kansas City area.

"As a metro, we cannot afford to miss this exceptional economic development opportunity," argued Robert J. Marcusse, president of the Kansas City Area Development Council.

Here are just a few of the other estimated economic impacts from the speedway:

· 224,000 overnight visitors annually.

· $63.7 million spent locally on construction materials.

· 3,378 construction jobs.

· $86 million impact on local payrolls.

· 390 permanent full- and part-time jobs once the track opened.

· $5.7 million spent in the local economy annually.

· $12 million annually in local, state, and federal taxes.

· $6.2 million in annual media exposure.

So what happened? In short, all of the predictions came true. In its first year, Kansas Speedway sold season tickets to the speedway's two annual NASCAR events in all fifty states. Every NASCAR Nextel Cup race ever held there has been a sellout. And not long after the speedway opened, the economic development that Mayor Marinovich had promised did indeed materialize. In fact, the local government bought four hundred acres adjacent to the new track and is reaping the benefits, too.

Today, shopping malls, restaurants, theaters, and a growing residential neighborhood surround the Kansas Speedway.

Arthur Bryant's, the world-famous Kansas City barbecue restaurant, is there. Nearly every chain restaurant in the country—McDonald's, Steak and Shake, Applebee's, Hooters—is there. Visitors find a slew of new hotels, including a Great Wolf Lodge with an indoor water park. And there are plans for Schlitterbahn, the hottest water park complex in America, to open there in 2007. The T-Bones, the local minor league baseball team, built their new stadium, Community American Ballpark, across the street from the racetrack. When they had the ribbon cutting for the new Nebraska Furniture Mart, another anchor store for the community, its owner, a somewhat successful entrepreneur named Warren Buffet, leaned over to Mayor Marinovich and asked, "Do you have any more of this property available?"

"It quickly became clear that the Kansas Speedway had created that economic spark that we'd hoped it would," Marinovich said.

When the speedway first opened, there were less than one hundred homes a year being built in the neighborhood. Today, there are more than five hundred a year going up. More important, the city used to collect about $15,000 a year in property taxes. Today, it takes in more than $7 million.

"New families are moving out there in droves," said Marinovich, who has since left office and now is a senior vice president at public relations agency Fleishman Hillard, a unit of Omnicom. "The shopping, restaurants, and entertainment venues draw ten to twelve million people a year."

The addition of Schlitterbahn is expected to continue the trend. The multibillion dollar project will include restaurants and river walk, more retail, and condos, and is expected to draw visitors from a dozen states.

"They would never have thought about Kansas City without the racetrack," she said. "It'll be one of the largest amusement park projects in the country. And it's just another example of the effect of the speedway."

Perhaps more important, the economic development spurred by the Kansas Speedway is starting to move eastward, toward some of Kansas City's more economically challenged neighborhoods.

"In some of our older neighborhoods, we're tearing down more homes than we're building," Marinovich said. "[The neighborhoods] have some of the lowest per capita incomes in the state. It's a hard sell to get developers in there, but if some of the speedway development can help that, it'll just be another boon to the community."

To put the economic impact—and cost—of a new NASCAR track in perspective, you have to compare it with the National Football League, the number one spectator sport in the country. Over the past two decades, more than twenty NFL franchises have built new or renovated stadiums. Most have been built with significant taxpayer help. Indeed, there is a widespread misconception that there is a broad trend toward privately financed stadiums in the NFL. While there are a few examples—Washington's FedEx Field and New England's Gillette Stadium—the fact is that the average taxpayer contribution for new NFL stadiums continues to hover at around 70 percent. How do NFL franchises, which earn hundreds of millions of dollars in revenue a year, get taxpayers to agree to pay for nearly three-quarters of the cost of a new stadium?

Along with stadium proposals come an industry of economic consultants who praise the benefits of a new stadium. New jobs, new income, more prestige for a community. But there are just as many economists and consultants not in the employ of the NFL or the local city council who can easily dispel the myths of these economic benefits. Nevertheless, taxpayers seem to have bottomless pockets when it comes to helping the local sports franchise build a new stadium or arena.

In a first-quarter 2001 *Kansas City Federal Reserve Bank Economic Review* article entitled "What Are the Benefits of Hosting a Major League Sports Franchise?" economists John Rappaport and Chad Wilkerson made a pretty compelling case that few—if any—of the economic benefits materialize from a new sports stadium. From 1995 through 2003, about $6.4 billion dollars, or an average of $304 million, was spent to build or substantially refurbish twenty-one NFL stadiums. The public contribution was about $4.4 billion, an average of $209 million, or roughly 69 percent of the construction costs. Another $1 billion was spent to renovate existing stadiums. As a result, by the end of 2004, nearly 70 percent of big-league sports franchises were playing in stadiums or arenas that had either been opened or were renovated in the previous ten years. For NFL teams, taxpayers paid for about $200 million, or 62 percent, of the $325 million average cost of a new stadium in 2001. And while generous returns were promised for these investments, few ever materialized.

For instance, when the Seahawks were lobbying for a new stadium, they told Seattle taxpayers that the team's presence increased local annual economic output by $69 million, personal income by $41 million, raised $3.3 million in state and local taxes, and created 1,264 jobs. Pro-stadium advocates in Cincinnati said that stadiums built for the football Bengals and baseball Reds would generate $1.1 billion in economic activity for the Cincinnati metro area and create 18,461 temporary jobs.

"These impact studies that justify stadium projects can be subject to a number of criticisms," the Kansas City Fed study said. "Many of the studies look at only the positive effects of hosting a major league franchise. Taking account of negative effects such as offsetting job losses, however, would produce much lower estimates of the net impact on local economic development. Moreover, the impact studies almost always fail to measure benefits in a form that can be compared with public outlays. While increases in output, increases in personal income, and job creation all measure increases in underlying economic activity, how should a metro area value these increases?"

A 1997 study by economists Robert A. Baade and Allen R. Sanderson entitled "The Employment Effect of Teams and Sports Facilities" looked at the subsequent growth of cities that acquired new sports teams between 1958 and 1993 and "found no significant increases in employment or output."

Another study found that per capita income actually fell in metro areas that added sports franchises. Economists Bruce Hamilton and Peter Kahn looked at the annual returns Maryland residents saw from the addition of the Baltimore Ravens. While the community saw a net economic impact of roughly $1 million, that paled in comparison to the $14 million of annual public cost to finance the new stadium.

In looking at the impact of stadiums overall on local economies, the authors of the Kansas City Fed study looked at two measures in particular: job creation and tax revenue benefits. They found that to accurately assess the impact of a professional sports franchise, one would need to measure not just the number of jobs created, but also the number of jobs lost.

"The presence of a professional sports team also creates job losses, because individuals who spend money to attend sports events have less to spend at businesses elsewhere in the host metro area," the authors said. "Less spending results in job losses."

King Banaian, chairman of the economics department at St. Cloud State University in Minnesota, agrees that in painting a rosy picture of promised benefits of new stadium construction, proponents rarely ever discuss the opportunity costs associated with building a stadium.

"You have to look at a piece of land and consider its uses now, for a stadium, or if you built a factory," Banaian said. "Is a stadium going to get you the best return? Is it the best use of that land? Usually not."

Banaian also points out that when a stadium is plunked down in a neighborhood, it becomes the predominant attraction in that neighborhood. That's good on the days that there are games, but what about the rest of the year?

"What kind of activity is there around the Metrodome [in Minneapolis, Minnesota] on days when there are no games?" he asks. "These places [stadiums and the surrounding neighborhood] become black holes when there are no events."

And cities—especially if they've lost a sports franchise—often give away the farm in outlandish revenue-sharing deals that would appall most taxpayers if they knew all the details.

For instance, the football Cardinals left St. Louis in 1987 after the city refused to give them $120 million for a new stadium. Yet less than three years later, voters approved $280 million in public funds for a new football stadium—before they even had a team to play in it. Depending on how you crunch the numbers, the Rams contributed only 20 percent of the total cost of relocating the team from Los Angeles to a new stadium in St. Louis, which some economists estimate cost taxpayers an aggregate $720 million. In exchange, the Rams get 100 percent of all concession revenues and 75 percent of advertising revenue (90 percent if it exceeds $6 million). Before the team even agreed to move, a local business group guaranteed that 85 percent of the suites and club seats would be sold and the Rams could keep all the revenue.

"There is the potential for the Rams to 'cover' the annual cost of their lease from the advertising they sell in the stadium built for them with taxpayers' funds," writes sports economist Mark Rosentraub in his book, *Major League Losers*.

When Baltimore lost the Colts to Indianapolis, the city gave away the farm to the Cleveland Browns and owner Art Modell. The new lease guaranteed the team—to be called the Baltimore Ravens—thirty years of free rent, plus a $50 million cash relocation bonus. The team also would get a 10 percent management fee for concerts and other non-football events. Tom Cushman, a columnist for the *San Diego Union-Tribune*, said that in terms of sweetheart stadium deals, "call this one the Demi Moore special."

And, of course, an economic analysis proved him absolutely right. In a 1996 Congressional Research Service Study, economist Dennis Zimmer estimated that the rosy scenario presented by stadium advocates overestimated the impact of the new Ravens stadium by 236 percent. Based upon public expenditures for the stadium, each job that was created cost the taxpayers about $127,000. By comparison, Maryland's Sunny Day Fund, an economic development program, creates jobs at a cost of about $6,000.

Zimmer also made the same arguments that St. Cloud State economist King Banaian did about opportunity costs. Zimmer said that any economic assessment of stadiums has to look at not just what the taxpayers got for their money, but what they didn't get.

"If an alternative generates $2 million of benefits net of subsidy and the stadium generates $1.5 million net of subsidy, the stadium can be viewed as imposing a $0.5 million loss on taxpayers, not a $1.5 million benefit," he said.

Cleveland, of course, was devastated with the loss of the Browns, the team that the city identified with more than any other. As John Cagan and Neil de Mause note in *Field of Schemes,* it was "perhaps the only time *The New York Times* has ever run a photograph of a grown man wearing a dog mask, smoking a cigar, and weeping."

So what did Cleveland do after being burned by the Browns, who moved to Baltimore, which was reeling from being burned by the Colts, who had moved to Indianapolis? It vowed to tear down Municipal Stadium and build a brand new, football-only stadium for $290 million, the majority of it financed by the city of Cleveland, the state of Ohio, Cuyahoga County, and the Regional Transit Authority. The new team, also called the Cleveland Browns, has a very generous thirty-year lease, gets all stadium rentals and pays for maintenance and operations but no property taxes. Upon hearing the terms of the deal, Modell, happily ensconced in Baltimore, said, "if they gave me half of what they're doing now, I'd still be in Cleveland."

As in other examples in this book, Cleveland ended up paying more for a new franchise than it was willing to pay to keep the old one. And it was willing to do so shortly after spending an estimated $350 million to $450 million—mostly from the taxpayers—for other pro sports teams. The money was used to renovate the central downtown market and build Jacobs Field for the baseball Indians and Gund Arena for the NBA's Cavaliers.

But perhaps the sweetheart of all deals—and the one with the most potentially dire consequences—was hatched about three hours south of Lake Erie in Cincinnati. In 1996, Hamilton County voters approved a five-cent sales tax that was supposed to raise more than $1 billion over twenty years. More than $450 million was earmarked for a new stadium for the Bengals, which team owner Mike Brown named after his father, legendary football coach Paul Brown. The thirty-year lease for the 65,000-seat stadium, which features 114 luxury suites and 7,620 club seats, allows the Bengals to keep all revenues from ticket sales, suites, advertising, broadcasting rights, and concessions. The team also gets a share of revenue for non-Bengal events.

What was the Bengals' contribution? The team kicked in $25 million from the sale of personal seat licenses toward the cost of the stadium—which came in $50 million over budget. The Bengals also will pay $11.5 million in rent over nine years of the thirty-year lease. The team will continue to pay about $1 million in game-day operating expenses, but Hamilton County will begin reimbursing the team in 2017.

That was the plan anyway. In August 2005, the fund that was earmarked for paying off the stadium debt and rolling back property taxes was expected to be about $8 million in the red by 2006.

"The deficit could hit almost $300 million by 2032, when the debt is to be repaid," the *Cincinnati Inquirer* reported.

The problem is that the county expected sales tax collections to grow by 3 percent a year. But from 2000 to 2005, receipts only grew by 1.3 percent. If the tax receipts continue to grow at a 2 percent rate, the deficit by 2032 will be an estimated $191.5 million.

At 3 percent, the shortfall will drop to just about $81 million. Either way, the taxpayers will be on the hook for a lot of money.

Hamilton County's troubles apparently weren't enough to deter the city of Glendale, Arizona, from spending $450 million to build a new football stadium for the Arizona—formerly St. Louis—Cardinals. In 2006, the team began play at the 63,000-seat stadium—expandable to 73,000—with eighty-eight luxury suites on two levels. The stadium has a retractable roof and features a club level that'll accommodate about seven thousand fans, with access to a private lounge area. The stadium's natural-grass field features a unique system that allows maintenance crews to roll the field out of one end of the facility to give it more sun. The "field tray" is 234 feet wide by 400 feet long and takes approximately 45 minutes to move into and out of the stadium. The 152,000-square-foot concrete stadium floor has a utility grid embedded in it so it can host conventions, trade shows, and concerts. The stadium is aligned along a northwest to southeast axis, so as to give maximum exposure to the sun for the grass field while keeping most of the patrons in the shade.

"An open roof will allow fans to take advantage of Arizona's world-famous climate and clear blue skies, but when closed will allow the building to host large conventions, trade shows, concerts, as well as other indoor events," according to the City of Glendale's website.

For all this, the team paid a mere 25 percent of stadium costs (plus any overruns), or about $109 million of the $450 million budget. The other 75 percent is being picked up by the Arizona Tourism and Sports Authority.

"During the construction phase of the stadium and site infrastructure there will be more than thirty-five hundred jobs and more than $400 million in economic benefits to Arizona's economy," the team claims.

In early 2007, the New York Giants and Jets announced that they planned to build a new stadium with taxpayer help. The cost? $1.4 billion.

So if the evidence that stadiums provide a paltry return to taxpayers is so overwhelming, why do cities keep playing this game?

"You can't unilaterally withdraw," said Minneapolis Federal Reserve economist Art Rolnick. "If Minneapolis doesn't build the Vikings or Twins a new stadium, someone else will. And it may be someone who's not in Minnesota."

And team owners aren't the only culprits. State and local government constantly engage in bidding wars for private entities, be it the Minnesota Vikings or 3M.

"Competition among states for specific businesses is commonplace and growing more costly," Rolnick and co-author Melvin L. Burstein wrote in the January 1996 issue of *fedgazette*, the Minneapolis Fed's monthly publication. "Competition for sports franchises is a drop in a big bucket of public money spent to subsidize businesses."

NASCAR isn't nearly as dependent on taxpayer financing as the NFL. On average, new NASCAR tracks look to the taxpayers to pick up about 20 percent of construction costs. But like NFL stadiums, new NASCAR tracks come with a bevy of economic experts predicting untold riches for the community that builds it.

NASCAR's track expansion during the 1990s mostly went off without a hitch. Yes, there were the occasional battles with community groups over environmental impact and noise ordinances, but most of those were quickly resolved. But lately, NASCAR has suffered two big setbacks in its track development.

NASCAR has been obsessed for more than a decade with building a track in the New York metropolitan area. Why? NASCAR is seeking a sense of legitimacy—the need to be accepted in the media capital of the world. It is the same sense that drove NASCAR to move its annual banquet to the Waldorf-Astoria on Park Avenue. I believe the drive to try and build a track in New York is irrational.

NASCAR's first foray into the New York real estate market was with Donald Trump. NASCAR officials and Trump worked for years on a project to build a racetrack in New Jersey's Meadowlands, near Giants Stadium. One year it looked like it was going to happen and the next it didn't. NASCAR eventually abandoned that plan and shifted its focus to a 675-acre piece of property it owned at the foot of the Goethals Bridge, which connects Staten Island to New Jersey.

In April 2006, the ISC attended a city planning commission hearing to detail its plans for a proposed eighty-thousand-seat short track, which would include retail development but no parking. The biggest argument against the NASCAR track was traffic congestion, so NASCAR said it would provide no parking so that fans would be forced to take mass transit to the racetrack. While that surely would have angered NASCAR fans, who are perhaps the biggest—and best—tailgaters in all of sports, it wasn't enough for the residents of Staten Island, either.

"The traffic implications for this project are such that it wouldn't work," said Staten Island Councilman James Oddo. "This is an island with essentially no mass transit; you have four bridges, three of which are overutilized or antiquated, and to put a project of this size into that realm, it didn't work."

In short, the project went nowhere. And NASCAR did all the right things to make it happen. Expert at working with city councils and mayors, ISC had hired beloved former Staten Island Borough President Guy Molinari to lobby on its behalf. It even had the labor unions—whose members would benefit greatly from the construction jobs and other union-mandated employment once the track was built—on its side. But the project was still a no go. The proposal was so contentious that the final Staten Island council meeting erupted in a brawl, with burly union negotiators, there on behalf of ISC, fighting with community activists. It was ugly. At the end of 2006, ISC announced that it had abandoned plans for the Staten Island project. On the upside, ISC owned the property, considered some of the most valuable real estate in the five boroughs. Rest assured, NASCAR won't get its Staten Island track, but it won't walk away empty-handed, either.

The other setback for NASCAR in 2006 was in the Pacific Northwest, a hotbed of stock car racing. During the 1980s and 1990s, NASCAR expanded significantly in the West. It added a race at Phoenix and Infineon Raceway in northern California's wine country just north of San Francisco. New tracks were built in Las Vegas and Fontana, California, just east of Los Angeles.

For the past few years, NASCAR has been trying to add to its western empire with a track in the Pacific Northwest. ISC, which earned huge kudos for the tracks it built in Kansas City and Joliet, Illinois, just outside Chicago, began to look at locations in Oregon and Washington State. In 2006, the site selection was narrowed down to Kitsap, just across Puget Sound from Seattle.

"We feel the Pacific Northwest is an untapped market as far as NASCAR goes," said NASCAR spokesman David Talley.

ISC had hoped to start racing in the Northwest by 2008. But then the negotiations got down to the usual sticking details, including acreage and infrastructure.

"If you are to build a facility with [seating for] eighty-five thousand people, you're going to need the roads to handle that many people," Talley said. "It's got to be the right fit. We're not going to build a five million dollar facility if it doesn't make sense."

The Puget Sound track proposal included some favorable tax treatment and help with roads and other infrastructure.

"They're not going to locate it here unless the state does something for them," Washington Lieutenant Governor Brad Owen said. Senator Tim Sheldon, a Democrat in the Washington Legislature, put forth legislation in January 2007. While he admitted that it was a form of public financing to help a private entity, he said it would be different than the means used to help build the Seahawks and Mariners stadiums in Seattle.

"We have to deliver when they pick a site," Sheldon said. "We can't sit around two years wringing our hands."

"I will support wherever NASCAR decides to go," said Snohomish County Executive Aaron Reardon. "I believe it's good for Washington State. It is a competitive process, and I plan on being damn competitive."

Jeff Boerger, president of Kansas Speedway, said he understands what local officials in Washington are facing in the struggle to land an ISC facility. He was on the economic development team that brought the company to Kansas.

"The Kansas taxpayer has about fifty million dollars invested in this project," Boerger said. "We saw an economic impact immediately during the construction phase, with two thousand new jobs and a construction payroll of fifty million dollars."

"We have sold out each of our races since day one," he added. "The impact has been tremendous."

The same is true for Chicagoland Speedway. The $130 million, 73,000-seat raceway on 930 acres has sold out every race since it opened in 2001.

The Checkered Flag Task Force, which includes officials from Washington State and from the Puget Sound counties under consideration by ISC, commissioned a study of the impact. Here are a few highlights:

· *Total Economic Benefits:* $87 million to $122 million
   regionally and $66 million to $98 million from a state
   perspective.
· *Jobs and Wages:* 1,325 to 1,846 new jobs and $38.3 million
   to $52.4 million in added income regionally and 1,061 to
   1,585 new jobs and $29 million to $42 million in income
   statewide.
· *Tax Benefits:* $2.5 to $4 million in annual revenue to the
   state and $3.7 to $4.5 million spread among multiple
   local jurisdictions.

The construction phase alone was expected to have an economic impact of $230 million. Once open, the track would generate an estimated $220 million in annual business revenue.

"It will be lucrative for almost anyone, whether it's in Washington of Oregon," said Paul Swangard, managing director of the University of Oregon's Warsaw Sports Marketing Center, which studies the business of sports.

When Seattle economist Dick Conway studied the impact of the Seattle Mariners, he found that the team brought nearly $142 million in business revenue and created 2,249 jobs. But only one-third of the revenue created by the Mariners is considered "new money, " or money from outside the area. By contrast, only 30 percent of NASCAR race attendees are local.

"The baseball crowd is largely, I think even today, from the central Puget Sound region," Conway said. "NASCAR tends to draw from a larger pool."

Even though Swangard is skeptical of some of the economic figures being cited, he said the opportunity is too tempting for any area to pass up. "It would still be worth going after," he said. "For what will amount to a low-impact development that will not be used more than a few times a year, the economic impact is significant."

Discussions continued as this book went to press.

CHAPTER EIGHT

SPEED DATING FOR DOLLARS

Inside the NASCAR B2B Council

On February 15, 2007, the grandstands at the Daytona International Speedway were packed to the rafters. Some eighty-thousand fans were eager to see the Twin 150s, the two qualifying races for the Daytona 500, which mark the official start of the NASCAR season. But five miles away, in a gold-leaf ballroom in the Daytona Beach Hilton, the NASCAR business season was getting underway. It was the first meeting of the year for the NASCAR B2B Council, the true driving force behind today's NASCAR sponsorships.

The B2B Council was founded in 2004. The impetus was an ultimatum from NewPage (then MeadWestvaco), the Fortune

500 paper and packaged goods company headquartered in Dayton, Ohio.

"We told NASCAR that we needed to sell fifty-thousand tons of coated paper in one year through our NASCAR sponsorship," said Greg Gruning, vice president of marketing at NewPage. "If we didn't meet that goal, there was no reason for us to be a NASCAR sponsor."

To make sure that it met that goal, NewPage convinced NASCAR to form the NASCAR B2B Council. The founding members were hotelier Best Western, Callaway Golf Company, NewPage, Sprint Nextel, and UPS. In just two years, the group has grown from a loose coalition of NASCAR sponsors to the hottest business proposition in sports. The group's goals are simple: identify potential business-to-business opportunities among NASCAR partners, compress the time and layers of corporate bureaucracy it typically takes to negotiate these deals, and learn how other companies leverage their NASCAR sponsorships. Sounds simple, but it is reaping incredible dividends.

"It's the dirty little secret of this business," Gruning said.

That's a bit of hyperbole. Today's NASCAR B2B play is neither dirty nor a secret. As noted in the preceding chapters, B2B has been the underlying driving force for NASCAR sponsorships since R. J. Reynolds first arrived on the scene in 1972. The B2B business model accelerated in the mid-1980s, with Folgers, Country Time, and Western Auto. But Gruning's correct that B2B in NASCAR has never been more prominent and successful than it is today. B2B isn't the underlying reason that Fortune 500 companies become NASCAR sponsors; it is *the* reason.

While a NASCAR team sponsorship today costs in the neighborhood of $20 million, some of these B2B deals can be worth five times that. In just two years, Gulfstream has already sold five business jets to fellow NASCAR sponsors. Because it's such a fertile place to do business, membership in the NASCAR B2B Council has grown from the five founding members at the end of 2004 to fourteen corporations at the start of 2007. At the NASCAR B2B Council meeting during the Las Vegas race in March, four new members were introduced: Bank of America, Coca-Cola, Home Depot, and Sirius.

"Sponsors are learning that they can pay their rights fees with just the B2B business they generate through NASCAR," said Denise Mays, motorsports marketing manager for NewPage.

These B2B meetings, which are held about once a quarter, typically start with a State of NASCAR address, which gives sponsors an update on NASCAR marketing programs, television ratings, and any other business developments. Then new sponsors—or old ones—give a thirty-minute presentation about upcoming sales and marketing promotions around their NASCAR sponsorship. They'll also give the B2B Council an overview of larger corporate initiatives and sales and marketing goals, in hope of garnering new business from B2B Council members. For example, at one B2B Council meeting UPS gave an overview of its logistics solutions business, something that very few companies knew it did.

The February 2007 B2B Council meeting was a little different. NewPage and xpedx, a division of International Paper, presented their 2007 strategy to account managers from NASCAR's New York and Charlotte offices. These NASCAR executives work directly with the sponsors, and NewPage wanted to outline its 2007 B2B goals. The company also gave the NASCAR executives a list of the sponsors it would be focusing on over the coming year.

"We just want you to be thinking of us, our companies, and potential B2B opportunities when you sit down with these sponsors," Gruning said.

It's a strategy that has worked before.

In 1996, NewPage was an associate sponsor on the Roger Penske–owned car driven by Rusty Wallace and sponsored by Miller Lite. The company used the sponsorship primarily to entertain corporate customers.

"It worked OK, but we wanted to take it to another level," Gruning said.

NewPage did just that in 2001. Instead of just bringing customers to the track, the company started giving away the rear deck lid on the Miller Lite-Penske car.

"We basically gave our best customers the sponsorship for the weekend," Gruning said. "The deck lid, the suite, everything."

This not only was a great marketing strategy, but it helped NewPage better measure sales leads from that customer, and, more broadly, to measure its return on investment in the NASCAR sponsorship. NewPage liked what it saw.

"It really showed us what we could do with this sponsorship, and how we could leverage it to improve our business," Gruning said. "People killed to be on that car. One hundred fifty thousand fans, television, a good car; it was a phenomenal success."

Since helping create the B2B Council in 2004, NewPage has used the forum to gain entry to the offices of chief sales and procurement officers at many of the Fortune 500 NASCAR sponsors.

"NASCAR is a direct conduit to the VP level of these companies," Gruning said. "Before you know it, you're sitting in a suite in the corporate offices of a major corporation, talking to exactly the right guy to get the deal done. It makes the whole sales cycle so much shorter and pays incredible dividends."

Early wins for NewPage have included UPS, USG, and Jackson Hewitt. In 2005, the first full year of the B2B Council, NewPage sat down with Jackson Hewitt, the tax preparer. Initially, NewPage was just interested in supplying the paper and printing the $10-off coupons that Jackson Hewitt mails out to potential customers. In the end, the deal resulted in much more. In exchange for Jackson Hewitt's direct-mail business, NewPage allowed Jackson Hewitt to put brochures in break rooms at its four major manufacturing plants, which employ seven thousand potential Jackson Hewitt customers. Jackson Hewitt also advertised on NewPage's internal corporate website. It has been such a successful partnership that neither company thinks twice about renewing it.

"It's almost become turnkey," NewPage Motorsports Manager Denise Mays said.

Another success story for NewPage—and testament to the deals that can get done through the NASCAR B2B Council—involves USG, the construction company. NewPage started talking to USG at the B2B Council meeting at Miami in November 2006. By the time SpeedWeeks at Daytona rolled around in February 2007, the two had already completed a deal. NewPage would use USG construction materials to build its new corporate headquarters in Dayton, Ohio, in exchange for the USG catalog and corporate communication printing business.

In February 2007, NewPage also began talking to DirecTV about supplying the paper for the tens of millions of promotional fliers that DirecTV sends out every year. And since earning some packaging business from Sprint Nextel in 2006, more than five hundred NewPage employees have been using BlackBerry wireless devices with service from Sprint Nextel. These are just a few examples of the networking potential of the NASCAR B2B Council.

During his presentation to the NASCAR account executives in Daytona, NewPage's Gruning noted that 2007 was a renewal year for NewPage's NASCAR contract. But few people in the room doubted that the company would be back.

"It's not the fuel I smell at the racetrack," Gruning said, "it's the dollars."

In short, the NASCAR B2B Council is a phenomenal success. It's also one area where NASCAR is head and shoulders above the NFL, the other major sports league to which NASCAR is so often compared.

In doing research for my book, *Tailgating Sacks and Salary Caps: How the NFL Became the Most Successful Sports League in History*, I learned that NFL sponsors aren't treated very well. There are so many of them, solicited at both the national and local level, that they often get lost in the media clutter. How does this happen?

The NFL recruits national sponsors and advertisers, such as Pepsi, which is the "official soft drink of the NFL." The NFL divides this national advertising and sponsorship revenue equally with all thirty-two NFL franchises. This guarantees that Pepsi will be able to buy preferred advertising time during NFL broadcasts, including the playoffs and Super Bowl, which deliver the biggest audiences, and use the NFL logo for marketing and promotions. But at the same time that the NFL is cultivating relationships with national sponsors like Pepsi, Chevrolet, and Motorola, NFL teams are courting their direct competitors on the local level and in many cases giving them more prominent space at the stadiums.

Traveling around the NFL over a full season, I found that national NFL sponsors were often overshadowed by local advertisers. Jerry Jones, the owner of the Dallas Cowboys, is the master of double dipping on NFL sponsorships. He was the first to figure out that if Pepsi was the official soft drink of the NFL, there was no rule against him selling pouring rights—and premier advertising space—to Dr. Pepper in Texas Stadium. What makes these local sponsorship deals all the more lucrative and attractive is the fact that NFL teams do not have to share locally generated revenue with the rest of the league. What they cultivate and earn locally is theirs to keep.

NASCAR, as a business, couldn't be more different. Yes, tracks have the right to secure local sponsors and vendors. But in terms of what's presented on the cars and during the NASCAR broadcast, the league is very protective of its corporate sponsors, the assets and rights they own, and the space they buy. Why? Because NASCAR understands that without its sponsors, there would be no NASCAR.

Furthermore, NASCAR doesn't look for short-term partners. It develops long-term relationships that sometimes last for not just years, but decades. For instance, NASCAR has a two-person office in Bentonville, Arkansas, that does nothing but work with Wal-Mart, which sells more than $500 million of NASCAR-licensed merchandise a year.

Because of this long-term focus, NASCAR is very selective about forming partnerships. It looks for companies that are willing to make a solid commitment to NASCAR, including significant advertising and marketing support. In exchange, NASCAR and its existing sponsors are willing partners, not competitors, with businesses that are new to the sport. This spirit of cooperation—unprecedented in major league sports—was the impetus for the B2B Council. It's also the reason that NASCAR works very hard to make sure that sponsors get as much—if not more—out of their sponsorship as they put in.

Here are just a few examples of the types of interwoven business relationships that have developed among some of the NASCAR sponsors as a result of this cooperative spirit and the NASCAR B2B Council:

NEWPAGE CORPORATION

Headquartered in Dayton, Ohio, NewPage Corporation is a leading producer of coated papers in North America. It has more than 4,300 employees working in integrated pulp and paper manufacturing mills from Maine to Kentucky and last year produced about 2.2 million tons of coated paper.

When NewPage looked at NASCAR, foremost in its mind was selling paper. How it could do that in NASCAR may be hard to understand at first, but you have to think of NASCAR as a business, not just a sport. Once you look at it through this lens, and think about the multibillion dollar, multinational corporations that are involved in NASCAR, you realize, as many NASCAR sponsors have, that the potential for new business is almost unlimited.

As a direct result of its NASCAR sponsorship and the relationships it has built through the B2B Council, NewPage sold more than 29,000 tons of paper in 2004 to NASCAR partners, including the following: International Speedway Corporation (800 tons for its annual reports); Levi's (100 tons); UMI Publications (260 tons); Caterpillar (475 tons); and Precision Publishing (250 tons). NewPage also has developed business partnerships with NASCAR sponsors Jackson Hewitt and USG, and provides the paper for the NASCAR.com catalog.

What's important to remember with NewPage—and every

other NASCAR sponsor—is that the partnerships it has built through its sponsorship and participation in the NASCAR B2B Council have been with companies with which NewPage had done little or no business before coming into NASCAR. More important, the transactions go both ways, with NASCAR sponsors both selling and buying products and services.

For instance, UPS is now NewPage's exclusive package delivery service. NewPage also buys golf equipment from fellow NASCAR sponsor Callaway, its employees are able to take advantage of discounts offered through Best Western's MVP rewards program, and NewPage contracts with Sprint Nextel for BlackBerry wireless service for its employees.

GULFSTREAM

A unit of General Dynamics, Gulfstream Aerospace became an official NASCAR partner in February 2005, just before the Daytona 500. Again, your first instinct may be, "What is Gulfstream doing in NASCAR?" Well, first off, the days are long past when drivers loaded up the hauler and took their turn at the wheel driving it back to the shop after the race. Today's NASCAR drivers helicopter into the track and fly in for race weekends on their own corporate jets. In fact, most NASCAR teams today have a small fleet of airplanes to ferry drivers, owners, and crews to and from the racetrack. Many NASCAR teams have full-time pilots on staff. When you understand that this is the world of NASCAR today, the Gulfstream sponsorship makes perfect sense.

Gulfstream executives will tell you that NASCAR is a fertile market for cultivating new business, both with race teams and with their sponsors. Gulfstream does just that every week, both by being a NASCAR sponsor and by hosting corporate hospitality events at select NASCAR events for its most important existing and potential customers. The company has even brought qualified buyers on test flights tied to the NASCAR race at Texas Motor Speedway.

"The Daytona 500 and NASCAR is a legitimate, substantial business-to-business opportunity," Gulfstream CEO Bryan Moss said. "We can get our airplanes in front of sponsor executives."

KODAK

An official NASCAR and team sponsor for more than twenty years, Kodak uses its race car and at-track opportunities to build business with NASCAR sponsors and its retail partners. In fact, Kodak has moved most of its sponsorship dollars from stick-and-ball sports into NASCAR because NASCAR produces results.

Kodak has followed the model developed by Country Time and Western Auto in the 1980s and 1990s. The Rochester, New York–based film manufacturer and digital imaging firm often puts the name of one of its retail partners—CVS, Eckerd, Rite Aid, Longs Drugs, Pathmark, Staples—on the rear deck lid of the No. 77 Kodak Ford at select NASCAR events. In exchange for the exposure, the retail outlets must feature two other Kodak product merchandisers in their stores.

Kodak also uses its NASCAR sponsorship to build its profitable entertainment imaging business. Some fans probably scratched their head when in 2004 the Kodak car was painted to promote the Lion's Gate Studio film, *The Punisher*. It's only when you realize that Kodak produces more than 90 percent of the film used by the motion picture industry that the special sponsorship and paint scheme makes sense. Indeed, every film to ever win an Academy Award has been seen on Kodak film. Lion's Gate was one of only two Hollywood studios that wasn't a Kodak partner before the special NASCAR promotion. Needless to say, Lion's Gate now uses Kodak film. The partnership has resulted in six thousand new movie prints being produced by Kodak.

Another example of the increasingly intertwined world of NASCAR sponsors is the partnership between Kodak and Sprint Nextel. On average, more than four hundred thousand fans a year visit the Nextel Experience, the company's interactive display that is set up on the midway outside every NASCAR race. Many of those fans get their picture taken with the Nextel Cup trophy—courtesy of Kodak Digital Imaging. Sprint Nextel collects data on some of these visitors—age, hometown, median income—and shares the information with Kodak. As a result of Kodak's NASCAR sponsorship and partnerships, its at-track events allow it to do five times the number of demos for 50 percent of the cost, said Kodak Motorsports Manager Tom Page. "NASCAR produces a return on investment in the forty to fifty percent range," he said.

DUPONT

The Wilmington, Delaware–based conglomerate that sponsors four-time NASCAR champion Jeff Gordon has one of the most sophisticated hospitality programs in all of NASCAR. DuPont brings more than twenty thousand customers, distributors, and partners to NASCAR races each year. During prerace hospitality events in its corporate suites and pit tours, Gordon signs autographs and takes questions from DuPont customers. This access makes NASCAR the only sport where fans can go into the locker room before the game and visit with the top players. These prerace hospitality events are literally the equivalent of going into the Indianapolis Colts locker room before the Super Bowl and visiting with Peyton Manning. Not only are DuPont and some of its innovative products—such as Teflon and fire-resistant Nomex—plastered across the hood of Gordon's car, but they're featured on his uniform as well. That's significant exposure for a company that gets 23 percent of its revenue from automotive-related products. But perhaps the most innovative display of DuPont and its products is in Dover, Delaware, just an hour's drive from DuPont's corporate headquarters. That's where fans will find the DuPont Monster Bridge at Dover Downs International Speedway. The bridge, which sits twenty-nine feet above the track, was built with twenty different DuPont products, including high-strength glass that is able to withstand a lug nut fired at it at two hundred miles per hour. DuPont provides four Monster Bridge seats at each race to its best corporate customers, who land at the track via helicopter, have breakfast with one of the NASCAR drivers, get to meet Gordon and his crew chief, Robbie Loomis, and watch the race from the bridge.

SUNTRUST

Before being replaced by Bank of America in late 2006, in line with NASCAR's strategy to partner with brands with a national footprint that can promote the sport coast to coast, SunTrust was NASCAR's official bank. Over the years, SunTrust has used its sponsorship to build relationships with NASCAR drivers, teams, tracks, and sponsors. The bank has built partnerships with the Women's Auxiliary of Motorsports (WAM), the organization of NASCAR Racing Wives, and Motor Racing Outreach (MRO), a Christian organization that helps organize church and faith-based programs within the racing community. These programs include a Sunday morning church service before each

NASCAR race for drivers and their families and a garage-area Bible study.

At the racetrack, SunTrust sets up a mobile bank in the exclusive parking lot where drivers, car owners, and crew chiefs park their million-dollar motor coaches on race weekends. SunTrust has an ATM in the lot, as well as a loan officer who can process loans, lines of credit, and other banking services for NASCAR drivers and team members who spend more time on the road than at home.

"The SunTrust brand was not well known in the NASCAR garage," said Brian Williams, senior vice president and director of SunTrust Entertainment Banking Group. "Early introductions by NASCAR to groups such as WAM and MRO helped us gain credibility and also helped guide us to an at-track servicing strategy that is making a difference in the NASCAR community."

WASTE MANAGEMENT

Since becoming an official partner of NASCAR in 2001, Waste Management has generated a significant amount of business with NASCAR tracks. The company has inked deals to provide comprehensive waste management and environmental services with Daytona International Speedway, Talladega Superspeedway, Bristol Motor Speedway, Dover Downs International Speedway, Chicagoland Speedway, Pikes Peak International Raceway, and Kentucky Speedway. Waste Management also is a service provider for many of the NASCAR Dodge Weekly Series tracks. The company uses these tracks for corporate hospitality and to take clients to the Richard Petty Driving Experience. The company has identified almost $10 million in annual revenue that it has won or maintained as a direct result of its NASCAR sponsorship.

A significant hospitality program has been at the heart of Waste Management's B2B program. The company hosted key customers at twenty-nine different events at twenty different NASCAR tracks during the 2004 season. Working through the B2B Council, Waste Management has picked up business from the Checkers/Rally's fast-food chain, which sells NASCAR's official burger. Waste Management also has the usual signage at the track and advertising during NASCAR broadcasts, so even though fans are unlikely to contract with a giant corporate entity like Waste Management—most of the local garbage pickup is negotiated by the city or county—the company has a presence that the fans see.

DOMINO'S PIZZA AND BEST WESTERN

The official pizza and hotel of NASCAR have teamed up on programs that help both businesses. Domino's "Official Pizza of NASCAR" logo has been featured on the key card at more than 2,300 Best Western hotels nationwide. Placards inside the rooms feature the phone number for the local Dominos.

Best Western has developed a dedicated sales team that assists NASCAR sponsors, teams, and other related businesses with their hotel needs. The company's Member Value Program allows employees of member companies to save 20 percent or more on hotel accommodations. For instance, NewPage has a web link on its in-house employee website to book rooms at Best Western's NASCAR discounted rates. Best Western also has MVP agreements with Tony Stewart Racing and the Tony Stewart Fan Club. And the hotel chain is thinking about placing NASCAR-themed Coca-Cola machines in all its locations, with the help of its partnership with Coca-Cola Racing Family driver Michael Waltrip.

Best Western also gives 5 percent of room charges to the Victory Junction Gang Camp, the NASCAR charity founded by Kyle Petty in memory of his son, Adam, who was killed while racing at New Hampshire International Speedway.

WHELEN ENGINEERING COMPANY, INC.

Based in Chester, Connecticut, Whelen Engineering Company, Inc. manufactures the emergency lighting systems used in police cars, fire and rescue vehicles, tow trucks, and airplanes. It supplies the warning lights on official NASCAR vehicles and is the title sponsor of the NASCAR Whelen All-American Series, which runs at sixty short tracks nationwide and is now seen on SPEED and HDNet. The company also sponsors a NASCAR Busch Series team and is the title sponsor for the Busch North Series race at Lee, New Hampshire.

Whelen is in NASCAR, Motorsports Director Phil Kurze said, because "the people who sit in the stands are our customers. The ones that race the cars, build the cars, pay to see the cars are cops, firemen, EMS people, construction workers, tow truck operators. If they see we are part of the sport they love, that we're helping to finance their sport, we feel they're going to be loyal and buy our product."

SPRINT NEXTEL

The title sponsor of NASCAR's premier racing series, Sprint Nextel, has designated an entire business development team to leverage all the assets of its title sponsorship. This commitment has led to a "return on investment (ROI) much faster than we expected," said Todd Weller, vice president of business development for Nextel. "We measure ROI by market penetration into the consumer segment as well as into the tracks and the track ecosystem; the drivers, teams, and owners, and other sponsors. We took on the title sponsorship because of the vast business-to-consumer opportunities, but clearly the B2B opportunities are equally impressive."

Sprint Nextel has four main B2B goals in NASCAR: finding new business at the track, capturing incremental sales to existing customers, retaining at-risk business, and serving the NASCAR community directly in innovative ways. The first three are pretty self-explanatory. Some of the ways Sprint Nextel has reached its fourth objective are by developing a radio frequency ID system for tracking tire inventory, telemetry applications for car data, and other wireless uses at the track.

In terms of working with NASCAR race teams, Sprint Nextel saw unit growth of 68 percent from 2004 to 2005, with 90 percent of NASCAR teams using Sprint Evolution Data-Optimized (EV-DO) products. Chip Ganassi Racing has converted all of its company-owned handsets to Nextel units. Usage by the team is more than double that of other NASCAR teams, with each unit generating an average of $150 a month. Joe Gibbs Racing uses Sprint Nextel's EV-DO products to send real-time stats from the garage out to the team while the car is on the track. The CIO of Gibbs Racing did a testimonial ad for Sprint that runs regularly outside of race broadcasts on CNN, MSNBC, and other cable networks.

Ingersoll-Rand represents a "multimillion dollar" account to Sprint Nextel, a direct result of the NASCAR B2B Council. The NASCAR relationship actually helped get beyond an issue in the proposal process: A request for proposal (RFP) was issued (via both a consultant and an online auction, which is becoming more common) on this business as part of Ingersoll-Rand's due diligence to ensure it was getting the most for its telecommunications investment. While the sales teams were very tight with the process, at the NASCAR B2B Council Sprint's Vice President Carolyn Rehling was informed of an issue with Sprint's RFP. In an environment where a consultant and online processes are being used, any issue might have quietly slipped through the process and left Sprint out of the running. Fortunately, through the high-level relationship afforded by the NASCAR B2B Council, Sprint was able to get behind the curtain, understand the issues, and address them. The result: a multimillion dollar, multiyear relationship was saved. And beyond that, incremental business was bid on and won—so the save also turned into increased business.

Nextel has sold tens of thousands of driver series phones to the employees of the companies whose driver is featured on the phone (e.g., Anheuser-Busch/Earnhardt Jr.; DeWalt/Kenseth; Home Depot/Stewart; Lowe's/Johnson).

Sprint Nextel credits its business partnerships with 116 NASCAR sponsors for a 25.2 percent sales growth rate in 2005. For instance, Sprint Nextel had a good relationship with Home Depot prior to becoming a NASCAR sponsor. But since then, Home Depot has expanded its wireless services with things like the Pro Business Toolbox, a mobile solution built to increase sales and loyalty in an important business segment. The toolbox targets pro-business customers to allow them to take advantage of unique Sprint Nextel offers and features. Service Connect is a Nextel BlackBerry that operates a mobile project management system that performs everything from scheduling to complaint management.

In 2006, Sprint Nextel grew its business with existing customer and NASCAR sponsor Cintas by becoming the wireless provider of choice and becoming Cintas's Wide Area Network (WAN) provider. In return, Sprint purchases first-aid equipment and uniforms from Cintas.

Sprint Nextel has also partnered with NASCAR sponsor NewPage. The two first met at the inaugural NASCAR B2B Council meeting in November 2004 and NewPage was invited to Sprint Nextel's corporate headquarters to visit its Center of Excellence. The relationship has led to the deployment of hundreds of Sprint Nextel–serviced BlackBerries throughout the NewPage organization.

Nextel focuses its business-to-business hospitality around NASCAR's all-star week, held in Charlotte each May. Nextel brought many top-level executives to its C-Level Technology Forum at the "NASCAR Nextel All-Star Challenge" in Charlotte in May 2005. The company entertained 150 A-list clients, representing such corporate giants as Bank of America, 3M, Waste Management, EDS, General Dynamics, Iron Mountain, Northrop Grumman, Sonic Automotive, US Airways, and Wachovia.

Business developed from these efforts includeed a relationship with Jackson Hewitt. The official tax service of NASCAR is now an endorsed vendor of Nextel products with all Jackson Hewitt employees receiving discounts on Nextel Service.

All told, Nextel can directly connect one million new subscribers to its Nextel sponsorship. And according to the company, the NASCAR fan is particularly valuable because they tend to use more enhanced services and airtime than the average customer.

I could go on, but I think you get the point. Literally billions of dollars of new business is generated in the NASCAR corporate hospitality suites and in the NASCAR B2B Council. While these companies each leverage their sponsorship in their own way, they all agree that among pro sports franchises, NASCAR offers some of the best returns on investment.

Americans love NASCAR for the action on the track, but the sport's status as one of the darlings of the Fortune 500 (and the incredible amounts of news coverage and public visibility that results) is due to NASCAR's revolutionary business-to-business sponsorship programs. Speed dating for business partners is just one of these behind-the-scenes activities that have made NASCAR one of this country's premier forms of sports entertainment.

CHAPTER NINE

SEE THE BROWN TRUCK GO

How UPS Took NASCAR to Mexico

T he United Parcel Service (UPS) is a relatively new NASCAR sponsor. It started as "the official package delivery service of NASCAR" in 2000 and a year later decided to sponsor Dale Jarrett in the No. 88 car. In 2007, UPS left Robert Yates Racing, as did Jarrett, and moved over to the brand new Toyota team owned by Michael Waltrip.

(The departure of UPS and Jarrett were big losses for the team, but don't fret for Robert Yates, one of NASCAR's savviest team owners. In late 2006, Masterfoods USA announced that it would become the only sponsor to have two brands from the same company backing one NASCAR team. The company said its Snickers brand would be on the Yates car driven by Ricky Rudd in 2007. Another Masterfoods brand, M&Ms, sponsored Yates driver David Gilliland for 2007. Those two cars sat on the front row for the start of the 2007 Daytona 500.)

While UPS has been a sponsor for just eight years, its relationship with NASCAR has grown significantly during that time, making it one of the most sophisticated sponsors in NASCAR today. It's also one of the sponsors that successfully utilizes all of the sponsor components of marketing and advertising, corporate hospitality, and team building. Along the way, it has figured out how to make a ton of money in NASCAR and build new business partnerships through the NASCAR B2B Council.

"We found this opportunity where we could own the category," said Patrick Guilbert, vice president of corporate sponsorships and events at UPS. Indeed, when UPS joined NASCAR in 2000, it was the only package delivery company. Since then, FedEx has come into NASCAR and was the sponsor of 2006 Rookie of the Year Denny Hamlin.

"Furthermore, it's a ten-month-long season," Guilbert said. "The opportunities to activate the sponsorship were almost unlimited."

It also didn't hurt that NASCAR was the fastest-growing sport in the United States and one where success was dependent upon teamwork.

"When you think about what we do and what NASCAR does—drivers, supported by a team—it just made sense for us," Guilbert said. "Speed and technology; that's what NASCAR's about and it's what we're about. All of which leads to a number of natural ties."

WHY NASCAR?

There are four primary reasons that a sponsor gets involved with NASCAR.

MARKETING AND ADVERTISING: With seventy-five million fans, the raw numbers alone are appealing to a NASCAR sponsor. NASCAR not only has the second-largest fan base in the United States behind the NFL, but it's also a nationwide sport that affords the opportunity for a company to build marketing and advertising programs both nationally and locally.

CORPORATE HOSPITALITY: NASCAR is truly a unique corporate entertainment environment, as you've already seen in previous chapters and will see again over the next few chapters. Businesses use it not only to entertain their most important clients, but also to reward employees and convince other corporate partners that NASCAR is a good place to do business.

TEAM BUILDING: For many corporations, a NASCAR team's focus on speed and accuracy is exactly what they're trying to instill in their employees. A NASCAR sponsorship is an ideal way to develop teamwork and camaraderie within a large, geographically diverse Fortune 500 corporation.

SELLING PRODUCT: As the previous chapter demonstrated, there are myriad opportunities in NASCAR—more than any other major league sport in America—for a company to sell its products and services to other businesses, as well as consumers. The potential for B2B deals has grown exponentially over the past twenty years. While it was once the icing on the cake for NASCAR sponsorship deals, today it *is* the cake for a wide range of different types of NASCAR sponsors. One thing ties all the sponsors together: NASCAR is a great place to do business.

The ties came with relative ease. Especially when it came to using NASCAR to foster and develop teamwork and excellence within UPS.

"We think we have one of the most integrated sponsorships in the game from an employee perspective," Guilbert said. "We really seem to be able to take this sponsorship across the segments within our business, from senior-level decisionmakers to district managers to administrative support staff, to drivers in the field, to the guys and gals on the street responsible for delivering the product every day."

One example of how UPS uses its NASCAR sponsorship to build teamwork within the company was the 2006 Employee Crew Award. In short, the entire company competed during the year to have the best safety record. The winners were a crew from Iowa, who won an all-expense paid trip to the 2007 Daytona 500.

"It's just one example of how we can use the sponsorship to promote teamwork and achieve goals throughout the company," Guilbert said.

UPS also hosted major hospitality events at seventeen NASCAR races during the 2006 season for its employees, as well as potential customers and existing business partners.

"We're very careful about the customers we bring to the race," Guilbert said. "We only bring those customers who we feel would benefit and enjoy being at the track. We bring existing customers and potential customers who we think appreciate the sport and appreciate how we're using it to build our business and make UPS better and faster."

In addition to being a great venue for the right customer, attending a race with corporate clients is an opportunity that

UPS executives rarely get with their most important and potential customers.

"You're with a customer for seven or eight hours," Guilbert said. "The discussion inevitably turns to business and generates discussions that spread well beyond race day."

A typical day at the races for these corporate clients usually starts with a police-escorted charter bus trip into the racetrack. From there, the clients go up to the corporate suites high above the grandstand and are usually greeted with a gift bag of NASCAR-related corporate goodies: a race program, a set of binoculars, a ball cap, or a collector car. All are embossed with the UPS corporate logo.

After a bit of relaxation and breakfast, the pit tours start. NASCAR sponsors are allowed to take small groups down to the pits and explain to them just exactly what will go on during the race. For many guests, this is their first time at the racetrack. For others, they know exactly what an air wrench is for and how to take out a round of wedge. But as many times as they've been on pit tours or watched a race from the corporate suites, it never loses its thrill.

After the pit tour, lunch is served. This is usually when the driver or the car owner comes up and spends a half hour or so with the guests. I was at the Brickyard 400 at Indianapolis a few years ago, doing a story on corporate hospitality with MBNA, the credit card company. The company had long been an associate sponsor on Joe Gibbs' car, something you'll hear more about later. MBNA's guests were upper-level corporate executives who had been on more than their share of corporate golf outings and all-expense-paid trips to the Super Bowl. But when Gibbs came in and took off one of his Super Bowl rings and let them fondle it, they were mesmerized. It was nearly the only thing these guests could talk about for the rest of the day.

This is the unique experience that a hospitality suite at a NASCAR race affords. It's the only sport where you can go into the locker room before the game and talk with the starting pitcher or quarterback.

The drivers all understand this, and go out of their way to be kind and courteous, no matter how many times they've heard the same questions. UPS thinks it has a winner with driver Dale Jarrett, who not only visits the corporate hospitality suite on race day, but also speaks at UPS marketing and sales seminars throughout the year.

"So many drivers that are in this game are really good at speaking with audiences, speaking with sponsor customers and employees," Guilbert said. "But there are a few who are at the top of that game. And I don't think there's any question that Dale Jarrett is at the top of that list."

There's a broader point here. One of the things that sponsors find particularly appealing about NASCAR is how easy it is to access the top players—drivers, owners, and crew chiefs. Furthermore, while many of today's drivers never had to mortgage their farm or write a check they knew they couldn't cover to buy parts and gas, they still understand the importance of the sponsors. They understand that without the sponsors, there would be no NASCAR. Accordingly, most are more than accommodating when a sponsor asks them to make an appearance or shake someone's hand.

"When we talk about the ease with which one might find entry to NASCAR, this is a perfect example," Guilbert said. "Dale Jarrett is a champion in his sport, yet he really works to ensure that he understands the audience that he's meeting with. He takes the time to develop a message that will be delivered effectively, and he makes it look quite natural. He really helps us to grow our business and to win new business. I'm quite sure that is not common in other sports."

One way that UPS leverages its NASCAR sponsorship is through the Team UPS Racing Employee Program, which rewards UPS employees with NASCAR incentives based on a scorecard that benchmarks all areas of package-delivery operations. In a typical NASCAR season, UPS hosts more than nineteen hundred employees and their guests and awards more than seventy-six hundred UPS Racing premiums. UPS also offers employees exclusive merchandise, discounts on regular UPS Racing gear, and special ticket discounts to races.

UPS also uses its NASCAR sponsorship to promote diversity through award-winning practices, and its NASCAR sponsorship provides the opportunity to extend these initiatives into motorsports. Through its position on the NASCAR Diversity Council, UPS helped build a network of NASCAR minority-owned merchandise suppliers modeled after the UPS Supplier Diversity Program. And since 2002, UPS has awarded scholarships to minority students pursuing careers in racing and automotive technology at the NASCAR Technical Institute (NTI). To date, fourteen minority students have received more than $230,000 in scholarships. Two former recipients and NIT graduates now work in the North Carolina racing community.

But team building and corporate hospitality is just the gravy of a NASCAR sponsorship today. Where it really pays off is in the business that's generated among sponsors, teams, and associates. The best example of this is UPS Trackside Services, a NASCAR business that was developed in 2002.

On any given weekend, thousands of packages—auto parts, contracts, licensed goods, even uniforms—arrive at the racetrack. Before 2002, the business was poorly organized and it was hard to find packages at the racetrack. More often than not, race teams, sponsors, and vendors had overnight packages delivered to their hotels rather than to the track.

In 2002, NASCAR gave UPS unfettered access to the NASCAR garage area, something it rarely did for a corporate sponsor. In exchange, the company formed UPS Trackside Services, a mobile delivery operation set up right in the garage area for NASCAR sponsors, teams, licensees, and media.

"We suggested that if we were allowed garage access, we could provide a service to reduce the complexity of having packages delivered to the track," Guilbert said. "We tested it over a three-race period and never looked back. Today, we have a team of UPS drivers and members who are directly responsible for the program."

According to everyone I have spoken to during the 2006 season, it literally transformed the way race teams ship parts to and from the track each weekend. In just the first ten races of 2002, UPS handled over thirteen hundred packages that were shipped to and from various NASCAR racetracks. The business has been a phenomenal success. As I noted in Chapter Two, UPS announced during Daytona SpeedWeeks that it had signed a new five-year agreement with NASCAR to continue as the official express delivery company through 2011. A week later, UPS said it was teaming up with Churchill Downs on a special Kentucky Derby promotion. A special Kentucky Derby paint scheme was featured on Jarrett's car at the Nextel Cup race at Talladega on April 29, a week before the Derby. The company also announced the "Off to the Races delivered by UPS Sweepstakes," an online contest that sent the winner to the Talladega race and the Derby.

"Trackside Services revenues have increased more than one hundred seventy-four percent since it was introduced," Guilbert said. "We've built a significant business in and off itself."

A business that's exclusive to UPS.

"We're the only one that can deliver in the garage," Guilbert said.

Over the past eight years, UPS also has developed or expanded business relationships with 242 NASCAR sponsor companies.

"Trackside Services have opened up a number of conversation opportunities for our sales force," Guilbert said.

For instance, UPS worked with M&M Mars in 2005 to promote the launch of its new dark chocolate–flavored M&Ms. The promotion was tied to the release of *Star Wars: Episode III*. The familiar UPS brown-and-white paint scheme was replaced during the April 23, 2005, Subway Fresh 500 with images from the film. Both Dale Jarrett and UPS Trackside Services had cameo appearances in the Disney film, *Herbie: Fully Loaded*, which featured the lovable bug in a NASCAR race. UPS has also developed an online partnership with NASCAR sponsor Callaway to sell Callaway-UPS Dale Jarrett racing merchandise.

Over the years, UPS Trackside Services has handled everything from auto parts and sponsor decals to in-car camera equipment and uniforms—even Richard Petty's trademark cowboy hats. In 2004, shipping was up 34 percent from 2003; 2005 saw double-digit gains as well. In 2005, UPS expanded its role in NASCAR and handled the logistics for the inaugural NASCAR Busch Series race at the Autodromo Hermanos Rodriguez in Mexico City. The company staged a two-day border crossing in Laredo, Texas, to transport a NASCAR Busch Series race outside the United States for the first time. UPS guided more than eighty team haulers, official trailers, scoring and template equipment, tires, emergency vehicles, and media trucks into Mexico. UPS Supply Chain Solutions coordinated the whole operation.

"Only UPS could bring the planning skills and trans-border resources together with existing NASCAR knowledge and relationships to coordinate this complex movement," Guilbert said.

The event required the synchronization of more than eighty trucks across the Mexico border, and back, in multiple convoys. UPS mapped the travel routes from both the Busch Series event in California and the race shops in North Carolina to Laredo, Texas, so that teams could swap equipment before the twenty-hour drive to Mexico City. The two-way move involved customs documentation and contingency planning, and required special provisions for "visiting" vehicles in Mexico.

The UPS sponsorship has not only generated business, but also increased brand awareness, something else businesses find appealing about a NASCAR sponsorship. According to a study from Joyce Julius and Associates, a market research firm that puts out quarterly and annual reports on NASCAR sponsorships and advertising, UPS ranks in the top ten among NASCAR sponsors for exposure time during race broadcasts. In 2004, UPS received more than seven hours of television exposure time and 112 sponsor mentions during NASCAR races. A

2004 independent study by the Center for Sports Sponsorship at James Madison University found that nearly 70 percent of respondents correctly identified UPS as the official NASCAR sponsor in its product category.

This in turn fueled sales of the company's licensed NASCAR merchandise, which in 2007 is approaching $1 million a season. The UPS sponsorship has also yielded tremendous business growth with other series sponsors. In 2000, UPS counted 40 percent of NASCAR-associated businesses as customers. Today, the company does business with 99 percent of the more than one thousand companies, teams, and tracks affiliated with NASCAR.

What's most interesting is that in 2000, UPS knew next to nothing about NASCAR. That's something I often heard from sponsors: They knew little about NASCAR going in, but since becoming involved with the sport it has become their most active—and valuable—sponsorship program.

NASCAR wasn't UPS's first foray into sports marketing. Before getting involved with auto racing, it was an NFL and Olympic sponsor. Since joining NASCAR in 2001, UPS has become the official package delivery company of the National Hot Rod Association and sponsors a team. It's also a sponsor of the National Thoroughbred Racing Association and the Kentucky Derby, which is run every year at Churchill Downs in Louisville, Kentucky, the worldwide headquarters of UPS's air delivery service. UPS also sponsors a local Italian soccer team and the Porsche Cup in Germany.

"I had zero knowledge of NASCAR when I took over this job in 2004," said Guilbert. "All I knew was that Dale Jarrett was our driver, mainly because I had seen him at a number of corporate sales and marketing events."

What impressed Guilbert from the very beginning was how open and accessible the drivers were—and not just Jarrett, the driver that UPS was sponsoring.

"NASCAR drivers are truly tuned in to just how valuable the sponsor is to the sport," Guilbert said. "They not only listen to what you have to say, but they give you a response that tells you they were not only listening, but understood what you said. It's really something that we have found is common to the principles in NASCAR."

The same is true of crew chiefs, owners, and other sponsors, Guilbert said.

"They're all open and interested in both the sponsor point of view and in helping us to understand their point of view," he said.

Guilbert credits NASCAR—the France family in particular—with this universal stance toward sponsors and their partners.

"I think they get it," Guilbert said. "They truly understand the value of the sponsor to the sport. More important, they understand how important it is to help brands align and not just get to new audiences, but keep them. As a result, there is a consistent approach to working with one another across the sport."

If you think the sponsors in the NFL, NBA, and Major League Baseball are treated like this, you are mistaken.

"I've not done a lot of work in professional sports, but I have met some executives who have and I've talked with other sponsors," Guilbert said. "They tell me that this is uncommon. This access that we afford one another, the genuine exchange of information, is a rarity in a professional sport with million-dollar paydays and multimillion dollar athletes."

What's more, it's this atmosphere of openness and cooperation that makes it so easy for new sponsors to come into the sport and hit the ground running.

"What I've found to be a significant learning opportunity is the chance to work with other sponsors with more experience than us, as well as others who are new to the sport," Guilbert said.

Although sponsors may have different levels of experience, the common denominator is the desire to grow their business through NASCAR.

"This open forum creates an opportunity for us to learn about [other sponsors'] businesses and for them to learn about ours," Guilbert said. "And from there, we look for opportunities to grow our business together."

Not only are these decisions made quickly because everyone's cards are on the table, but there is almost a laissez-faire attitude about doing business in NASCAR.

"No harm, no foul," Guilbert said. "If it works, it works. If it doesn't, it doesn't."

In 2006, UPS had some fun with its sponsorship and raised its hipness quotient on Madison Avenue by creating one of the most memorable ads of the NASCAR season.

It started with a father and son, standing near the fence going into Turn One, watching NASCAR practice. First to zoom by is Tony Stewart in the Home Depot No. 20, then Elliott Sadler in the No. 38 M&Ms car. As the cars streak by, the son pumps his fist, cheering them on. So far, nothing out of the ordinary.

Then they look up into Turn Four and see headlights in the distance. Stock cars don't have headlights. The camera zooms in and a big brown UPS delivery truck is screaming down the track, its engine making the same throaty roar as the other race cars. The truck zooms by—easily as fast as Stewart and Sadler—and creates such a draft that the kid's feet lift up off the ground, his father holding on as tight as he can as the kid's whole body waves in the wind by the draft that's created. The commercial closes with another closeup shot of the truck, and the words "Go Dale Go."

No doubt, it's a pretty clever commercial. But it also tells you a lot about the sponsor. Whoever approved that commercial knows a lot about NASCAR.

The NASCAR audience is Middle America and often multi-generational, with a parent or grandparent passing on the traditions of the sport to the youngsters. For many, just watching the cars go around the track is a thrill. You can see it in the way the father and son from the commercial watch the cars—and it's only practice. You can almost smell the exhaust and tires as the cars—and the UPS truck—go roaring by.

When I interviewed Guilbert, the first thing I said was: "Great special effects on the commercial. It really looked like the truck was going that fast."

"That wasn't special effects," he said.

Indeed, what many people don't know is that UPS had a delivery truck body put on a race car chassis. The big brown truck in the commercial is really going about one hundred sixty miles per hour.

"We could have hired a special effects studio to do the commercial for us using a digital UPS delivery truck," Guilbert said. "We didn't."

Apparently it worked. According to Ad Track, of those

familiar with UPS's NASCAR ads, 26 percent like them "a lot," compared with the Ad Track average of 21 percent. The ads are considered "very effective" by 19 percent of respondents, compared with an average of 20 percent.

But as you'll see in the next chapter, the UPS delivery truck ad was not the most famous NASCAR ad of 2006.

CHAPTER TEN
FANTASY ACCIDENTS

Allstate's All-Star Ad Campaign

Without a doubt, the award for best NASCAR advertising campaign of 2006 goes to Allstate, a sponsor of Kasey Kahne's No. 9 Dodge and the Allstate 400 at the Brickyard at the Indianapolis Motor Speedway. If there was an award for best new sponsor in NASCAR, Allstate would probably win that, too.

Allstate's 2006 ads featured three everyday women who are representative of NASCAR's 40 percent-plus female fan base. Like the women you find in the grandstands every week, the women are race fanatics, and often have these elaborate fantasies about their favorite driver, Kasey Kahne. That's where they get into trouble. Their daydreaming leads to hilarious mishaps, which ties the whole thing back to one of Allstate's core businesses, auto insurance, and its most direct connection to NASCAR.

"Actually, the idea of a fantastical accident started with the 2004 Olympics," said Lisa Cochrane, vice president of marketing for Allstate.

One of Allstate's Olympic commercials featured a shot putter who hurls the shot outside the stadium and into the parking lot, where it hits a bunch of parked cars. It ended with the tagline, "Are you in good hands?"

The combination of the Olympics media buy and the highly creative ads from a company in a rather dull industry put Allstate on Madison Avenue's radar screen.

"When we announced our NASCAR sponsorship, we said to our advertising agency, Leo Burnett, that this formula works," Cochrane said. "So we asked them, 'Can we do a tasteful accident in NASCAR and make it work?'"

The agency, which, like Allstate, is based in Chicago, came up with what it calls the "girl's day out" series.

"We were looking for women who were like me," said Cochrane, who admits she's fifty-one but still feels (and sometimes acts) like she's in her late twenties. "We wanted these women to be like every woman. They're not Bo Derek, but they could be our friends. They're three girlfriends. They're ageless, anywhere from late twenties to fortyish. We can identify with these women."

More important, they were exemplary of the typical female NASCAR fan, many of whom know as much about the sport as their husbands and fathers and are just as fanatical about their favorite drivers.

The first ad in the campaign that started in 2005, entitled "Victory," didn't feature the women at all. It was a dream sequence, with Kasey Kahne popping the cork on a bottle of champagne, celebrating a race win. Like the Olympic shot put spot, the cork goes careening around the garage area, bouncing off cars, breaking windows, "doing far more damage than a normal cork could ever do," Cochrane said. Again, it closed with Allstate's signature tagline, "Are you in good hands?"

The first "girls' day out" ad debuted August 7, 2005, and featured a group of women driving to the racetrack. As they look for a parking spot in the infield, they spot Kasey Kahne near his hauler. Distracted, they back into an infield light tower, knocking it over onto a bunch of parked cars.

The ads were an instant hit.

"We only show them two times over a four-hour race—sometimes four," Cochrane said. "But they worked, so we said, 'Let's keep it going.'"

The latest ad in the 2006 season featured the Allstate women going to a Kasey Kahne autograph session at a local garage. As they pull into the parking lot, they see him and each has their own dream sequence. In one scene, Kahne is racing down the front straight during a NASCAR race. When the camera zooms in, one of the girls is in the car with him, cuddling, as he drives nonchalantly with one hand. Another features one of the Allstate women on a dollie under a car in the repair shop. When she scoots out, there he is. Kahne reaches down and wipes a smudge of grease off her face. She spontaneously pulls him down onto the dollie, kissing him as they roll back under the car.

The ad ends with the women waking up from their dream as they knock a seven-ton tire off its perch onto one of Kahne's show cars. Like the UPS delivery van commercial, Allstate didn't go with flashy special effects.

"We literally dropped a seven-ton tire on his show car," Cochrane said.

"A lot of the creativity you see in the ads is [the actresses] hamming it up and ad libbing," Cochrane said. "Grabbing him, kissing him, rolling back under the car. That was a total ad lib."

The ads were the number one downloaded NASCAR video on YouTube in 2006. They also finished ninth in *Ad Age's* annual survey of most downloaded ads across all categories.

"When you think that we only run them during NASCAR races, that's pretty impressive," Cochrane said.

Indeed, so impressive that Allstate debuted two new ads during the broadcast of the 2007 Daytona 500 and plans to continue the campaign through the 2007 season. One of the ads features Kahne being pulled over by a police car. He's told to put his hands on the trunk and then a female officer tells him to move his hips. The camera zooms into the car, and there are the Allstate girls, giggling. The woman police officer says, "This is the last time I let you ride with me."

As stunning as the ad campaign and its success are, equally stunning is what Allstate has done with its NASCAR sponsorship in just two years. To see just how creative and successful the company has been with its NASCAR marketing program, all you needed to do was try to find a place to park outside the Indianapolis Motor Speedway and the Allstate 400 at the Brickyard in late July 2006.

As any NASCAR fan can tell you, people who live near a NASCAR track make a killing selling parking space in their yards and driveways during race weekends. That's especially true for Indy, which is in a residential neighborhood and had three big race weekends in 2006—the Indianapolis 500 in May, the Allstate 400 at the Brickyard in July, and the U.S. Grand Prix Formula One race in September. On those weekends, lawns are dotted with handmade signs that read: "Park Here—$25."

In 2006, Allstate took the local parking enterprise upscale by creating preprinted signs that read "Park Here" and a blank space where residents could fill in the price with a magic marker. Of course, the signs were all branded in Allstate colors and featured the Allstate logo. In short, that little promotion made sure that every race fan—some two hundred fifty thousand—knew the title sponsor's name before they even stepped inside the track. Pretty smart.

The whole Allstate sponsorship is fairly unique. Yes, sponsors have been buying the naming rights to races—and racetracks—for decades. But the Indianapolis Motor Speedway had never before sold naming rights to any of its races.

"We tried to figure out how, with all the clutter in NASCAR, we could make ourselves memorable and notable, with a limited budget," Cochrane said.

That issue of clutter is not insignificant when it comes to NASCAR. With all the Fortune 500 brands in NASCAR today, it's hard to distinguish one's self.

Sponsoring a driver or a car are the top two ways to jump-start a NASCAR sponsorship. Allstate did that by signing on as an associate sponsor with Ray Evernham Motorsports and driver Kasey Kahne in 2005 (Dodge is the primary sponsor on the car). Another way is to attach the corporation's name to a racetrack or race.

"We are a very big brand, so we looked for a track affiliation that would be large," Cochrane said. "That brought us to the Indianapolis Motor Speedway."

At the time, Indy was not shopping for a sponsor for the Brickyard 400, which since its 1994 debut has grown to be Indy's single-biggest event of the year, eclipsing even the Indy 500. But because of the entrée that a company gains by becoming a NASCAR sponsor, the doors to the Indy executive offices were opened.

"What we figured out was that we [Allstate and NASCAR] were two very solid Midwest brands," Cochrane said. "We were both first-class organizations, delivering a first-class product to consumers."

Not bad for a company that two years before didn't know anything about NASCAR. Indeed, before Allstate started its NASCAR sponsorship in 2005, it looked at its entire marketing and advertising portfolio.

"We realized that in a highly competitive business like insurance, it's important to find new ways to reach potential customers," Cochrane said. "We felt that if we focused on two sponsorships where we could engage people who are passionate—a fan base—we could do that."

NASCAR was particularly appealing because of its core male fan base in the twenty-four- to thirty-six-year-old age range.

"NASCAR was a sport we thought we could grow with," Cochrane said. "NASCAR fans are a particularly loyal fan base when it comes to sponsors and brands. Particularly when it's a product that's relevant to racing. They're not only loyal, but will switch to that brand."

In 2005, after looking at sponsorships as diverse as rock concerts and Broadway musicals, Allstate chose NASCAR and college football as the focus of its marketing, advertising, and branding campaigns. The company became the official auto, home, life, and retirement insurance provider of NASCAR, aligned itself with Evernham and Kahne, and bought the naming rights to the Brickyard 400.

"It was the best venue for the one question we ask every consumer in all of our advertising: 'Are you in good hands?' " Cochrane said. "Through our sponsorship, we have, in essence, affiliated our customers with the best drivers in the world— NASCAR drivers."

Beyond the hype of a promotional campaign, Allstate has a legitimate legacy of being associated with safe driving. It championed the use of seat belts in the 1950s and 1960s. Later, it lobbied the government for air bags and crash-resistant bumpers. Today, Allstate is one of the biggest advocates for electronic crash avoidance systems, the next wave in automotive safety technology. But like a lot of new sponsors, Allstate knew next to nothing about NASCAR.

"I didn't even know what NASCAR stood for," Cochrane said. "But I knew it could be used as a very effective marketing tool and I learned about the fan base. Most important, we had a chance to go to a race and see the kind of people who went to these races."

Like a lot of NASCAR sponsors, from R. J. Reynolds in the 1970s to DuPont and Kraft Foods in the 1980s, and Nextel and Best Buy today, Allstate learned that the NASCAR audience was mostly made up of people they work with every day: their customers.

"It was moms and dads holding kids' hands," Cochrane said. "It was a polite crowd that was interested enough in NASCAR to commit a full weekend to it. They were regular Americans. Moreover,

NASCAR and its audience fit well with our corporate image. We want to be where America is, and America is into NASCAR."

Indeed, it's usually after going to a race and digging deep into the NASCAR demographic data that sponsors get sold on the sport. Yes, NASCAR is the fastest-growing sport in the United States with a fan base of seventy-five million. But it's also a family sport that can be leveraged both nationally and locally.

"We can craft a successful national advertising campaign, but it's also something that can be used locally by our 13,500 Allstate agents across the U.S.," Cochrane said.

Like a lot of sponsors, Allstate leverages its NASCAR affiliation in a variety of ways. The Allstate 400 at the Brickyard is, in many ways, its signature NASCAR event of the year. In 2006, Allstate brought more than one thousand employees and customers to the race. The company runs contests in its claims and service centers across the country, with employees, many of them rabid NASCAR fans, competing for tickets and all-expense-paid weekends at the Allstate 400. Allstate also uses the corporate hospitality suites at Indy to entertain important existing clients and potential new ones.

"We use it as a sales incentive for our agents and regional sales managers," Cochrane said. "We also use it to entertain business colleagues and clients."

In addition to employees who get to go to the track for free, as part of an incentive bonus, the company also offers discounted tickets to employees throughout the company. Allstate also brands all the key cards at local hotels with its logo, buys extra garbage cans for the city of Indianapolis with its logo on the side, and buys advertising on billboards along the roads leading to and from the track. The Allstate Foundation, the company's charity arm, also brings kids from the local Boys and Girls Club to the race.

"We plaster the city for the entire weekend," Cochrane said. "There are very few places you can go and not see our logo or brand."

Beyond the Allstate 400, the company uses its relationship with driver Kasey Kahne in a variety of venues. He does traditional meet and greets in the corporate hospitality suites at select NASCAR events. Like UPS, Allstate uses him to speak to agents and to CEOs and CFOs of important business partners and at senior leadership meetings.

Allstate also used Kahne to kick off its promotion, "Kasey Wins, You Win." In both 2005 and 2006, people who called into an Allstate service center for a rate quote heard an automated greeting from Kasey Kahne. After they received their quote, they became eligible for a free trip to the Allstate 400 at the Brickyard. The winners got to meet Kahne before the race, and if he won the race, they would win $400,000.

In 2005, Allstate almost had to pay out the $400 grand. Kahne finished a close second to Home Depot driver Tony Stewart. In 2006, he was in top contention early on in the race, but then faded.

"We also use him a few times a year for local appearances around NASCAR races," said Stacey Zipse, marketing manager for Allstate's NASCAR programs. "We show clips that demonstrate how his good driving connects to Allstate."

That's the theme that runs through all of Allstate's NASCAR promotions, and the reason it became involved in the sport in the first place.

"It's why NASCAR is a good fit for us," Cochrane said. "It's all about good driving, making good choices."

The "You're in good hands" tagline has been ranked number one for the past ten years in terms of consumer recognition. The natural extension to NASCAR includes a new tagline, "We'd like to sponsor your car, too."

So how does Allstate know that this is money well spent?

The insurance industry is one of the most guarded with its data. But Cochrane said that the company has a variety of metrics that tell it that it's getting a good return on its investment.

"We have a national monthly tracking study where we measure lots of brand [promotion] and advertising [efforts]. We watch that very carefully," she said. "We also have tools that help us break it out by demographic groups, and we have very sophisticated modeling and measuring within our marketing group."

Allstate is also able to measure the impact of the sponsorship locally. For instance, local agents near a NASCAR event will often use the NASCAR sponsorship to drive new business. All of the leads that are generated via NASCAR or mention the sponsorship are recorded.

"We measure number of inquiries, leads, other metrics," Cochrane said. "Anything that's related to or driven by the sponsorship."

Allstate measures the number of leads generated at the racetrack, as well. Like a lot of sponsors, Allstate has kiosks throughout the grandstand and midway area. Its agents are there throughout the race weekend, handing out promotional and marketing material. Sometimes the agents do driver appearances to drive traffic.

Allstate also measures the press coverage it receives.

"We measure earned media, media mentions," Cochrane

said. "And we don't just measure press clippings, but degree of coverage. Whether it's positive, negative, or neutral."

"The truth is," Cochrane said, "we're still very new at this. It's still building. There hasn't been enough time to see how much it has been embedded in the American public. But we're seeing very positive trends."

"We've been very strategic about our NASCAR sponsorship programs," she added. "Strategic and focused."

CHAPTER ELEVEN

WHAT'S DLP?

Educating the Public at 200 Miles Per Hour

While Allstate and its "You're in good hands" tagline had remarkably good brand recognition before it ever became a NASCAR sponsor, DLP got into the sport because almost no one knew what it was or what it did.

You've probably seen DLP's commercials. The little girl with the elephant. "It's all about the mirrors."

DLP is a division of Texas Instruments. It consists of three business units: one focused on cinema, one focused on front-screen projection technology for conference rooms and home theater, and one focused on the home market for high-definition television (HDTV).

"The technology has actually been in commercial production since 1996," said Doug Darrow, brand and marketing manager for DLP.

The technology was invented in the late 1970s, but it wasn't commercialized until the mid-1990s. Over the past ten years, the company has been focused on marketing and selling the technology to its three core markets. Over the past decade, DLP grew its business to the point where it is working with all major brands in all three market segments. Despite that success, very few people knew what it was or what it did.

Darrow has been with Texas Instruments for more than twenty years. He started out working in the company's military optics division and eventually moved into business development and marketing for the company. About nine years ago, he started with DLP, first working with its cinema unit, getting its digital projection technology in about two thousand theaters worldwide. As a result, most major films produce copies in high def for those venues.

About two years ago, he took over all marketing and branding for DLP, focusing specifically on where the brand was in terms of consumer awareness for HDTV technology. What he saw didn't look good.

"We felt that we were behind the other major technologies, most notably plasma and LCD technologies," he said. "We also found that when we educated people about DLP, a high percentage became owners of DLP HDTVs. In short, we needed to get our message to the consumer."

This was especially important because HDTVs, which had once been something that only Hollywood directors had in their home theaters, were becoming mainstream consumer products.

"Price points were dropping twenty percent to thirty percent per year," Darrow said. "As a result, the big-screen TV market was growing thirty percent to forty percent per year."

Indeed, Forrester Research found that 41 percent of HDTV buyers had household income of below $50,000. HDTV was becoming a must-have for all income levels in U.S. households.

"It's not just the wealthy anymore. When it was a product that cost five thousand dollars, yes, but not now. We'll see fifteen hundred dollar TVs this year, probably even pressing the nine hundred ninety-nine dollar barrier," he said in late 2006.

HDTV was becoming mainstream because of price as well as programming. Almost all sports programs today are broadcast in high def. In 2005, NASCAR started broadcasting all its races in HDTV.

"People buy TVs now like they buy cars," Darrow said. "They ask, 'What's my payment? I'm going to get the biggest TV I can fit [in] my living room.' "

With prices dropping, broadcasts increasing, and competition intensifying, DLP had to find a way to get its name out there and educate consumers about the DLP technology and why they should buy it.

"NASCAR was interesting to us because it allowed us to tap into the consumer who's going to be thinking about DLP over the next several years," Darrow said. "We looked at that and saw an opportunity to connect with very loyal fans in the second-biggest sport in the U.S. We thought we could accelerate awareness with an audience like that."

Like a lot of sponsors, the NASCAR demographic was what sold DLP on the sport.

"The fan base is so big," Darrow said. "The demographics with the NFL overlap fairly closely. Typical fans are very much the same. These people buy big screen TVs for watching sports and movies. It just provided a unique opportunity to get our message out to the people who were going to be buying. It matched the other large targets that we focus on, as well."

Like Allstate, DLP jumped into NASCAR with both feet. It became the primary sponsor on the No. 96 car driven by Tony Raines and owned by Roger Staubach and Troy Aikman, the founders of Hall of Fame Racing, a team new to NASCAR. The sponsorship alone probably cost the company $20 million.

"It's a very expensive endeavor," Darrow said. "However, there are few places you can go and have your brand represented as prominently and be supported so strongly by the sport and the fan base.

"I can't put my logo on the jersey of a football player," Darrow said. "I can make my logo part of the competitive aspect of a race team and it translates to on-air measures and exposure. It's a unique combination that no other major sport provides in a similar way. It's very appealing to someone trying to connect to a large audience."

Proof that it was money well spent will come from increased brand awareness.

"Do more people know about DLP?" Darrow asked. "Do they make it part of their purchase?"

The company was also attracted by a NASCAR sponsorship's ability to improve relations with existing business partners and develop new relationships through the sport, particularly the B2B Council.

"While our primary customer is the consumer, we definitely looked at our NASCAR sponsorship as an opportunity to work with other retailers and develop joint promotions," Darrow said.

DLP has done exactly that, doing joint promotions around NASCAR races in key markets with retailers such as Ultimate Electronics, ABC Warehouse, and Circuit City. NASCAR sponsorships also help companies to woo important customers—sometimes at the expense of others. Both Circuit City and Best Buy are NASCAR sponsors, but DLP chose to work specifically with Circuit City on NASCAR promotions in 2006.

"We didn't do the same thing with Best Buy, but did it with Circuit City because it allowed us to take that investment and make it work for us," Darrow said. "Circuit City was a partner we needed to grow with, and partnering with them through NASCAR helped us do that."

While it's fair to say that B2B has been the primary focus of DLP's sponsorship during its first year, the company hasn't forgotten about the consumer segment. DLP had an eighty-foot-by-eight-foot mobile display on the NASCAR midway at thirty races in 2006. It's literally a mobile theater where consumers could go in and watch a film on HD that explains the business and technology behind DLP.

Through its NASCAR sponsorship, DLP also became the exclusive provider of HDTVs at the racetrack for International Speedway Corporation, which owns Daytona; and Speedway Motorsports Inc., which owns Charlotte, Texas, and Las Vegas facilities, plus the Indianapolis Motor Speedway.

DLP also hosted hospitality events at about twenty races in 2006, including a big event at Texas Motor Speedway, just down the road from Texas Instruments's corporate headquarters. And while most any hospitality event is a thrill for customers, the DLP suite takes on a unique aura when team owners Roger Staubach and Troy Aikman are there.

"When you bring a customer or business partner inside NASCAR, show them what we're doing, and you get that behind-the-scenes look, it's like nothing else," Darrow said. "Having Roger and Troy there as the team owners is a great plus. [Our guests] get to meet two of the legends of pro football. Several times during the 2006 season, I heard guests say, 'That was the best weekend of my life.' It made such an impact, such an impression with important customers like Samsung, Mitsubishi, Toshiba, and RCA.

"Because we're a primary sponsor, you can give people a behind-the-scenes look like no other sport," Darrow said. "We can put them in pits, watch a pit stop, every weekend. I can't put somebody behind Bill Parcells and watch him call the Cowboys game. That is a unique benefit."

DLP also advertises during NASCAR race broadcasts. According to company internal surveys, it has increased brand awareness among consumers.

"In terms of on-air exposure—car, team, mentions, etc.—DLP is in the top five along with Lowe's, Cingular, Home Depot, and Budweiser," Darrow said. "In terms of brand awareness, we measure it constantly and see it increasing."

That's sometimes difficult in NASCAR, which Darrow said is a "noisy environment," especially the midway in front of the track.

"There are a lot of companies bombarding the fans with images and promotions, trying to get their message out," Darrow said. "Seven of the top ten Fortune 500 companies have a presence in NASCAR. That's some tough competition."

But so far, it's working for DLP. Part of the reason is the fact that NASCAR fans are at the track for three days. They pretty much stay in their seats on Friday, watching practice and Nextel Cup qualifying. But if Saturday is a down day, with just second-round Nextel Cup practice and a Busch or ARCA race, that's when they'll spend some time strolling the midway, looking at all the displays set up by the sponsors.

"It's not like a football game where people show up for a few hours, watch the game and go home," Darrow said. "NASCAR fans are there for three days, looking for something to do."

As our next sponsor will tell you, some fans even sign up for the biggest commitment of their life.

CHAPTER TWELVE

THE MILITARY MARCHES IN

Recruiting at the Racetrack

"I just ain't got the words to express it," said National Guard Staff Sergeant Quinton Martin. "I'm just an ole country boy and I'm not used to all this attention."

Who is Sergeant Martin? Did he just save a busload of school kids in Iraq? Was he decorated by his commanding officer? No, he was the first ever winner of the National Guard's Hero of the Year award, sponsored by Jackson Hewitt Tax Service. In February 2007, at the second NASCAR race of the season, Sergeant Martin's image was displayed on the hood of the No. 25 National Guard/GMAC Chevrolet. Martin served in Iraq with the 1108th

Aviation Support Detachment and has been a member of the National Guard for twenty-four years. The fifty-one-year-old Mississippi Guardsman is from the tiny town of Seminary, just north of Hattiesburg. The company flew Martin and his family to California to be trackside during Sunday's race. It was the first time the hood of a NASCAR vehicle carried the image of a regular guy. Only celebrities have had the honor in the past.

Martin was scheduled to deploy to Kuwait in support of the war in Iraq when Hurricane Katrina hammered the Gulf Coast on August 29, 2005. His base in Gulfport, Mississippi, was hard hit. His unit, the 1108th Aviation Classification and Repair Activity Depot, was put on hurricane duty. As that assignment was wrapping up, Martin volunteered to go to Kuwait.

The military has always had a pretty strong connection to NASCAR. Many of the early NASCAR drivers who raced around dusty half-mile clay ovals in the South in the 1940s and 1950s were World War II vets. Bud Moore, one of the most successful car owners in the history of NASCAR, served with Patton's Third Army at the Battle of the Bulge. In the 1980s, long before there were NASCAR mechanic schools, many pit crew members received their training in the military and then came home to the Carolinas to find jobs with the local race team. Bart Creaseman, the jack-of-all-trades truck driver for Bobby Hamilton's Country Time team in the early 1990s, had been an Army Ranger and parachuted into Grenada. Another well-known pit crew member during the 1990s was nicknamed "Rambo," both because he was built like Sylvester Stallone and had served in the U.S. Army's Special Forces.

When the Gulf War came along in the early 1990s, Humpy Wheeler, president of the Charlotte Motor Speedway and the undisputed P. T. Barnum of NASCAR, staged a scene from the war in the infield before the start of the 1991 Coca-Cola 600. He even had a façade of the battleship U.S.S. *New Jersey* rise above the retaining wall in Turn Three and fire a couple of salvos against Saddam's mock forces.

With Fort Bragg, home of the 82nd Airborne, less than one hundred miles to the east of the Charlotte track, the military has become a common theme to Humpy's prerace extravaganzas. Over the years, Rangers have parachuted into the infield and Black Hawk helicopters have hovered long enough to allow Special Forces troops to rappel down to the start/finish line. When country music glommed onto NASCAR in the 1990s, the patriotic streak only got wider and a deeper shade of red, white, and blue. In short, honoring our military just fit with the culture of NASCAR. With all this patriotism surging through the NASCAR garage area, it only seemed natural for the armed forces to become full-time NASCAR sponsors.

The U.S. Army became the first armed forces full-time NASCAR sponsor in 2003, spending a reported $16 million in the first season with MB2 Motorsports, which agreed to change its car number from 36 to 01 to coordinate with the service's "Army of One" ad campaign. Soon after, all five active-duty services and the National Guard followed with full-time sponsorships either in the Nextel Cup or Busch Series. They even became part of the "silly season," the period toward the end of each NASCAR season when sponsors hop from one team to another. During the 2006 off-season, the National Guard team announced that it was leaving car owner Jack Roush's stable and teaming up with longtime car owner Rick Hendrick. In 2007, the National Guard and GMAC jointly sponsored the No. 25 Chevrolet driven by Casey Mears in the Nextel Cup Series.

"NASCAR continues to be a vital component of our recruiting and retention programs, and we believe this new relationship will further enhance our involvement in the sport," said Colonel Mike Jones, chief of the Army National Guard's Strength Maintenance Division.

The Air Force also re-upped with Wood Brothers Racing and Ken Schrader for the 2007 season.

Considering the changing demographics of NASCAR—more affluent, more female, more educated, more urban—why does the military continue to target this audience?

"We're trying to reach the influencers," said Senior Chief Jeff Priest, thirty-seven, a twenty-year career recruiter who heads up the U.S. Navy's NASCAR sponsorship. "The moms, the dads, the uncles. We're trying to let them know what the Navy is all about and why it might be a good place for some of their kids to start their career, earn money for college, whatever."

Even though the NASCAR demographics might not appear on the surface to be a good fit with the armed services, all the recruiters say they are.

"According to our research, seventy-two percent of the NASCAR fan base fits in our target market," Priest said. "That's age seventeen to fifty-five. The upper end of that are the influencers."

You're probably getting tired of hearing this of every influential NASCAR program manager that's been introduced in this book, but here it is again: Before taking over the Navy's NASCAR program, Priest didn't know much about NASCAR.

"I knew they went in circles. I knew the names Jeff Gordon and Dale Earnhardt Jr. But I had never been to a race or watched a race."

When he finally did go to a NASCAR race, he had the same epiphany that many of NASCAR's business sponsors have had.

"I went and said, 'This is just like what the Navy does.' It's high-tech. Speed and accuracy is important. You have to be concerned with the minutest details: tire pressure, tire wear, shocks, aerodynamics. This is not just a bunch of guys going around in circles."

The Navy went NASCAR racing in 2001 with Roush Racing and NASCAR Craftsman Truck Series driver Jon Wood. In 2003, a new admiral took over the Navy Recruiting Command, liked what he saw from the NASCAR program, and decided to turn it up a notch.

"He said, 'We're going to do this right. We're going to make it a Navy awareness tool,'" Priest said.

Campbell Ewald, a motorsports public relations firm, sent out a proposal to the Busch Series, looking for open sponsorships. But why not Nextel Cup?

"We're in the business of developing young men and women into productive citizens," Priest said. "That's sort of what the Busch Series does."

The Navy signed on for just ten races in 2003 with FitzBradshaw Racing and driver Casey Atwood. At the end of the season, it exercised its option for the 2004 season and all thirty-four Busch races. It renewed the sponsorship again in 2005. Then the Navy was approached by one of the few names that Priest knew before getting involved in the sport: Dale Earnhardt Jr.

"He contacted our ad agency because he knew we had done an open bid the last two years," Priest said. "We knew what was out there, what was available. Dale Jr. wanted the Navy to be the sponsor for his first Busch team. He's a military history buff, attended military school. It was a good fit for us and for him."

Earnhardt Jr. isn't alone in the NASCAR garage in his admiration for the armed forces.

"NASCAR has the most patriotic fans of any sport I've ever seen," Priest said. "It means something special to these guys in the garage to represent a branch of the service. That's our base. Those patriotic fans, drivers, and crews."

The military clearly has a strong presence in NASCAR. In addition to providing color guards and jets to accompany the National Anthem at the start of every race, all the armed services have display booths set up along the NASCAR midway, the area behind the grandstand where souvenir trailers and promotional booths are lined up. While these kiosks are meant to entice new recruits, they're often where the services learn just how successful their NASCAR programs are and how they resonate with the NASCAR fans. During the last week of the 2006 NASCAR season, Priest and his other recruiters had a woman walk up to them at Homestead-Miami Speedway and thank them for their service and their sponsorship.

"She literally had tears in her eyes and thanked us for what we were doing for our country," Priest said. "That, right there, says a lot about what we're doing and why we're in NASCAR."

So how exactly do the Navy and the other armed services leverage their NASCAR sponsorship beyond putting their name and colors on the hood of a stock car, setting up a kiosk along the very crowded NASCAR midway, or bringing in a flight simulator to entice young seventeen-year-olds? Like the major corporations that are NASCAR sponsors, the armed services are very targeted and strategic in their approach.

"We looked at lead generation, the parts of the country where recruiting was low," Priest said. "So in 2005 and 2006, we focused on eighteen tracks and thirty-five races." Places like Daytona; Talladega, Alabama; Richmond, Virginia; Fontana, California; Kansas City; and Sparta, Kentucky, which is the only stand-alone Busch race that has sold out every year.

The Navy also "sailorizes" the race team, including the driver, owner, and crew chief. What does that mean? They take crew members to various Navy facilities during the season and let them see just what life is like in the Navy. It's akin to putting actors through a mock boot camp before they make a military film.

"We've taken team members to the Great Lakes boot camp just north of Chicago, to fly with the Blue Angels, out for a day on a submarine," Priest said. "It gives them a greater appreciation and understanding of what our sailors do every day."

This is especially important when team owner Dale Earnhardt Jr. and driver Shane Huffman talk to the media.

"They can talk about what it means to be a sailor with honor, courage, and commitment," Priest said. "And that's the way we run the team and the sponsorship. It's more of a partnership than a business relationship."

Priest knew the Navy training had rubbed off when, during an August 2006 interview, team owner Dale Earnhardt Jr. said, "I'm not selling soap, I'm selling a way of life."

It's tough for the armed services to measure exactly how many leads they generate and how many people actually join the service because of a NASCAR sponsorship. But the Navy is sticking with its focus on under-represented markets in 2007.

"Kansas City is one of those markets that is often forgotten about," Priest said, especially for the Navy. "It's in the middle of the country, about as far from the ocean as you can get, but we recruit sailors from there all the time."

While the number of recruits that NASCAR exposure generates is hard to measure, there's the occasional anecdotal evidence. At the Talladega race in May 2006, Priest had a young kid walk up and shake his hand. He told the recruiter he had signed up for the Navy to be a nuclear engineer and was due to ship out to boot camp in October. What made him join?

"He talked to one of our recruiters at the track, was impressed that we were associated with NASCAR, and decided to join," Priest said. "There was no way to track him and attribute it to the program. But we know it's happening."

And while NASCAR's diversity program has been hit and miss, it's another area where the Navy's goals and NASCAR's goals are one in the same.

"We want to hire you for your ability to perform a job," Priest said. "When you look at NASCAR, the face of the fan base is changing. It's becoming a more diverse crowd. There are almost as many female fans of NASCAR as there are males. We're constantly looking for females as well, for nontraditional jobs. We're not hiring females to be secretaries. We're looking to hire females to be mechanics."

In fact, the shock specialist at Junior Motorsports is a woman.

"That fits in line with what we're talking about," Priest said.

The Air Force is convinced that its NASCAR sponsorship is having a positive impact on recruiting.

In 1999, the Air Force fell short of its recruiting goal for the first time. General John W. Handy saw NASCAR as a way to turn that around. In 2001, the Air Force signed on as an associate sponsor of Elliott Sadler's No. 21 Motorcraft Ford. By May, the Air Force had reached its recruiting goal for the full year.

"I'd like to think it's rocket science, but it isn't," Air Force Vice Chief of Staff John W. Handy told *Sports Illustrated*. "We had a recruiting/retention task force looking at a long list of opportunities for the Air Force to market itself to the American public. It didn't take much market analysis to tell us what we all know today. NASCAR was a sport on the rise. The traditional sports were flatlining or declining, as far as TV and audience participation.

"It's important to understand that NASCAR is a speed sport," Handy continued. "There's tremendous teamwork required between driver and pit crew. There is a crew chief. If you look at the Air Force, it's very high tech, very high speed. The relationship between the pilot and crew chief is similar to NASCAR. One of the skills we need most is mechanical skill. The average NASCAR race has one hundred fifty thousand in attendance and the audience for TV is in the millions. That all combined in the picture."

The NASCAR connection became clear to the Air Force after the 2000 Coca-Cola 600, which is always held on Memorial Day weekend. The Air Force colors were on Dale Jarrett's car for the race, part of a special promotion. Charlotte, like the rest of the country, had been behind in its recruiting goal. But for the three months immediately following the Memorial Day race, recruiters saw a spike in enlistments.

"With NASCAR, you get a real patriotic crowd out there," said Master Sergeant Randy Fuller, who oversees the Air Force NASCAR sponsorship. "They might have a propensity over some people to join the Air Force."

"I think all the services, ever since the elimination of the draft, have had to be innovative," said former Georgia Senator Max Cleland, a Vietnam veteran, member of President Jimmy Carter's cabinet as head of the Veterans' Administration, and an avid

NASCAR fan. "They're going after the same cohort, seventeen- to twenty-one-year-old males, basically. But more and more it is a high-tech force. It's a force that thrives on adventure and excitement and technology and speed. And in some ways, NASCAR may be more in that zone than most. Whatever seems to work, the services have to try it.

"Right now, they are struggling for visibility, for just coming into the mind of a young person," Cleland continued. "In effect, the services are like many other commodities, I guess. You've got to break through what one of my friends in the advertising business used to call it, the 'boredom barrier.' And if that means at halftime of sporting events or between NASCAR races all of sudden paratroopers are coming out of Air Force planes, dropping to the middle of the infield, that at least breaks the boredom barrier. You've got to get people's attention first. So then you can say, 'Hey, this might be cool.' "

The NASCAR connection for the Air Force is particularly strong. The vast majority of its recruits go on to receive some sort of mechanical training to keep multimillion dollar fighters and bombers flying. To tap into that interest in mechanics, the Air Force brings its show car to high schools, malls, and other teen hangouts, as well as the racetrack. It also doesn't hurt that Air Force planes are often the ones that do flyovers during the National Anthem at NASCAR races.

"It's been great to be represented by the U.S. Air Force," said driver Elliott Sadler. "That is pretty cool. And the way they just rolled out the red carpet for us. I've been to the Pentagon with them, been to a few Air Force bases. They took up a few of my crew members and owners in F-15s and F-16s. What they've done for us is unbelievable. There are only like eleven or twelve four-star generals in the whole United States, and I think I've already met seven of them."

Given all that, it only makes sense that the Air Force would return to the Wood Brothers and drivers Ken Schrader and Jon Wood, who will split the driving duties for the 2007 season. It will mark the seventh consecutive season that the Air Force has been with the Wood Brothers.

"Having a chance to represent the United States Air Force is an honor for me," said Jon Wood, who will be behind the wheel for all of the primary sponsorship races. "To me, it means getting a chance to represent the men and women who put their lives on the line around the world every day so that we can enjoy the freedoms we do."

According to U.S. Air Force Senior Master Sergeant Mike Rowland, who oversees the Air Force's NASCAR-related programs, the service's association with the Wood Brothers/JTG Race team has brought extended benefits to its recruitment efforts over the years.

"We target four million graduating high school seniors each year by seeking the same target audience that follows the high-octane sport of NASCAR," Rowland said. "This program has been exciting and successful for us and we're looking forward to a great relationship with Jon Wood and the twenty-one team next year."

While Wood will share the driving duties with Schrader on the Nextel Cup circuit, he will still drive full-time for his family-owned No. 47 team in the Busch Series with Air Force backing.

Either way, the military has a strong presence at every NASCAR race. At 2007 Daytona SpeedWeeks, military color guards—from all the services—were part of every prerace ceremony. The 82nd Airborne glee club sang prior to the start of the Daytona

500. As country duo Big & Rich hit the final notes of the National Anthem, U.S. Navy F-14 Tomcats screamed overhead. The patriotism pulsing through the stands was palatable, and I'm sure making some teenagers—and their parents—think about stopping at one of the kiosks on the way out and asking, "Where can I sign up?"

CHAPTER THIRTEEN

BRINGING THE BIG SHOW TO THE LITTLE STORE

How Associate Sponsorship Changed the Game

Rather than pony up the full price to sponsor Rick Hendrick's No. 25 car for the 2007 NASCAR Nextel Cup season, the National Guard decided to share the sponsorship with GMAC. A lot of companies do that, or opt for an associate sponsorship, which costs about half the price of a full sponsorship. An associate sponsorship gives a company less space and exposure, but allows the company to tap into the NASCAR market and fan base for considerably less money. For others, an associate or title sponsorship allows them to set up a promotional kiosk at the racetrack, offer free samples of their product, or link the sponsorship to national sales or marketing promotions. For many companies, it's a better deal than paying for a full-time Nextel Cup sponsorship.

While becoming an associate sponsor on the No. 25 Hendrick cars in 2007 may seem like a step back for the National Guard, it really isn't. Some of the biggest, most successful corporations in America opt to be associate sponsors on Nextel Cup teams or affiliate sponsors of NASCAR in general.

What are the advantages of an associate versus a full-time sponsorship? The two big ones are affiliation and entry fee. You get all the affiliation of a NASCAR sponsorship at about half the cost. Depending on the deal you strike, your name is either on the car all the time with smaller placement—say the right rear quarter panel—or you get the whole car for a few select races or just one event, like the All-Star race at Charlotte in May. Regardless of your position on the car, the NASCAR affiliation is all a lot of these companies are looking for. It allows them to use the team and driver in their advertising and tap into that seventy-five million-member fan base. Other sponsors merely get to say they're the official whatever of NASCAR. Costs for the program range anywhere from $5 million to $10 million, while a full-time NASCAR Nextel Cup sponsorship in 2007 cost between $20 million and $25 million.

A good example of a major corporation that's an affiliate sponsor is Coca-Cola. The Atlanta-based soft drink company has been around NASCAR for decades. In the mid-1970s, Coca-Cola sponsored driver Bobby Allison. It has sponsored the Coca-Cola 600, the longest race of the NASCAR season that's run every May in Charlotte, since 1986. And it has long had individual advertising and pouring rights contracts with various NASCAR tracks. But in 1998, Coca-Cola took a whole new tack to affiliate sponsorship. It created the Coca-Cola Racing Family.

"We didn't want to do what everyone else had been doing, which was sponsoring a team," said Bea Perez, vice president of sports and entertainment marketing for Coca-Cola. "We didn't need awareness; we're one of the best known brands in the world. What we needed was to create a connection between Coca-Cola and the NASCAR fan."

When the marketing team at Coke sat back and put its thinking caps on, it realized that one common theme running through NASCAR is family.

"There have been generations of families involved in NASCAR," Perez said. "Our brand is about family. There are generations of people who've consumed Coca-Cola. It was a hook that no one had focused on."

So Perez and her team created the Coca-Cola Racing Family, starting with the multigenerational families that had helped to build NASCAR. In 1998, the first year the marketing effort was launched, the team included Dale Earnhardt, Dale Jarrett, and Kyle Petty.

"We looked at that and said 'We have something special with that foundation of family,'" Perez said. "It helped us reach a cross section of multigenerational fans, as well as appeal to the new families that were discovering NASCAR."

From a marketing and advertising perspective, this was a very shrewd move. First off, it didn't tie Coca-Cola to one team. It meant that fans didn't have to cheer for just one driver, but had a family of drivers from which to choose. In 2007, the Coca-Cola Racing Family was made up of Greg Biffle, Jeff Burton, Carl Edwards, Kevin Harvick, Dale Jarrett, Bobby Labonte, Mark

Martin, Jaime McMurray, Kyle Petty, Elliott Sadler, Tony Stewart, and Michael Waltrip. Seven of those twelve drivers are either members of well-known multigenerational NASCAR families, or have other close family members in the sport, like Michael Waltrip and his brother Darrell.

But the big payoff for Coke came as a result of the healthy B2B environment in NASCAR. Because Coke didn't affiliate itself with just one driver, the sponsorship opened up a whole slew of partnership opportunities with the primary sponsors of the Coca-Cola Racing Family drivers. Coke could partner with them and do special promotions, create special brands, and do other cross-marketing promotions. And that's exactly what Coca-Cola has done.

"What the Coca-Cola Racing Family did was allow us to work across multiple customers, geographies, and channels," Perez said.

For instance, in 2006, Coca-Cola created a special orange flavor of PowerAde for Tony Stewart. It was sold exclusively at Home Depot stores, Stewart's primary sponsor, in NASCAR-branded vending machines.

In addition to the marketing program, Coca-Cola was able to build a public relations program around the new flavor. The company was able to bring Tony Stewart to Atlanta, where Home Depot is also headquartered, to launch the new PowerAde flavor at one of Home Depot's flagship stores. Coca-Cola also used Stewart for a satellite media tour during the NASCAR season.

"That is one of the benefits with a NASCAR sponsorship," Perez said. "It's one of the few places where your team plays every week, year-round. There's a loyalty factor, in that the fans are incredibly brand loyal and reward the NASCAR sponsors with that loyalty. And it allows us to work across a variety of channels and outlets. All of that makes a NASCAR sponsorship very powerful."

Coca-Cola is doing other cross promotions with the primary sponsors of the Coca-Cola Racing Family, such as driver Carl Edwards and his primary sponsor, Office Depot. But it's also taking the sponsorship beyond NASCAR and tying it into other sports. For instance, last year, Coca-Cola created Flava 23, a special flavor of PowerAde tied to Cleveland Cavaliers star LeBron James. The company took over Coca-Cola Racing Family driver Bobby Labonte's car for the race in Bristol, Tennessee, branding it with Flava 23. Coca-Cola also did in-store promotions around the race and the launch of the brand, and brought James to the racetrack to shoot hoops with the NASCAR drivers. For every basket he made, Coca-Cola donated money to the Victory Junction Gang, the charity in memory of Kyle Petty's son, Adam.

"We received one hundred sixty-nine million impressions off of that program alone," Perez said. "It also tied in well with NASCAR's Diversity Program and created exposure for NASCAR and the NBA beyond their traditional markets and consumers."

Coca-Cola is also a primary sponsor of the television show, *American Idol*. It has been able to cross promote that property within NASCAR by bringing an *American Idol* winner to Charlotte every year to sing the National Anthem at the Coca-Cola 600.

"That's the beauty of the system," Perez said. "It's a wonderful portfolio of marketing assets that allows us to bring these platforms together."

MBNA, which was acquired by Bank of America in 2005, is another NASCAR partner that has had great success with its affiliate and associate sponsorships.

For better or worse, MBNA in many ways started what became the NASCAR midway. The Wilmington, Delaware–based credit card company started coming to NASCAR races in 1994 and setting up small kiosks where fans could sign up for credit cards. In exchange for signing up, they received some small token, like an MBNA/NASCAR-branded bobble head, T-shirt, or hat.

"For the first few months, we were the only business set up behind the grandstand other than the souvenir trailers," said Bob Boyles, who managed publicity for the MBNA NASCAR account for nearly a decade. "That was the beginnings of the NASCAR midway, which today is filled with gigantic tents where fans can test DeWalt drills and saws or see how fast they can change tires."

Boyles was first mentioned in this book in Chapter Five. He was one of the first employees to be hired by Tom Cotter after he left the Charlotte Motor Speedway to start his own motorsports public relations agency. Boyles oversaw the Gwaltney and Hardee's accounts that sponsored up-and-coming driver Ward Burton in the Busch Series. He also created the first spokesman training program to teach drivers like Michael Waltrip, Sterling Marlin, and Burton how to answer tough questions from the media and mention their sponsors without it sounding forced or rehearsed.

Boyles left the Cotter agency in the mid-1990s to work with Burton. He eventually migrated over to MBNA full-time, where he worked with driver Bobby Labonte and car owner Joe Gibbs. Boyles retired from MBNA in 2005 when it was acquired by Bank of America and has since followed his other passion: college football. He and coauthor Paul Guido wrote *50 Years of College Football*.

Over the years, MBNA went through the full evolution of NASCAR sponsorships. It started out as an affiliate sponsor signing up fans for credit cards at racetracks. It went on to be a primary sponsor of Jeff Burton in the Cup Series and Jason Leffler, Mike McLaughlin, and Coy Gibbs in the Busch Series, an associate sponsor of Bobby Labonte in the Nextel Cup Series, a title sponsor of races, as well as a sponsor of NASCAR awards and contingency funds.

The NASCAR credit card program was actually the brainchild of Dave Elgena, a South Dakota banker who had had success signing a few branded credit card deals—called affinity programs—with several NBA teams.

"Because of his personal interest in racing, he signed up NASCAR," Boyles said. "At the time, NASCAR was still very much an underappreciated sport for most bankers."

MBNA soon became the first official nationwide credit card issuer of NASCAR in 1994. By then, Elgena had moved on to MBNA, a fast-growing, Delaware credit card lender. It had been the vision of MBNA Chairman Charley Cawley that had created the affinity credit card concept a few years earlier. Cawley started by signing the alumni association of Georgetown University, his alma mater, and the concept had grown to more than three thousand organizations. NASCAR would consistently be among the top ten of MBNA's endorsing groups.

"Charley knew that people would flock to a credit card product that displayed their first love," Elgena said. "It allowed them to show their loyalties, as well as support the group by having some of the royalties go back to that association, team, or school. As far as MBNA getting into NASCAR, it helped a great deal that Charley loved racing and was a devoted collector of classic cars."

Geoff Bodine was the first NASCAR driver to have an MBNA card with his image on it.

"Dave knew that the program wouldn't succeed unless we could put the drivers on the cards," Boyles said.

Indeed, for several years NASCAR had a credit card affinity

program that featured some of its racetracks. But it was never as popular as the driver cards that MBNA offered.

"People don't really have the loyalty to Daytona International Speedway that they do to Dale Earnhardt," Boyles said.

Earnhardt, Richard Petty, and Bill Elliott were some of the first drivers to sign up for the program.

"Earnhardt very quickly became a business unit all to himself," Elgena said. "He did extremely well, and was good to MBNA as a result."

And MBNA was good to him. When Dale Jr. emerged onto the NASCAR scene, it created some hard feelings in the Earnhardt family. Dale's other son, Kerry, who is the spitting image of his father, was trying to break into racing as well, but wasn't having as much success as his half-brother, Dale Jr. At the eleventh hour, Earnhardt Sr. came to MBNA and asked if it would sponsor Kerry in the 2000 ARCA support race at Daytona.

"Dale made a real point when he was interviewed to talk about MBNA," Boyles said. "He also went to a couple of private functions for MBNA, as a favor to Dave for helping Kerry."

Earnhardt went on to become the single most successful NASCAR affinity card that MBNA ever offered. Other popular— and profitable—NASCAR drivers included Jeff Gordon and Davey Allison. In fact, after Allison died in a July 1993 helicopter accident at Talladega Superspeedway, his cards continued to be popular. MBNA worked with his widow, Liz, to have royalties go to Allison's trust for his family.

The typical affinity credit card deal involved the driver getting a retainer, as well as a percentage of the interest and fees earned off the card. But like a lot of NASCAR, the business became more complicated over time.

Part of the challenge, Elgena said, was that a lot of drivers didn't always know how much money they made from the affinity credit cards. They would often sign up, knew there were credit cards out there with their face on them, but didn't bother to keep track of their income.

"I would make it a point at Daytona or Charlotte to lay out the portfolio for each driver and say, 'Here's what you made this year, last year, the number of cardholders that were added, etc.' " Elgena said. "A lot of them would look at the statement and say, 'Wow!' "

While the affinity cards made perfect sense for MBNA, sponsoring cars came about purely from Chairman Charley Cawley's interest in motorsports. MBNA had a suite for the last race of the 1994 season in Atlanta and brought a slew of its corporate partners along. As almost an aside, Cawley turned to Dave Elgena and asked, "How much does it cost to sponsor one of these cars?"

During the Atlanta race, Bobby Labonte wrecked and Cawley was impressed that car owner Bill Davis was right in the thick of things, wrenches in hand, trying to fix the car and get it back on the track. Sponsor Maxwell House was leaving the Bill Davis team at the end of the season. Labonte left to drive for Joe Gibbs and the car was driven for most of the 1995 season by Randy LaJoie with MBNA sponsorship. After twenty-one races, Ward Burton moved over from the Hardee's Chevrolet. The team finished fourth in its second race together.

A few weeks later, Burton, Davis, and MBNA celebrated the first Winston Cup victory for each of the three race partners. Burton bypassed a late-race pit road controversy to pull away for victory at the fall Rockingham race. The three would not win another race together, and when MBNA's agreement came to its conclusion, Caterpillar became the primary sponsor on the car in 1999. MBNA left the team, but didn't leave the sport.

"After 1998, we were ready to leave the sport in terms of sponsoring a race team," Boyles said.

Indeed, although it was no longer the primary sponsor for Bill Davis Racing, MBNA was still very deeply involved with NASCAR. In fact, it was a cash cow for the company. MBNA was the sponsor of both NASCAR weekends at Dover Downs International Speedway. In fact, the company owned the whole weekend for the fall races, sponsoring the truck, Busch, and Cup races, something very few sponsors did back then. MBNA also was an associate sponsor for Joe Gibbs and driver Bobby Labonte, and it helped Gibbs' sons, Coy, who was an aspiring driver in the Goody's Dash Series, and J. D. Gibbs, who raced in the Busch Series. It turned out to be a good partnership.

In 2000, Joe Gibbs and Bobby Labonte won the Winston Cup championship. In 2002, J. D. Gibbs, who had since retired from driving to become a very successful team manager, won the title with Tony Stewart. MBNA was an associate sponsor on both cars.

Interstate Batteries was the primary sponsor on Bobby Labonte's car. MBNA would buy the hood for five races a year. By sheer luck, the five races MBNA negotiated for the 2000 season were the two Dover and Pocono races and Miami, which then was the next-to-last race of the year. It turned out to be the weekend where Labonte mathematically clinched the Winston Cup Championship. Norm Miller, president of Interstate Batteries, said good-naturedly to MBNA, "If I had thought of this, I never would have let you have Miami."

So what exactly did MBNA get for its associate sponsorships over the years?

"It's most important for an associate to maximize their relationship with the driver," Boyles said. MBNA did just that with drivers Bobby Labonte and Tony Stewart, and car owner Joe Gibbs.

One of the best examples of a sponsor maximizing its driver relationship today, Boyles said, is Subway and Greg Biffle. In 2006, Subway ran an advertising campaign that featured a 1950s-style, film noir, police car chase. When the cops finally catch the driver, it's Greg Biffle, trying to get his Subway sandwiches home while they're still hot.

"That's a great campaign," Boyles said.

Associates sponsors also usually get to use drivers for personal appearances. As already noted, MBNA was able to use Dale Earnhardt because he was a member of the company's affinity credit card program. Associate sponsors also usually have access to a driver for personal appearances at off-track events and for at-track hospitality. In MBNA's case, Hall of Fame coach Joe Gibbs was often a bigger draw than drivers Bobby Labonte and Tony Stewart.

"Where else can you fondle a Super Bowl ring?" Boyles asked. "That was the key benefit of Joe Gibbs's team: Joe. He's a charming, funny, smart, sincere guy who can mingle and talk with anyone. He's very personable and very genuine."

Boyles thinks that as NASCAR continues to evolve, there will be more people involved who are famous for something other than NASCAR. A good example is the DLP team, which is owned by Hall of Fame Dallas Cowboys quarterbacks Roger Staubach and Troy Aikman. Another example is Coca-Cola and the *American Idol* finalists who sing the National Anthem at the Coca-Cola 600.

And, of course, there's the obvious marketing and advertising opportunities for associate sponsors. When Rick Hendrick's cars finished 1-2-3 in the Daytona 500, Quaker State Oil, which was just an associate sponsor on the Hendrick cars, ran ads all year long saying it was the motor oil that finished 1-2-3 at the 500.

MBNA also has leveraged its NASCAR affiliation by sponsoring the mid-race leader award. Initially, the driver who had led at the halfway point the week before would come onto the stage during driver introductions the following week and get a check from MBNA. At the NASCAR banquet in New York, MBNA would again present a check to the driver who won the most mid-race leader awards over the year. But over time, MBNA turned it into a consumer campaign.

"We started using cardholders who won a promotional contest," Boyles said. "They'd go onstage and present the check instead of one of us from MBNA Motorsports."

MBNA would have a photographer take their picture, run it as part of a print ad, and present a laminated plaque of the ad to the cardholder, forever memorializing their fifteen minutes of NASCAR fame. But ever mindful of the real reason the company got into NASCAR—to distribute credit cards and earn fees and interest—MBNA eventually tied the promotion to cardholders with a certain amount of MBNA NASCAR points.

"One of the challenges we always had was that a few people would apply for the card at the racetrack, get the card, and never use it," Boyles said. "Because the credit card had a picture of their favorite driver, they would frame it and hang it in their NASCAR-themed hobby room. Having the promotions based upon award points helped fix that."

The problem today, though, is that almost every NASCAR sponsor has an awards program or some kind of promotion that features real fans instead of just the drivers. It's just one more element that has added to the clutter of NASCAR marketing.

One way to get around that clutter is to have brand exclusivity—especially if it's in a somewhat obscure category where you won't have much competition. One example of this is Tissot, the Swiss watchmaker that is most famous for its Swatch brand of sport watches. In February 2006, Tissot became the official timekeeper of NASCAR.

The company has been around since 1853, but most people in the United States don't know about the Swiss watchmaker. It became a NASCAR sponsor to try and fix that.

"We wanted to increase our market penetration in the U.S.," said Olivier Cosandier, brand manager of Tissot U.S. "NASCAR was a natural fit."

That's because Tissot is the official timekeeper of seventeen motorsports championship events around the world, including MotoGP and the Asian Games.

"NASCAR also had a demographic appeal for us," said Anthony Migliazzo, sponsorship manager for Tissot U.S. "Tissot hasn't had a strong brand presence in the U.S. and NASCAR offered an opportunity to reach out to a number of Americans in our target demographic."

The message Tissot hopes to get out to the NASCAR fan base is that it has a watch for everyone.

"Our core price range is two hundred to eight hundred dollars," Migliazzo said. "We have a wide variety of products. The NASCAR community has a little bit of everyone in America. There are seventy-five million NASCAR fans with a fairly diverse mix of males and females. The people who are spending money on NASCAR merchandise are spending the amount of dollars that would allow them to afford our product."

"I had no clue about NASCAR when we started to look at a partnership," Cosandier said. "A lot of people—especially in New York—still have the impression that NASCAR is a southern redneck sport. That's absolutely not true."

Furthermore, when Tissot talked to some of its U.S. partners, it realized that many of them knew about NASCAR and the opportunities it afforded to reach a core demographic. But what really sold Tissot on NASCAR were the opportunities that existed through the NASCAR B2B Council.

"That allowed us to jump start our sponsorship," Cosandier said.

Tissot began by becoming an associate sponsor of the Bud Pole qualifying award. It gives a $1,100 Tissot watch to the pole winner at every NASCAR race. But what Tissot quickly learned, like so many NASCAR sponsors, was that there were opportunities beyond the racetrack.

Through the NASCAR B2B Council, Tissot met Budweiser, a company it had never done business with before. After sitting down with Budweiser, it started providing watches to the St. Louis brewer for corporate giveaways, promotions, and other events.

"Since then, they have come back to us with other opportunities," Cosandier said. "Not just watch orders, but we've partnered with them for advertising in Times Square. They also sell our watches on their corporate website."

Tissot also met NASCAR sponsor Motorola through the B2B Council. Tissot discovered that Motorola was having trouble coming up with a battery for its next generation of cell phone. Tissot has a core competency in miniature battery technology, something it uses in every one of its watches. Thanks to the introduction through the NASCAR B2B Council, Tissot is now supplying batteries to a new generation of Motorola cell phones. Tissot also makes radio frequency identification chips that are now used in security systems made by another NASCAR sponsor, Ingersoll-Rand.

On the consumer side, Tissot has developed a line of NASCAR-branded watches that will be priced from $200 to $1,200. Two of them were top-twenty sellers in 2006, and the company projects them to be in the top five by the end of 2007.

But like a lot of NASCAR sponsors, it's not all about consumer marketing. As Tissot builds its line of watches, it expects that some of the NASCAR sponsors it's partnering with will help with distribution.

"Our target is not to have twenty or thirty NASCAR-specific watches," Cosandier said, "but to get six to eight references per year from NASCAR sponsors."

Other sponsors look to leverage the Busch Series or Craftsman Truck Series to promote their products. The price of entry is about half that of a Nextel Cup sponsorship, and if done right it can reap significant benefits. Furthermore, while they're lesser-known support series, they still carry the NASCAR name.

An example of a corporation that has found a home in the Busch Series is Kimberly-Clark. Around since 1994, it is the longest running primary sponsor in the Busch Series. To promote its product—Kleenex—the company is using the tried-and-true methods developed by Tom Cotter and Ed Several in the 1980s and perfected by Darrell Waltrip and Van Colley at Western Auto in the 1990s.

"We leverage our sponsorship by going directly to our partners," said Steve Abdo, associate director of customer marketing for Kimberly-Clark. "You buy X amount of our product or a full-page ad in a NASCAR market, and we give you a menu of promotional opportunities to choose from. Simulator. Show cars. We'll even put the retailer's name on the back rear quarter panel of our car. Whatever they want."

The biggest user of the Kleenex show car is Wal-Mart, which used the car more than two hundred times during the 2006 NASCAR season, mostly around new store openings in NASCAR markets. But like the NASCAR marketing pioneers in the 1980s and 1990s, Abdo quickly learned that just putting the show car in front of the store doesn't work.

"You have to promote it," he said. "Make it special."

For Kleenex, that includes having a product promotion to drive sales or a driver appearance to drive traffic.

"The bottom line is that it drives cases to Wal-Mart," Abdo said.

Like many NASCAR marketing programs, it's hard to precisely measure just how much product the sponsorship is selling. Like a lot of sponsors, Abdo cites the fact that NASCAR fans are incredibly brand loyal.

"Can we sway the consumer?" he asks. "Just by sheer numbers, NASCAR gives you seventy-five million chances to try."

Most of Kimberly-Clark's promotions are away from the track at retail, but the company is looking at some at-track promotions for the 2007 season. The company is also having a broader, unexpected impact at the racetrack. Many of the partners it has brought in to do promotions have become NASCAR sponsors themselves. The best example is Dollar General.

"We did a number of promotions with Dollar General," Abdo said. "Today they are a full-time Busch Series sponsor."

Kimberly-Clark also runs employee contests tied to its NASCAR sponsorship. Because many of its paper mills are in the Southeast, it's a natural tie-in to reward employees who meet sales or productivity goals with free tickets to a NASCAR race. The Kleenex car and driver also come to the company's corporate headquarters once a year and spend the day with employees.

Kimberly-Clark will also re-brand the car for an important corporate partner or to promote other Kimberly-Clark brands. For instance, during 2006, Kimberly-Clark's Huggies Pull-Ups brand was on the car.

Kimberly-Clark does a fair amount of charity work with its NASCAR team, as well. In 2006, its Viva paper towels brand took over the No. 27 Busch Series car and was painted pink to promote breast cancer awareness.

"Everything Viva will be colored pink, from the car, to the driver, Casey Atwood, to the entire pit crew," Kimberly-Clark said in a September 2006 press release. "Viva will also donate a minimum of one hundred thousand dollars to the Breast Cancer Research Fund (BCRF) and will host an online auction of NASCAR memorabilia with proceeds benefiting BCRF. Even Viva paper towels will sport special prints and pink packaging during October, designed to heighten consumer awareness." The special promotion was held at the Yellow 300 at Kansas Speedway and the Dollar General 200 at Lowe's Motor Speedway.

The tie-in was, unfortunately, a natural for Kimberly-Clark because car owner Clarence Brewer Jr.'s family has been hit by breast cancer. His grandmother died in 2000 after a five-year struggle with breast cancer. He also has two aunts who are breast cancer survivors.

The larger point here is this: Associate sponsorships offer companies the same opportunities to leverage the NASCAR brand at about half the cost. And associate sponsorship must be working, because even when longtime sponsors leave, they are quickly replaced.

In late 2006, Anheuser Busch announced that it would stop being the title sponsor of the Busch Series after the 2007 season. It was rumored that Busch was paying $10 million to $12 million for the title sponsorship. That was considered a bargain. NASCAR expects to get three or four times as much from a new title sponsor.

CHAPTER FOURTEEN

TEACHING OLD BRANDS NEW TRICKS

A Wunderkind Helps Goodyear Leverage Its Legacy

O ver the past chapters, you've learned how the business of NASCAR has evolved. From the days when a major sponsorship was a case of oil and gas money to the $20 million deals today. Over the past twenty years, NASCAR sponsorships have also become increasingly sophisticated. They're now pure B2B plays with clever marketing and advertising campaigns, on-site promotions, and corporate hospitality at every NASCAR race. Fortune 500 corporations hold their worldwide sales meetings at race shops or in the suites above the Daytona Speedway. Given how far the business of NASCAR has come, you would think it would be safe to assume that corporate America has this NASCAR sponsorship thing nailed.

Not so fast.

There is an entire industry of sales, marketing, public relations, and image consultants built up around NASCAR. They earn six- and seven-figure contracts for helping NASCAR sponsors get the biggest bang for their buck. Those corporations that take their NASCAR relationships seriously don't want to leave opportunities on the table, so many seek these third party experts to maximize their investments.

"Goodyear has been involved with auto racing since it began," said Roger Rydell, vice president of Global Business Communications for Goodyear. "But developing racing-informed technologies and constructing strategic marketing programming around racing properties are two different things. Just look at how much NASCAR has grown in just the past five or ten years. It is one of the most sophisticated, far-reaching, and, in some ways, complicated business models in sports. Given how much it has changed, how much it has grown, with so many tentacles branching off in so many different directions, we thought it was smart to bring in somebody from the outside to help ensure that we are getting everything we can out of our NASCAR relationship."

One of those firms trying to help NASCAR sponsors get it right is Wunderman, of Y&R Brands, one of the largest integrated marketing agencies in the world. Wunderman offers expertise in retail, online, promotional, direct, and, most important for its NASCAR clients, event marketing. The agency services clients that include some of the biggest and best-known NASCAR sponsors: Sears Craftsman, title sponsor of the NASCAR Craftsman Truck Series; Burger King; the Texaco/Havoline unit of Chevron; and one of the most venerable brands in the history of auto racing, the Goodyear Tire and Rubber Company.

It's important to note that Goodyear is a rare breed of NASCAR cat. Unlike any other sponsor (with the exception of Sunoco that provides fuel for races), Goodyear provides products to NASCAR that are integral to its operation—namely tires and selected engine parts. So along with wanting to leverage its NASCAR relationship from a marketing standpoint, Goodyear has very real operational issues to consider every time a green flag is waved.

So what exactly does Wunderman do for Goodyear and its other clients?

"Simply put, we support their sports and event marketing efforts," said Jim Rappel, a senior vice president and group account director in Wunderman's Chicago office. "This means that we help our clients maximize their NASCAR investments through a customized, integrated approach that includes strategic planning, activation, program management, and evaluation."

At first glance you're probably wondering why these companies with their own full-time, in-house sales, marketing, and communications departments sometimes numbering into the hundreds of employees, need to hire marketing consultants to help them manage their NASCAR sponsorship. But the fact is, NASCAR is a complex entity that continues to evolve. Therefore, even a company like Goodyear can benefit from outside counsel, even with its rich racing heritage and long history at the track. One could argue that no other company has a longer racing résumé.

Indeed, in 1901, an upstart young automaker named Henry Ford worked out a deal with Goodyear sales manager Charles

Seiberling to get a special set of tires—at cost—for a race at the one-mile Detroit Driving Club oval in Grosse Pointe, Michigan. What resulted was Goodyear's—and Ford's—first racing victory.

A year later, Goodyear developed its first racing tire. As speeds climbed to forty and fifty miles per hour, Goodyear had to find something more durable than the square woven fabric used in early tires. It developed cord fabric.

In 1905, Goodyear hired legendary race car driver Barney Oldfield to test its new straight side detachable tire. He won seventy-two consecutive races in fifteen months without a problem. In 1919, Goodyear scored its first Indianapolis 500 victory with driver Howdy Wilcox. In winning the race, Howdy only used seven tires. Two of the tires he never changed from start to finish. Altogether, twenty-three of twenty-seven drivers in the 1919 Indy 500 rode on Goodyear tires.

Indy was just the beginning, as 1919 turned out to be a pretty good year for Goodyear. Every major auto race won that year was won on Goodyear tires. Ralph DePalma also broke nearly every land speed record on the sands at Daytona Beach, including a 150-mile-per-hour run. He did it all on one set of Goodyear tires. Pressed by an increasingly depressed U.S. economy, in 1922 Goodyear withdrew from racing, saying simply that there was "nothing left to prove."

Even though the Akron tire maker had pulled out of racing, drivers continued to use its products. A southern race car driver by the name of Bill France drove a Ford coupe in a 1935 Daytona Beach race. Local garage owner Glen Brooks sponsored France with free gas and a set of Goodyear passenger car tires.

In 1954, Goodyear returned to racing, helping NASCAR drivers test at Darlington, where the rough track surface ate tires like locusts ate crops. Goodyear partnered with Chrysler and car owner Carl Kiekhaefer, whose Chrysler 300s were driven by NASCAR legends Buck Baker and Tim Flock and rode on Goodyear Police Special tires. In 1957, Goodyear hired Lee Petty to test tires on a quarter-mile oval in West Palm Beach. What resulted was the first set of Stock Car Special tires. Baker clinched the 1957 NASCAR Grand National title and Petty won it a year later, both on Goodyear tires. Tire tester Jim Reed also won the Southern 500 at Darlington at a record speed of 111.836 miles per hour. In 1959, when the new 2.5-mile Daytona International Speedway opened, Lee Petty won the inaugural Daytona 500 on Goodyear tires. The rest, as they say, is history.

In 1965, Goodyear worked with Richard Petty and NASCAR to develop the first inner-liner tire, a tire within a tire that helped drivers maintain control and get back to the pits on super speedways. They became mandatory at all super speedway races. Along the way, Goodyear developed the racing slick—a tire with no tread, but incredible grip and control—and the first fuel cell, a rubber inner-liner for gas tanks that helped prevent fuel leaks and fires. By 1974, it was all too much for Firestone, Goodyear's primary competitor. Firestone withdrew from the USAC, Formula One, and NASCAR circuits.

In the late 1980s, Hoosier, a small tire maker from Indiana, challenged Goodyear in the NASCAR Winston Cup Series. Hoosier was challenging Goodyear on the sprint car short tracks in the Midwest and thought it could make the leap to NASCAR. It was a short-lived competition that ended when Goodyear introduced the Eagle radial tire. In 1994, Hoosier tried to make a comeback, but it was ill-fated. By the time Hoosier left stock car racing for good, the score was Goodyear: twenty-eight victories; Hoosier: three.

April 1995 marked Goodyear's one thousandth NASCAR win with Jeff Gordon at the tough half-mile bullring known as Bristol Motor Speedway. Two years later, concerned that future tire wars could endanger drivers, NASCAR named Goodyear the exclusive tire supplier to the Winston Cup Series. Today, Goodyear is the exclusive tire supplier to the Nextel Cup, Busch, and Craftsman Truck Series. The contract was extended in early 2007 and will ensure Goodyear's "official" and exclusive status through the 2012 season.

During its long association with NASCAR, Goodyear has used racing themes in a variety of marketing and advertising programs. For example, the company was the first to use NASCAR drivers, including Richard Petty, to demonstrate the performance characteristics of its tires.

However, while Goodyear has been good at innovating on the track, it readily agrees that it could probably have been more effective with its NASCAR-related marketing and advertising efforts off the track. And it's not alone.

For every NASCAR sponsor, there are myriad choices, and not all of them are the right ones. Indeed, Jim Rappel at Wunderman's argues that a lot of the NASCAR sponsors make the same mistakes.

"The most common mistake they make is having a brand manager or marketing manager in charge of the sponsorship," he said.

That's because brand and marketing managers often know their own product very well. But very few of them understand the depth and breadth of NASCAR.

"Before bringing Wunderman on board, we realized that we had a huge asset that was not being fully activated," said Joey Viselli, Goodyear's director of marketing services in the company's

North American tire division. "If you don't know the property—and know it well—you can suffer," he said. "That's because the nuances of a NASCAR sponsorship are significant. You have to understand not just consumers, but the consumers and their personal and collective relationship with NASCAR."

Moreover, properly managing a fully integrated NASCAR sponsorship today is a full-time job—and not just for one person.

"Most of our clients are so busy with so many other business matters, they know that in order to properly leverage and fully activate a NASCAR sponsorship they need to engage experts," Rappel said. "That's why they engage us. We have the resources to focus on the property. They may not be able to hire five people to focus on NASCAR, but they can hire an agency that does have adequate resources."

Further complicating the equation is the fact that unlike Goodyear, many sponsors are conglomerates that have multiple product lines with myriad corporate identities and strategic goals. Many times, only one of those brands is a NASCAR sponsor. As a result, many employees of those conglomerates—including marketing and advertising executives—often don't know a company is even sponsoring a NASCAR team.

"That's because there are often silos within a multibranded corporation," Rappel said. "What we've found with many of our clients is that an agency is instrumental to breaking down those walls, which leads to a more integrated and encompassing activation plan."

That's especially important with a NASCAR program, where the opportunities are many and the entry fee astronomical.

Then there's the problem of clutter—the noise—of NASCAR. Perhaps the best example of this is the sponsor midway. After taking just one walk through the midway set up outside the Daytona International Speedway in February 2007 for the Daytona 500, I was dizzy. There were so many images, so many products, and so many pitches thrown at me in the span of five hundred yards that very few left a lasting impression. I'm not alone.

"Some of the mobile marketing displays make sense," Rappel said. "But it has to be more than just an experience where someone comes in and looks around. You have to engage the consumer with your product and create a memorable experience that leads to a call to action."

There were at least one hundred booths, kiosks, and interactive displays set up outside the Daytona International Speedway and, honestly, a lot of them didn't succeed. Wunderman has done post-exit surveys of NASCAR fans on the midway and found that most people can't remember half the exhibits they went through.

"You have to engage them in a way that's relevant to NASCAR and their everyday life," Rappel said.

Again, this makes for a very cluttered and noisy marketplace. It's further complicated by the fact that *everyone* wants to be associated with NASCAR. Getting brand recognition amid this cacophony is often difficult.

Goodyear is one rare example. Since 1997, there has been no other brand of tire on a NASCAR Nextel Cup car. But look at the other sponsor categories. In cell phones, Nextel, Cingular, and Alltel are all NASCAR sponsors. Among retailers, there's Best Buy, Target, and Circuit City. In the home improvement category, Lowe's, Home Depot, and Menards are all sponsors. Yes, Lowe's distinguished itself in 2006 as the sponsor of Nextel Cup Champion Jimmie Johnson, but the same could be said about Home Depot in 2005 when Tony Stewart won the title.

The more important question is this: Of all those brands I just mentioned which one is the official "whatever" of NASCAR? Beyond Goodyear's status as NASCAR's "official tire," I doubt many fans know.

Because of these difficult challenges, many NASCAR sponsors fall back on the tried-and-true methods: branded show cars, a modest advertising or marketing campaign, and corporate hospitality.

"While this approach may seem strategic for a NASCAR sponsor, to me it's too limiting and needs to be more integrated," Rappel said. "Entertaining your important B2B clients is just one element of activation, but it's certainly not the end all and be all of a modern NASCAR sponsorship."

One corporation that is distinguishing itself in the NASCAR market—both in advertising and its mobile marketing kiosk—is DLP, the HDTV unit of Texas Instruments. DLP has succeeded in both its mobile entertainment complex that it sets up at each NASCAR track, and its offbeat, engaging advertising campaign featuring the little girl with the elephant who simply tells viewers, "It's all about the mirrors." DLP has also launched an aggressive corporate hospitality program, fueled by the fact that the team is owned by Hall of Fame Dallas Cowboys quarterbacks Roger Staubach and Troy Aikman. It has also used its NASCAR relationship to buy advertising on other Fox Sports broadcasts.

"The primary goal of many NASCAR sponsors is to expand awareness of their products," Goodyear's Viselli said. "Whether it's on site, at retail, or through media—online, TV, radio, or print—any of those, in and of themselves, is not a valuable activity. What's essential is getting people to care enough to *buy* your products. The marketing and communication surrounding a NASCAR sponsorship has to be fully integrated and reach consumers in as many touch points as possible with salient selling propositions. It doesn't mean every single one has to be an equal investment, but you have to engage consumers on all possible levels so they get your message."

This further illustrates just how forward thinking the General Foods sponsorship was in the late 1980s. Ed Several and Tom Cotter created the Country Time Tool Box, which featured a variety of sales and marketing tools. A business partner could use those tools to activate its sponsorship and leverage the Country Time, Maxwell House, and Kool-Aid brands. That business partner, then, would be doing exactly what Rappel and Viselli are saying is necessary to effectively leverage a NASCAR sponsorship today. The difference is that General Foods was doing this almost twenty years ago.

So what is Wunderman telling Goodyear?

"You can't just do television ads or on-site promotions," Rappel said. "You have to do pieces of it all."

For Goodyear, according to Viselli, that starts with asking why the company is in NASCAR to begin with. The short answer is technology and innovation. This is especially true for a company like Goodyear, which not only uses NASCAR as a marketing and advertising vehicle, but also supplies products to race teams that are integral to those teams' success. But in the retail sector, the key to a successful NASCAR sponsorship is making a solid connection with consumers between Goodyear's success on the racetrack and the products it sells at the tire shop. For a time, when there were competing tires screaming around NASCAR tracks, the mantra at Goodyear's retail establishments was, "Win on Sunday, Sell on Monday." Performance claims in advertising that linked tires to NASCAR wins were common. However, as noted earlier, the decision was made to go with a single tire provider to cut down on any perception that safety might take a back seat in the quest for bragging rights following any given race.

Since then, the direct connection between track and road has been less direct.

Adding to this separation is the fact that for decades, Goodyear tires said nothing more than "Goodyear" on the sidewall. There was no direct connection between the race tires and the brands that were being sold at retail.

That started to change in 1981. That's when Goodyear started branding its race tires as Goodyear Eagles. That same year, Goodyear put Eagles on the new Chevrolet Corvette.

"The Eagle GT brand was developed specifically for the Corvette, based upon the technology that went into our NASCAR tires," said Bob Toth, marketing manager for Goodyear Brand Auto Tires. "Before we launched the tires, we said, 'Boy wouldn't it be great if we could rebadge all of our Blue Streak racing tires and make them Eagles? That way, we could create a family of performance tires that had a direct connection from the track to the street.'

"Well, that's exactly what we did. That was the genesis of the Eagle family of tires."

Goodyear built an entire ad campaign around the Eagle brand, featuring drivers A. J. Foyt, Dan Gurney, and Richard Petty.

"That seemingly subtle change made it all gel," Toth said. "It gave us a platform to make that direct connection between the racetrack and the street."

Since then, Goodyear Eagles have been the only tires that have gone on the Chevrolet Corvettes coming out of GM's Bowling Green, Kentucky, plant. More important, Goodyear used the concept to build a whole family of performance tires. To make the connection even clearer for consumers, Goodyear put together a television ad campaign that built off of that theme. One featured a Winston Cup stock car that morphed into a passenger car. "The only performance tire so important that it comes with an owner's manual," said spokesman Darrell Waltrip. Another television ad featured Dale Earnhardt saying, "I've won seven Winston Cup championships on Goodyear Eagles. That should tell you something."

Goodyear even had some fun with the campaign, playing off of A. J. Foyt's legendary temper.

"They wanted me to wear a tux, but I told 'em I don't wear tuxes," Foyt deadpanned into the camera.

Since then, Goodyear has built on that theme of developing technology for the racetrack, proving it, winning with it, and then transferring it to passenger car tires. For instance, the Goodyear inner-liners for stock cars were the technological precursor to the run-flat consumer tires the company sells today.

"It was an innovative approach," Toth said, "because the last thing that anyone in the tire business wanted to talk about was a flat tire. But they're facts of life. And it's a direct descendant of our efforts in NASCAR."

In the 1990s, Goodyear introduced the Eagle GT HR, a consumer tire that featured the same race wrap technology that the company uses to make Nextel Cup tires. Goodyear also developed a new way to laminate the Goodyear name onto the sidewall. It made the letters crisper and easier to see. The company also developed a set of performance tires for passenger cars that features the rainbow-colored NASCAR logo. While they weren't big sellers, they were popular with gearheads who put them on their hopped-up retro Chevrolet Monte Carlos and Buick Grand Nationals.

Goodyear also changed the color of its logo on the race tires from a pale yellow to "championship gold." That crisp gold became associated with the Eagle brand—and winning. So much so that then–CEO Stanley Gault directed the company's blimp operations team to change the colors of the Goodyear Blimp.

Unfortunately, gold-lettered tires were popular with the street rod crowd, but not mainstream consumers.

"White-letter tires are more acceptable to the street," Toth said. "But it's still just a niche market."

As a result of all this, the Eagle brand is the most successful signature brand tire that Goodyear has ever produced. It celebrated its twenty-fifth anniversary in 2005. It has "grown into an icon brand and has been extremely successful in terms of marketing, sales, and profit," Toth said.

"The Eagle brand was a huge step forward for our company," said Stu Grant, general manager of Worldwide Racing for Goodyear. "Prior to Eagle badging, you could develop technology in racing, but from a marketing standpoint all you had was the generic Goodyear name."

And it wasn't just NASCAR. Tires used for drag racing, Indy, Formula One, were all rebadged as "Goodyear Eagle."

"We really took advantage of that in marketing our Eagle high-performance line," Grant said. "It was the first time we told consumers that the tires you can buy for your Chevy Camaro look very similar to and use the same technology as the Goodyear Eagle at the Darlington racetrack."

Goodyear has also used its NASCAR sponsorship to leverage its relationship with the automakers that are also NASCAR sponsors.

"There are few companies in the world that make automobiles and are successful without being involved in racing," Toth said. "Eagle opens the door for us because all of those manufacturers, if they want to get serious about being dominant, they need good tires. Our tires, our technology, are second to no one."

This is especially true with domestic U.S. automakers.

"Can you imagine a Monte Carlo on anything but Goodyear Eagles?" Toth asked. "Our NASCAR relationship and success on the track opens the doors to the manufacturers' design rooms when they're thinking about leveraging their racing programs to the street. That's a huge positive for us. It gives us credibility and stature when it comes to the design teams."

Despite all the success of the Eagle brand, its support campaign has been hit and miss over the years. Often, Goodyear only advertised its Eagle success in niche auto racing newspapers and magazines. Or the ads were only run during auto races. In short, there never has been a large-scale, mainstream consumer sales and marketing effort to drive home the connection between Goodyear's success on the racetrack and the tires it sells at retail. That's what Goodyear and Wunderman are hoping to change.

"What Goodyear is doing requires focus," Rappel said. "But that focused effort needs to be leveraged in as many places as possible."

Finding that focus and applying that leverage was a difficult proposition for Goodyear over the past several years as the company transitioned from a traditional manufacturing mindset to the marketing organization it's becoming today.

"Goodyear clearly values the NASCAR relationship that we have," Goodyear's Viselli said. "We particularly value the sixty to seventy million NASCAR fans that can have a huge impact on our topline. We need to tap into the loyalty that NASCAR fans have for the products that NASCAR sponsors sell, because we know that effort can move product off the shelf."

"In short, we got into this sport fifty years ago to race, and we've proven ourselves beyond any measure," he said. "Now we have to see it as a mechanism to sell more tires at retail."

One of the ways Goodyear is going to do that is by educating its customers: tire dealers and their sales staff.

"All too often, a consumer will go into a tire shop, intent on buying a set of Goodyear tires, and the salesman turns them toward another brand," Viselli said. "It's not that the salesman has anything against Goodyear, but maybe they're not the tires on sale this week or the brand offering the biggest sales incentives."

The way you fix that is by targeting the sales person.

"We have to educate them on the power of NASCAR and build in some sales incentives tied directly to Goodyear sponsorship and our products' performance," Viselli said. "Then when someone walks into the tire shop wanting to buy a set of Goodyear tires, the salesman doesn't talk them out of it, but reinforces that decision. In fact, at our dealers' conference last year we gave our dealers the opportunity to tape TV commercials with former NASCAR drivers, legends of the sport, who were in attendance. These segments were then provided to the dealers to splice into their respective TV spots. Believe me, it was a huge success and made the NASCAR relationship come to life."

If Goodyear does its job really well, that salesman not only reinforces the consumer intent on buying a set of Goodyear tires, but convinces the consumer who isn't committed to a specific brand, that Goodyear is the tire for them.

"A very large portion of the tire buying decision is made by the person behind the counter," said Ed Markey, vice president of public relations for Goodyear's North American tire division. "We have to use our NASCAR relationship to make the connection with those experts."

Goodyear works on that by bringing tire dealers on test drives to compare Goodyear tires to its competitors. It also runs dealer group sales contests and brings important retail tire customers and partners to the track for hospitality.

"We have to make sure customers know that we're in NASCAR," Markey said. "Goodyear is the sole tire provider for all three NASCAR series. If we do that, we can show them that we are the provider of tires for the premier racing series in North America, and that that level of performance translates to the products they put on their own vehicles.

"Frankly, we've got tons of awareness. More people know the Goodyear brand name than any other tire brand in North America. What [customers] need to feel is a compelling reason to purchase our products. We can't just have them be aware of Goodyear, we've got to give them tangible reasons to purchase Goodyear."

"I think Goodyear has a tremendous opportunity," Wunderman's Rappel said. "They just need to use the tools of their NASCAR sponsorship as much as they possibly can. As we've said, Goodyear doesn't need to build brand awareness. It's one of the best-known brands in the world. Our opportunity lies in developing more of a grassroots focus, targeted to specific regions and tied to the product."

Goodyear will also try and leverage its relationship with other NASCAR partners, especially the automakers and their dealer network.

"There's a group within our company that works exclusively with the automakers," Viselli said. "What we've found is that consumers are increasingly going back to the dealerships for their second set of tires. Therefore, we will create promotions and incentives through NASCAR, the automakers, and their dealer networks. This is an area that's a great opportunity for creating synergies through our NASCAR relationship."

Wunderman is working with Goodyear to differentiate other in-house brands, in much the same way Goodyear did with Eagle. Goodyear has four premium brands: Assurance, Eagle, Wrangler, and Fortera.

"If you ask consumers what tires run on Nextel Cup cars, they'd say Goodyear. Many don't know that it's Eagle—and maybe that's not all that important," noted Goodyear's Markey. "What we're more interested in is making sure that all of our brands benefit from our association with NASCAR, the venue from which we're bringing our learning to our new product development." To that end, Goodyear has started focusing on the track-to-consumer connection for its other distinct brands, like the Wrangler tires that are used exclusively in the NASCAR Craftsman Truck Series.

Another area where NASCAR is helping to achieve a key Goodyear goal is in the area of marketing to women.

"More than eighty percent of tire purchases today are either made by or are influenced by women, whether they're single or a stay-at-home mom," Viselli said. "There is a huge female fan base in NASCAR, but to leverage that we have to understand and speak to women differently than we speak to men. And once again, we need to communicate in ways that make a connection between NASCAR and the consumer's car."

To sum all this up, there is a perception that the marketing link between Goodyear and racing—especially NASCAR—has been maximized and lacks any significant new opportunities. In reality, there's lots of opportunity out there.

"Goodyear and its products are well known in the racing community, and they're even better known at the consumer level," Rappel said. "Making the link between the two is the key objective."

Indeed, Goodyear's reputation has been built on its products and the learning it has derived from, among other sources, racing. Now Goodyear has to focus on taking that success and marketing it effectively.

"Goodyear makes great tires and people buy them," Rappel said. "What Goodyear has to do now is become an even more savvy marketing company. There's no disputing that they're the number one tire company. Now they have to become the number one marketing company in their category."

And that goes for more than just tires. Very few know that Goodyear makes an array of engineered products for use in cars, including a brand of performance belts that are used in NASCAR and sold at retail.

For twenty-five years, Goodyear has supplied racing belts to NASCAR teams. And in 2002 it introduced Gator-back Poly-V belts. By the end of that year, every major Cup Series team was using Gator-back products to drive water pumps and other engine accessories. It's the same belt that consumers can purchase at auto retailers and installers.

But in 2006, Goodyear began working with NASCAR teams to develop a new timing belt. Engine performance demands were increasing during the season so Jim Wall, director of engine engineering for Hendrick Motorsports, contacted Goodyear looking for a timing belt that would tolerate a significant increase in horsepower.

It was determined that a performance jump of the magnitude Hendrick Motorsports was seeking would increase the demand on the belt by 50 percent. So Goodyear began working with the engine builders and crews at Hendrick and Evernham Motorsports and developed the new Gator-back line of timing belts with a rubber compound loaded with carbon fiber. They debuted at the Coca-Cola 600 in Charlotte in 2006 and Evernham driver Kasey Kahne won the race. Shortly after the race, NASCAR deemed the belts ready for competition and released them to the rest of the NASCAR field.

"The Gator-back cam drive belt is constructed with a revolutionary fabric treatment that is resistant to heat buildup, has a very low coefficient of friction, and displays excellent wear characteristics," said Mike Gregg, chief engineer of Goodyear's power transmission belt products. "The belt, with its eight-millimeter design, withstands temperatures of three hundred degrees Fahrenheit and permits smooth tooth engagement at very high speeds and loads."

Goodyear also developed the new Super Torque oil pump drive belt. It consumes less power and requires less space.

"The new five-millimeter Goodyear Super Torque uses smaller pulleys, which reduces the size of the drive system," Gregg said. "That adds up to less space needed for the belt and pulley and less energy needed to power it."

The new belts give engine builders a greater choice of ratios between oil pump drives and engines.

"The slower the oil pump drive operates, the less energy it requires," Gregg said.

It is these technical innovations that Goodyear has to figure out how to translate into effective sales and marketing campaigns at the retail level.

"In NASCAR, you see things that are actually on the cars, in the cars, part of the cars," said Tim Toppen, president of Goodyear engineered products. "It's a whole different opportunity. For example, Riddell manufactures helmets for the NFL but isn't going to be able to market them to the mass consumer market the way Goodyear can market products through its NASCAR relationship."

"We're still learning," he added. "But we feel we've benefited from our NASCAR involvement."

Goodyear's engineers have benefited as well.

"Toyota, Chrysler, Ford, and GM are all heavily involved in NASCAR," Stu Grant said. "Every weekend, our technical guys and their technical guys meet at the track. They share in a mission. Our guys are there living with their guys."

"A young race tire engineer learns a lot in a very challenging environment like NASCAR," he continued. "And he's got to come back with a solution to a problem, not in three months but by tomorrow morning. I can't tell you the number of times I've seen our guys go back to Akron, make tires overnight, and drive them to the track the next day.

"Eventually, these guys move onto our passenger car division and work with the OEMs. That NASCAR environment helps them grow up fast. The auto manufacturers do the same thing. Their young hot shots are working on racing, and in a decade, they're working on a new chassis program. And the two meet. [NASCAR] really does offer an environment where we can challenge our guys beyond the day-to-day. It forces us to do things outside the box; things that we wouldn't do ordinarily. That's how you plow new turf."

And plow new turf is exactly what Goodyear will have to do in the next few years.

"Our hope in 2007 is to have a year to do some real targeted type of marketing, in media, retail, to the consumer, and to dealers behind the counter at the tire store," Goodyear's Viselli said. "We're going to use this year to set the ship on the right course."

And Viselli isn't just talking about North America. The fact is that Goodyear has also gone international with NASCAR. At the start of 2007, it was already looking at ways to leverage new NASCAR driver Juan Pablo Montoya in the Latin American market. The company also runs a Busch race each year in Mexico City where it overlays a complete and integrated marketing program that connects the NASCAR halo to Goodyear's light truck tires, which dominate the market. Goodyear is also keeping close tabs on NASCAR's acquisition of CASCAR, the Canadian stock car circuit, and has its sights on other related properties throughout the Latin American region.

"We're going from zero to fifty in 2007 and hope to be full throttle in 2008," Viselli said.

"Two things work in our favor," said Goodyear's Stu Grant. "We've been [in NASCAR] for fifty years, and we have access to everyone in the garage area. We don't have one car; we have forty-three."

CHAPTER FIFTEEN

WE'RE AN AMERICAN BRAND

Toyota Comes to NASCAR

W alking through the agricultural building of the 2006 Texas State Fair, I saw the usual displays: prize-winning cows and ears of corn, blue-ribbon pies and cakes, award-winning marmalades and jams, and a Toyota Tundra pickup truck.

If that last item seems a bit out of place to you, you're not alone. But more surprising than the fact that the Tundra was even there is the prominent placement the pickup truck was given. It wasn't relegated to some far-off dingy corner, where Texans, many of them lifelong Ford and Chevy owners, could walk by and sneer in disgust before quickly ushering their families out of the building. It was smack dab in the middle of the Caterpillar display. And its placement was a direct result of the NASCAR B2B Council.

"I couldn't buy placement like that," said Jim Farley, vice president of marketing for Toyota Motor Sales USA.

No, he couldn't buy it, but he was able to negotiate it thanks to Toyota's NASCAR sponsorship. And the truck's placement, alongside one of the most accepted brands in America, goes directly to the heart of Toyota's NASCAR strategy.

"Our primary goal—with NASCAR and everything else we do—is to get into the heartland of America," Farley said, "to convince people that we are an American car company."

That's no small task. In 2006, Farley and his staff spent an entire afternoon trolling the parking lot outside of the California Speedway in Fontana, just east of Los Angeles. Amid all those cars, trucks, and SUVs, they found just one Tundra.

"We have almost a thirty percent share in the southern California market," Farley said. "It's one of our strongest markets in the country. But I can tell you that there isn't another place in that market—or most of the rest of the country for that matter—where I could find only one Tundra. That tells me that even in a traditional loyalist market, the NASCAR fan is an incremental Toyota customer at best."

Convincing Americans that Toyota is very much an American car company shouldn't be so difficult. In the 1980s, Toyota partnered with General Motors to build the NUMMI plant in Fremont, California, the first U.S./Japanese joint auto-manufacturing venture in the United States. A few years later, Toyota's Georgetown, Kentucky, plant opened, making it Toyota's first wholly owned manufacturing plant in North

America. It produces more than five hundred thousand Camrys, Solaras, and Avalons, including the Camry Hybrid, as well as four-cylinder and V-6 engines. Toyota's Princeton, Indiana, plant produces the Tundra pickup, the Sequoia full-size SUV, and the Sienna minivan. The company's Buffalo, West Virginia, plant makes four- and six-cylinder engines, as well as a variety of transmissions. And in late 2006, Toyota opened a second Tundra manufacturing plant in San Antonio, the heart of Texas truck country. This Texas location is a sign of Toyota's commitment to go after multigenerational Ford and Chevy truck owners in one of the most traditional truck markets in the country.

Toyota also has plants in Canada and Mexico, which together produced 1.5 million vehicles, 1.3 million engines, and 400,000 transmissions in 2006. Toyota bought $28 billion worth of goods and services from suppliers in North America in 2006. Toyota has deep North American ties, and the dollars spent on its products circle back into the domestic market.

Despite its huge presence in North America, Toyota is still fighting prejudice against foreign car companies. Toyota's NASCAR sponsorship and the partnerships it has built with some of NASCAR's very American sponsors has helped Toyota begin shift its brand image, both within NASCAR and beyond.

"I can't begin to emphasize how important that placement was for us with Caterpillar at the Texas State Fair," Toyota's Jim Farley said. "Forget about any biases these buyers have about a Japanese truck maker. Some of these people have been buying Fords and Chevys for generations. No matter where your product is manufactured or your company is headquartered, that's an incredible hurdle to overcome. But we think NASCAR is one way to do it. It opens the door a crack with those customers, and gets them to give us a second glance—not a look, but a glance—that we otherwise might never have gotten."

Indeed, just rubbing shoulders with some of the iconic American sponsors in NASCAR helps Toyota improve its image among U.S. consumers. Budweiser, M&Ms, Coca-Cola, McDonald's, Sears; those are brands Americans have trusted for decades.

"There's not one brand that's important to Middle America that isn't in NASCAR," Farley said.

Because of the relationship that Toyota has developed with Caterpillar through the NASCAR B2B Council, Tundras were featured as part of the Caterpillar display not only at the Texas State Fair, but also at every major agricultural show and fair in the country.

"Without Caterpillar, many of those consumers would simply pass us by. They wouldn't have given us a second look," Farley said.

Beyond trade shows and state fairs, Farley knows that Caterpillar is on every construction site in the United States.

"The people we want to sell Tundras to trust the Caterpillar brand," he said. "Just associating with Caterpillar gets them to give me time and attention that I wouldn't otherwise get."

Toyota has also done promotional rides and drives at the Caterpillar Proving Ground in Arizona, and is working with UPS, another partner that it met through the NASCAR B2B Council.

"UPS has one hundred thousand people who drive pickup trucks and sort packages every day," Farley said. "Getting in front of that audience is huge. Moreover, it's indicative of the kinds of cross-promotional benefits you get from being in NASCAR."

Indeed, talk to any chief marketing officer at any of the major NASCAR sponsors and they'll tell you that the relationship building that's facilitated through NASCAR is almost immeasurable.

"It's something we didn't even calculate when we got into NASCAR," Farley said. "But we know it's paying dividends for us, especially in working toward our core goal of acceptance as an American brand."

But Toyota clearly has its work cut out for it. There is much focus on Toyota in 2007 because it marks the automaker's entry into the NASCAR Nextel Cup and Busch Series. While a sliver of xenophobic NASCAR fans are alarmed that a foreign brand would be allowed to pollute the pristine American waters of NASCAR, many of them don't know that Toyota has been in NASCAR for nearly a decade. More important, Toyota is a textbook example of how to initiate, activate, and, in many ways, maximize a NASCAR sponsorship. Just as the automakers in Detroit are copying the Toyota Manufacturing System to improve the quality of the cars they produce, any new NASCAR sponsor would be wise to study how Toyota has developed, grown, and leveraged its NASCAR sponsorship.

"A lot of fans know that we've been in the NASCAR Craftsman Truck Series since 2004," said Les Unger, national motorsports manager for Toyota. "But our involvement with NASCAR actually started four years before that in 2000."

Toyota had long been involved with motorsports. It was the title sponsor of the Toyota Atlantic Series, a feeder circuit for Champ Car and the Indy Racing League. And it had a strong presence in off-road racing.

"As successful as we had been in those series, by the late 1990s it was hard to ignore NASCAR," Unger said.

So Toyota started talking to NASCAR in 1998. As it turned

out, just as Toyota came knocking on NASCAR's door, NASCAR was looking for a new engine supplier for its Goody's Dash Series for late-model stock cars. Historically, the engines had been inline four-cylinders and NASCAR wanted to move up to V-6s.

"That was our first partnership together," Unger said. "NASCAR thought it was a cool idea because it brought another manufacturer into the series."

So instead of plunging headfirst into the Nextel Cup Series, like a lot of sponsors do, Toyota began with baby steps. Toyota Racing Development (TRD), the manufacturer's racing entity, modified a V-6 overhead-cam engine to meet NASCAR's specifications and became an engine supplier for the Goody's Dash Series for the next three years.

"From a technical perspective, it enabled us to learn about NASCAR, how they operated," Unger said. "Conversely, it allowed NASCAR to work with TRD and learn what we were all about. But most important, it established a trust, a rapport, between NASCAR and Toyota."

Indeed, the project demonstrated Toyota's technical expertise to NASCAR and to some in the garage who looked askance when Toyota first came in. It also earned Toyota its first NASCAR championship in 2003 when driver Robert Huffman took the season title in a Toyota Celica.

A year before Huffman captured the Goody's Dash Series championship, NASCAR had already started talking to Toyota about stepping up its involvement and competing in the NASCAR Craftsman Truck Series. About the same time, Toyota executives decided that if the Tundra was really going to compete with the Ford F-150 and Chevy Silverado, the company needed to build a second truck plant in North America. And it needed to do it in Texas, the heart of American pickup truck culture.

"It was a pretty big deal for NASCAR to extend an invitation to us to compete in the truck series," Unger said. "It was also a huge deal for TRD because it meant that we had to develop, from scratch, a pushrod V-8 engine."

Indeed, unlike the Goody's Dash Series, which merely required Toyota to convert an existing engine to meet NASCAR specs, Toyota had to start from scratch and develop a new engine for the truck series.

"It was a huge challenge for TRD, a huge challenge for Toyota," Unger said.

But a year and a half later, in February 2004, Toyota debuted at Daytona in the NASCAR Craftsman Truck Series.

"We wanted to utilize NASCAR and the truck series as a marketing lever to increase exposure for our full-size truck," Unger said. "It was an awesome opportunity to appeal to a fan base that was interested in our truck and remind them that the Tundra is an American-built truck."

It also was an opportunity for Toyota to grow its NASCAR exposure beyond the Goody's Dash Series, which primarily ran in the Southeast.

"The truck series was a nationwide series. The races were broadcast nationwide on the SPEED Channel," Unger said. "We could reach a lot more fans who may not know that we had a full-size truck for sale in this country."

Because of that, Toyota's entry into the truck series was "one hundred ten percent focused on nameplate exposure and increased awareness of the Tundra," Unger said.

Many in the media speculated that Toyota had bigger plans. They were right, but for the wrong reasons.

"We made the announcement that we were going to get into the truck series in February 2003 at the Chicago Auto Show," Unger said. "Quite a few members of the media looked at that announcement and said, 'We understand. You're going to use trucks as an opportunity to learn more about NASCAR, but in a year or so you're going to drop trucks and go to Busch and Cup.' That was not the case.

"Yes, we continued to explore and expand our involvement with NASCAR," Unger said. "However, a lot of people felt that when we made the decision to move up to Nextel Cup, we were going to drop trucks. We haven't done that. In fact, we've since built a truck plant in Texas. That's our second U.S. truck plant. The decision we made in '02 and '03 to get involved in the truck series makes more sense now than it did then. We are in the truck series for the long haul."

Indeed, Farley will tell you that the move into Nextel Cup is not about selling more Camrys, but about selling more Tundras.

"We're in NASCAR to sell Tundras, not Camrys," he said. "That goes for the Nextel Cup and Busch Series, as well as the truck series. The Camry has been the best-selling car for six or seven years. We're racing Camrys to sell Tundras because that's what we want to see in the parking lots at NASCAR races."

But that's easier said than done.

"One of the hurdles we've faced in NASCAR is that many people still see us as a foreign manufacturer," Unger said. "We knew there was going to be flack; NASCAR knew that. But one of our objectives was to showcase our ability to not only be a competitor, but to have good teams driving Tundras."

The obvious way to do that would have been to partner with an established, successful team owner like Rick Hendrick, Richard Childress, or Roger Penske. In fact, Unger said, the fans and the media expected it. They expected that Toyota would come in, partner with a well-established Cup or truck series team, and, in essence, buy success or even a championship.

"We very purposely went in the opposite direction," Unger said. "We went with rookie teams."

Rookie to the truck series, anyway.

In 2004, Toyota partnered with Bill Davis Racing and Darrell Waltrip Motorsports. Bill Davis had successfully competed in both the NASCAR Nextel Cup and Busch Series, notching a combined sixteen wins, including a victory in the 2002 Daytona 500 with driver Ward Burton. When he first entered the sport in the mid-1980s, Bill Davis worked with fellow Arkansan Mark Martin before hiring a young kid named Jeff Gordon, who went on to be the 1991 Busch Series rookie of the year. Other Davis drivers in both Cup and Busch over the years have included future NASCAR champion Bobby Labonte and Scott Wimmer.

Waltrip's résumé is well known. He is a former NASCAR champion who traded in his driving shoes for a set of wing tips and a seat in the broadcast booth. The truck series was Waltrip's way of keeping his hand in the game.

At the end of that first season, Toyota finished tied for last in the manufacturers' points standings with just four wins. In 2005, Tundra finished second in the manufacturers standings with nine wins, just one behind series winner Chevrolet. And in 2006, in just its third season, Toyota won the Craftsman Truck Series Manufacturer's Championship with twelve wins, compared with eight for Ford, five for Chevy, and zero for Dodge.

Toyota driver Todd Bodine was the 2006 NASCAR Craftsman Truck Series champion. In fact, Toyota drivers filled out the top six positions in the truck series season-long points standings. Toyota driver Mike Skinner finished tenth, giving Toyota seven of the top ten spots in points.

Furthermore, the Toyota sponsorship is not as much of a factory effort as you would think. Certainly not the way factory teams were run in the 1960s and 1970s.

"These teams have to generate their own sponsorship," Unger said. "If you don't have sponsorship, too bad, so sad. We are not in the team-cash sponsorship business. TRD will provide you with technological expertise, but that's it."

And even though Toyota is the primary sponsor of one of the Bill Davis Racing teams, it spreads the wealth. The TRD engineers that work with the teams share engine data, but it's up to each team as to what to do with it.

"Every one of the teams running Tundras get exactly the same degree of technical support," Unger said.

Toyota operates the same way with its Busch and Cup programs. There are some teams, like Bill Davis Racing, who have their own engine shop. They get basic parts from TRD, but assemble the engines themselves. Other teams, like Michael Waltrip Racing, get complete engines designed and assembled by Toyota. At-track support and data sharing is the same among all the Toyota Cup teams.

"A high tide lifts all boats," Unger said.

For all its success in the truck series, Toyota still has a long way to go.

"Whether you talk to a Tundra owner or a Camry owner,

they don't necessarily know at this point that we're involved in NASCAR," Unger said. "We do know that because NASCAR is such a significant part of the motorsports landscape, our being involved is a net gain."

What impact has Toyota's involvement in NASCAR had on Tundra recognition and sales?

"That's impossible to measure," Unger said, "but anecdotally, we hear from fans and owners all the time."

Unger tells a funny story about a guy walking up to him at the final race of the 2005 season in Miami.

"Are you from Toyota?" he asked Unger.

"I thought I was going to get punched out," Unger said. "Turns out he was a longtime Ford owner, but our involvement in NASCAR got him to test drive and eventually buy a Toyota truck."

Again, that's anecdotal evidence that the NASCAR sponsorship is working. But when you think about it, the only way Toyota can go is up when it comes to selling trucks in America. Today, Toyotas account for about 6 percent of U.S. truck sales.

"It's going to be a long-term commitment to convert those people," Unger said. "We're trying to win over people from Chevrolet and Ford who have thirty, forty, fifty years of loyalty. It's also tough because, honestly, the Silverado and F-150 are quality products.

"We're at the point where it's not about buying," Unger said. "It's just getting them to go look. It's all we can do. Increase the percentage of competitive owners to consider the purchase of a Toyota full-size truck. If we're successful in increasing the consideration, it's up to the dealer to close the deal."

But with more exposure has come more criticism from some NASCAR fans who consider Toyota a foreign intrusion.

"Any negative reaction to us getting involved in NASCAR has been a little more vocal as we've moved into Busch and Cup," Unger said. "We expected that and so did NASCAR. In Busch and Cup, you're talking about a more fervent fan. They follow the sport more closely. That's a challenge we want to address, as does NASCAR."

The opposition is not as fervent and outspoken as you'd expect. For one thing, the NASCAR audience has matured significantly from the days when fans would throw beer bottles onto the track if they were angry with a driver. This was borne out when NBC's *Dateline* news program planted Muslim and Arab-American people accompanied by hidden cameras in NASCAR audiences in 2006 in an effort to measure anti-Muslim sentiments. The investigation failed, as the fans simply didn't react at all. In the end, it was a major embarrassment for NBC News and its parent company, which was a NASCAR broadcaster in 2006.

And while many of the fans may not drive their Toyota Camrys to the racetrack, you can bet that a lot of them either own one or don't have an issue with a foreign nameplate on the grille.

"We know that over time the NASCAR fan is going to see that Toyota's participation is a plus for the sport," Unger said.

And while Toyota is again partnering with Bill Davis Racing, two of the three teams fielding Toyota Camrys in the Nextel Cup and Busch Series in 2006 are new teams, including Michael Waltrip, who's a veteran driver but a first-time owner.

"We're bringing new blood to the sport," Unger said. "We know, from a competitive perspective, it's going to be extremely difficult. Our teams are going up against some hall of famers. Jack Roush, Rick Hendrick, Chip Ganassi, Roger Penske, Joe

Gibbs, Robert Yates. They've been here for decades. It's not going to be easy."

And if some NASCAR fans think Toyota is going to try and come in and buy a championship, that's just plain wrong.

"A lot of the negative comments always focus around speculation that we'll bring tens of millions of dollars into the garage and we'll win all the races," Unger said. "The irony is that if you know anything at all about NASCAR over the past fifty years, that isn't the way things happen. There are very tight rules; no one team or manufacturer gets any long-term advantages. So those criticisms simply aren't valid."

And those rules got tighter in 2007 with the introduction of NASCAR's new Car of Tomorrow. As one observer said, the Car of Tomorrow was built for all the right reasons, but many doubt it will resonate with fans. The car, designed and built by NASCAR, is primarily aimed at improving safety. Its many benefits include the following: a reduction in spiked G forces; enhanced cockpit protection; a roll cage that is two inches taller, four inches wider, and three inches further back in the car; left-side door bars covered with steel plates and reinforced to take greater impacts; a driver's seat moved four inches to the right; a fully enclosed drive shaft tunnel; enhanced fire protection; and, a smaller (17.5 rather than a 22 gallon), stronger gas tank.

NASCAR said that teams will have fewer cars in inventory. Currently, top-flight teams have a different car for almost every track, and some teams have different cars for different races at the same track, such as spring and fall Charlotte cars (and a third for the All-Star race). The intention for NASCAR's Car of Tomorrow is for the rig to be a "universal car" to be used in Cup racing. As NASCAR's website explained, "NASCAR would like to use the exact same car at every track by only adding and subtracting simple bolt-on pieces."

Some critics are calling the Car of Tomorrow "a flying brick." Among aerodynamic concerns are straighter headlights and a more upright windshield, both of which will more closely match production models but make the race cars more wind resistant. In addition to designing the car, NASCAR also designed an infrared, 3-D inspection system that will cut down on cheating on spoiler heights, trunk lid angles, and the like. And in a nod to the modern era, NASCAR has also designed in-car camera pods to broadcaster specifications.

All in all, it's a big change for NASCAR and the manufacturers. The Car of Tomorrow debuted at Bristol in April and will run sixteen races over the 2007 season. In 2008, it will probably be run at every race.

Some critics say that it will dumb down NASCAR stock cars to the point that they're nothing more than a generic box with a front nose clip to distinguish whether its a Chevy, Dodge, Ford, or Toyota.

"They're a generic box today," Unger said. "But it'll definitely be safer."

The two issues for Toyota and the other manufacturers are these: Will the Car of Tomorrow look like a NASCAR race car and will the fans accept it?

"Because it's so different looking, there's no doubt it's going to have an impact on the fan," Unger said.

The initial concern for manufacturers was that the Car of Tomorrow would not look like the car models dealers are trying to sell in the showroom. Many are worried that it flies in the face of that old NASCAR adage, "Win on Sunday, Sell on Monday."

"It's very troublesome for the automakers," said Chris Economaki. "How do you sell a car on Monday when the one that wins on Sunday is a generic box engineered by NASCAR whose only distinguishing characteristic is Chevy or Ford headlights."

"I think all four manufacturers have gotten that issue resolved with NASCAR," Unger said. "Everyone seems to be fairly happy with the fact that the front will resemble that particular manufacturer's car. So that initial issue—brand identification—isn't so much of an issue anymore."

Only time will tell.

The Car of Tomorrow is perhaps the greatest technological challenge that NASCAR and the manufacturers have faced. And it would be wrong to look at Toyota and not talk about the technical expertise it has gained from being involved in NASCAR. While its Toyota Manufacturing System is the envy of the automotive world, and Toyota brought a fair amount of technical and engineering expertise to the NASCAR garage, you can't discount what Toyota has learned. Furthermore, Toyota's experience further illustrates how NASCAR isn't a one-way street for the manufacturers. It's not just what they put into it, but what they get out of it in terms of design, technology, and automotive engineering.

Again, Toyota isn't new to racing. Toyota Racing Development was not created when the company came into NASCAR in 2000, but has been around for nearly thirty years. Until 2006, it was the only company of its kind.

Initially, TRD was set up to focus on aftermarket products for Toyota. But over the past twenty years, it has evolved into one of the most sophisticated and high-tech race shops in the world. For much of that time, TRD was an engine tuner for sports car, road, and endurance racing. In 1995, Toyota moved into open-wheel racing, first with CART (champ cars) and then with the Indy Racing League (IRL) in 2003. At the peak of its open-wheel program, TRD had 225 employees, including about fifty engineers.

"We won in virtually every venue that the company was associated with, whether it be sports cars, drags, midgets, Goody's Dash, off-road racing, and, of course, now the Craftsman Truck Series," said Lee White, who has headed up TRD for more than a decade. "We have won championships in every single venue."

Since coming into NASCAR, TRD has played an increasingly important role as a NASCAR technical partner. For instance, when Toyota decided to go truck racing, NASCAR couldn't—or wouldn't—tell Toyota exactly what was in the garage area in terms of engine technology.

"In 2003 we had to go out and buy Dodge, Ford, and Chevrolet engines and reverse engineer them so that we could determine what was in the garage," White said. "NASCAR didn't know. Now, as a result of our submission process, NASCAR has a very good understanding of what's in the garage. They understand what the dimensional limitations are."

When Toyota decided to go Cup racing, it had to take everything it knew about the truck engines and apply it to Cup.

"In our case, that was a very natural thing for us to do," White said. "This is all we do, fifty-two weeks a year."

NASCAR, which White said gives his employees a performance review every Sunday, also helped Toyota to expand its racing expertise beyond just engines.

"Historically, we've supplied the engines and left the vehicles up to the race teams," White said. "In NASCAR, we learned how to design, engineer, build, and perfect the complete car."

Indeed, over the past four years, Toyota has been fostering a group of engineers specifically to help the Toyota Cup and Busch teams with aerodynamics, computational fluid dynamics, damping, tire dynamics, and suspension geometry. Toyota has since developed a group of twenty engineers who just focus on what they call race vehicle engineering. In this group are subsets that specialize in Cup, Busch, and truck racing.

"It's a very unique approach," White says. "It isn't something that the other manufacturers have."

Indeed, what Chevy, Dodge, and Ford have done historically is pick a few successful multicar teams and write them a check. Those teams then spend the money on engineering and development.

"The difficulty with that approach is that most of the benefits end with the teams," White said. "The Toyota approach is to invest in TRD to provide constant engineering improvement of the racing product and dispense it equally and fairly to all the Toyota teams."

Over the past three years, you've seen the real-world results of this strategy in that the Toyota teams racing in the truck series are usually bunched together. They're either all near the top, in the middle, or at the back of the pack—if the Toyota engineers haven't missed something.

"What we've found over the past two or three seasons is that this approach works for you more than against you," White said. "That's how we got seven Tundra drivers in the top ten in truck points in 2006."

So how has Toyota's strategy of moving up through the

NASCAR ranks worked? Very well. Toyota has learned a lot about the design, construction, and engineering of NASCAR race cars. But more important, it has learned the inner workings—the politics and subtleties—of NASCAR.

"NASCAR is an organization that's driven by relationships," White said. "You can't come into NASCAR and buy your way to the front. You have to get to know the people, and position yourself so that you're comfortable dealing with NASCAR and NASCAR is comfortable dealing with you."

This is exactly what Toyota has done as it has progressed from the Goody's Dash Series to the NASCAR Craftsman Truck Series to Busch and Nextel Cup. It was all about building a foundation with NASCAR and then going up from there.

"We started the NASCAR program in 2000 with a budget of less than two hundred thousand dollars," White said.

Toyota partnered with driver Robert Huffman and NASCAR garage maven Don Miller, a veteran engine builder for several of NASCAR's feeder series (but not the same Don Miller who partners with Roger Penske and Rusty Wallace). For the next three years, Toyota went to school and learned all it could about NASCAR and how it operates.

"We spent three years working with the NASCAR Competition Group, developing personal and professional relationships," White said. "Now, when we tell those people that we will do something, they trust us."

That's because, again, NASCAR, for all the big business that goes on, is very much about personal relationships. That's the number one lesson that should be learned by any company that's thinking about getting involved with NASCAR. It's not about what you say or how much money you spend, it's about what you do.

"NASCAR is very much about trust," White said. "It is, in my experience, driven by personal relationships. And they don't develop overnight."

As an example, White talks about how Toyota actually got involved with the NASCAR Craftsman Truck Series. It wasn't part of an overarching, elaborate strategy that NASCAR and Toyota had formulated in 2000, when Toyota first came into the Goody's Dash Series. It started as a casual conversation White had with some NASCAR officials about DaimlerChrysler, whose Dodge brand had returned to Nextel Cup, Busch, and the truck series.

"I made the point that they didn't have a pushrod engine, they didn't sell a rear-wheel-drive car in America, and they're foreign-owned," White said. "I said I thought there might be an opportunity for Toyota to fit into that category."

After six months of feasibility studies and one-on-one discussions with NASCAR, "Bill France said we were welcome to compete. A lot of that stemmed from the foundation we'd built in the Goody's Dash Series."

Toyota and NASCAR agreed that Toyota would follow the Dodge model. That meant two or three years in the truck series, before moving up to Cup. That would give fans time to become comfortable with Toyota, and time for NASCAR to make sure that Toyota could be competitive at that level.

"Looking at it from that perspective, our time in the truck series has been immeasurably valuable," White said. "It has given the fans time to learn a little bit about Toyota and for us to learn a lot about NASCAR."

The personal relationship portion of a NASCAR sponsorship cannot be overemphasized. It really is the oil that makes the NASCAR business engine run smoothly.

"NASCAR, in my experience, from bottom to top, is an organization in which it is absolutely fundamental to develop one-on-one respectful, courteous, and friendly personal relationships," White said. "The very best thing that anyone can do on any given weekend at the races is just sit down and say 'Hello.' I do it every week. It's an investment that has paid off one-hundred-fold. Because at any point in time, this thing can be a challenge, and whenever it becomes a challenge, we have never once asked for consideration or help and been turned away. We've always had a courteous reception. And it's not because we wrote a big check; it's because we've invested in NASCAR. It is a family, far beyond the France family."

Toyota is betting that membership in that family will help it sell Tundra pickup trucks. But it won't happen overnight.

"You can't change the fans' minds with a thirty-second commercial," Toyota's Farley said. "You can only change it in person."

And while "Win on Sunday, Sell on Monday" is one of the NASCAR marketing mantras, it has always been tougher for manufacturers to connect with fans than traditional sponsors.

"There is no example of a car company fully leveraging NASCAR like Home Depot does," Farley said. "What's on the track is almost incidental. It's an opening. A door that squeaks open a couple of inches."

What a manufacturer does with that opening—that connection—makes all the difference. And even if it is less successful than it expected in leveraging its sponsorship, many still don't walk away from NASCAR.

"When we were considering moving up to Cup, the first question we asked was, 'How are we going to pay for this?'" Farley said. "I got on the phone with the chief marketing officers of some of the biggest sponsors I knew and I was shocked at what I heard. They all said to me, 'You have no idea how big this is. If there's one thing I don't drop from my budget, it's this.' "

WHAT'S NEXT FOR NASCAR?

So what challenges will NASCAR face going forward? First consider the challenges it has faced over the past twenty years. I don't want you to put this book down thinking that the past two decades have all been days of wine and roses for NASCAR. While it has been a period of tremendous economic growth, it hasn't been without its speed bumps. This was particularly true in the late 1980s and early 1990s, when corporate America really began to exert its influence.

Back then, the majority of NASCAR fans were blue collar. For the most part, they worked middle-class jobs and led middle-class lives. They drove American-made cars, drank beer, and had never been on a corporate hospitality junket in their lives. A trip to the Daytona 500 or the Saturday night race at Bristol was their once-a-year splurge. Because they had seen their share of tough times, they respected drivers like Dale Earnhardt, Rusty Wallace, Geoff Bodine, and Ken Schrader. These guys were once middle class, too (or even poorer). They had fought their way up (literally) through the weekly racing series in the Carolinas, Upstate New York, and the Midwest. They had paid their dues on no-frills tracks in places like Pevely, Missouri; Middletown, New York; and Greenville, South Carolina. Long before they had million-dollar contracts, million-dollar crew chiefs, and million-dollar motor coaches, they were the driver, crew chief, tire and chassis specialist, fabricator, roustabout, and truck driver. Somewhere along the way, probably more than once, they too had taken a Ned Jarrett-like gamble. They had mortgaged everything they had—including relationships with wives and children—to buy parts and a chance to prove to the world that they had a special talent and a drive to win. They had seen more than their share of hardscrabble times, but they eventually made it. They had achieved their lifelong dream—a seat in a Winston Cup stock car, sitting on the starting grid of the Daytona 500, and a chance to win the biggest race in all of stock car racing.

The majority of NASCAR fans in the 1980s saw these drivers as no different than themselves. They had come from nothing, which made it OK for fans to spend their entire tax refund, or empty their bank account, to sit in the grandstands and cheer on these men who had once been just like them. These drivers were their real-life heroes.

This all started to change when a young, brash kid from California with a cheesy moustache came along in the late 1980s. Jeff Gordon had grown up in California, not Carolina. He had raced go-karts since he was in grade school. Yes, he'd had his struggles. But his career had been funded by his stepdad, who spent every last cent he had to make sure that his very talented son realized his own dreams of racing glory. But in many fans' eyes, Gordon hadn't worked hard enough. He was too good, too soon, and he'd had too much help along the way.

Despite these criticisms, which I'm sure were stinging for a twenty-year-old kid, Gordon persevered. Through the resounding boos from the grandstand, and despite being and labeled an outsider and an interloper, Jeff Gordon became one of the winningest drivers in NASCAR history.

In 475 races through the 2006 season, Gordon had seventy-five victories. That means he has won 15.9 percent of the races he's competed in. In more than half of them, he's finished in the top ten. Through the end of 2006, he had won more than $80 million.

Yes, by every measure Jeff Gordon should be NASCAR's new reigning superstar. And in some ways he is. He drives for Rick Hendrick, one of the best and brightest car owners in all of NASCAR. His team has one of the biggest budgets and is one of the most technically savvy teams in NASCAR. He is funded by a company—DuPont—that epitomizes the new breed of NASCAR sponsors. He even married the trophy girl.

But it was not to be. Jeff Gordon came along at the wrong time. He challenged the wrong guy—Dale Earnhardt—for supremacy. And in the eyes of the predominant fans of the day, he had the wrong pedigree. Instead of being the darling of the sport, he came to epitomize everything that the old guard said was going wrong with modern NASCAR racing: the money, the slick corporate polish, the new sponsors. It was all changing, and many of them didn't like it. In 2007, when Gordon eclipsed Earnhardt in total number of wins, it was greeted more with derision than applause.

I think that one day Jeff Gordon will be seen as the most underrated, under-appreciated driver in NASCAR history. He will also be seen as one of the most talented drivers ever—and rightly so. I say that as an Earnhardt fan, who pretty much lost interest in the sport after he died.

But looking at NASCAR today, it's clear that Jeff Gordon ultimately won. He was the beginning of a new era, not the end of an old. And while you can quibble about the ever increasing shadow that corporate America casts on the sport, NASCAR is clearly better off in 2007 than it was in 1987. Moreover, those fans who loved Earnhardt, Wallace, and Martin have either evolved or left and have been replaced by a multitude of new fans who don't remember "the good old days" and love the NASCAR of today. In short, the carpers who long for the bygone era of fistfights, fender banging, and two-fisted drinking are in the minority, replaced by a more sophisticated, more upscale, more media-savvy audience that loves the NASCAR of today.

To see how the sport and the fans have evolved, just look at 2006 NASCAR Nextel Cup Champion Jimmie Johnson. He didn't cut his teeth on the clay ovals of the Midwest or the South, but on the dirt bike tracks of Southern California and the off-road racing circuit, where there were more cacti than corporate sponsors. Sure, he spent a few years in the Busch Series, but he was anointed from day one.

Today, he too drives for Rick Hendrick, in a car owned by Jeff Gordon. He doesn't live in Mooresville, North Carolina, but in Manhattan's uberhip Chelsea neighborhood with his wife,

Chandra, a former New York model. In many ways, he is a carbon copy of Jeff Gordon. But there have been very few complaints about who he is, where he's from, and where he learned to race. In essence, Johnson proves that NASCAR has made the transition from a lower-middle-class regional sport to a more upscale, wealthier nationwide sensation.

That's not to say that NASCAR doesn't face any challenges. The biggest question for the sport is whether it's peaked, a legitimate question.

While it has long been called the fastest-growing sport in the United States, NASCAR has been stuck at seventy-five million fans for several years now. Indeed, NASCAR enjoyed phenomenal growth over the past twenty years, but in 2006 there were signs that it had slowed. Television viewership declined by 6.5 percent in 2006 from 2005. Ratings dropped in thirty-two of thirty-six races, averaging 7.8 million viewers per weekend. The one exception was the Daytona 500, which gets about twenty million viewers ever year, with as many as forty-seven million watching at least part of the race. At NASCAR tracks across the country, attendance was down as well in 2006. Less than half the races sold out. One of Fox Sports' highest-rated racing broadcasts was a rain delay at Talladega (Alabama) Superspeedway.

While NASCAR is hoping to grow in 2007, in some ways it has already grown too much. NASCAR is hurting smaller weekly racetracks all over the country. Why? Because it's so expensive and because it's so accessible.

Tickets to the Daytona 500 are $200, and the only way you can get them in advance is to buy a package that includes tickets to the Craftsman Truck Series and Busch Series races, which are each at least $50. Hotels in Daytona are $300 a night, with a four-night minimum stay. Add in airfare, a rental car, meals, and souvenirs, and before you know it a family of four is looking at some serious coin. Good seats at other tracks around the country are about $100. As a result, many race fans are opting to go to one or two big NASCAR races a year instead of going to their local racetrack two times a month. And while it's more expensive, it's a reasonable option because every NASCAR track isn't packed into the Southeast anymore. If you live in Denver, the tracks in California, Chicago, Kansas, and Phoenix are all within a twelve-hour drive or a two-hour plane ride. You don't have to travel clear across the country to see a NASCAR race anymore. As a result, small tracks across the country are struggling to fill the grandstands every week. Some are simply closing.

"I don't think we've plateaued at all," NASCAR CEO Brian France said in his State of NASCAR address during Daytona. "We don't get too hung up on [ratings]. We look at it over a long period of time—two, three, four, five years trending the right way. My expectation is we'll be up in TV ratings in '07."

NASCAR is counting on some big changes in 2007 to make that happen. Toyota is a new competitor, and I think they'll draw more fans than they'll drive away. If this was 1987, I wouldn't feel that way. But as I showed in the last chapter, Toyota has been smart in how it has eased itself into NASCAR. The Daytona cheating scandal aside, Toyota coming into NASCAR has been sort of a so-what event.

NASCAR's also revamped the points system for the Chase for the Cup to—hopefully—make it more interesting. And NASCAR is betting that the return of ESPN after a six-year hiatus will boost ratings.

EPILOGUE

"I'm absolutely thrilled that ESPN is involved with NASCAR," Fox Sports Chairman David Hill said. "The amount of commitment that they contribute is absolutely terrific."

One problem NASCAR still has to overcome is the fact that its Chase for the Cup ten-race season finale bumps up against the undisputed king of professional sports, the NFL. And while NBC (Nothing But Commercials, as some fans called it) was chastised for not promoting its NASCAR broadcasts, ESPN reaches 19.2 million fewer households than NBC. ESPN is in 92.3 million homes, while NBC reaches 111.4 million. ESPN will televise all Busch Series races, but it will cover only seven Nextel Cup races from July 29 through September 2. ESPN on ABC will finish out the season, including all the chase races.

NASCAR may have hit a wall in terms of track expansion as well. While most of its previous new track proposals went off without a hitch, NASCAR suffered a big setback in New York City in 2006. Frankly, I think NASCAR is unduly obsessed with having a track in New York. If you can't get a track proposal passed with the labor unions and Guy Molinari, Staten Island's favorite son, on your side, then you should give up. Even if the deal had worked out, the logistics would have been a nightmare. And it's not like NASCAR is going to lose money on the deal. It still owns the land, which is considered some of the most valuable undeveloped real estate in the five boroughs. And finally, it's not as if New York City NASCAR fans can't get to a race. Within easy driving distance are Dover, New Hampshire, Pocono, Richmond, and Watkins Glen.

NASCAR's real estate troubles continued in 2007. As this book went to press, it looked increasingly less likely that the Washington State Legislature would OK funding for a NASCAR track in Kitsap Country, on the Washington Peninsula across Puget Sound from Seattle. In late February 2007, Washington Governor Chris Gregoire said NASCAR's proposal appeared dead. She suggested moving the NASCAR project about ninety minutes south of Seattle. A statewide poll in early 2007 also showed little support for public financing of sports venues. Citizens for More Important Things, an activist group, was pushing for a public vote, saying subsidies are needed only "because billionaires need welfare."

Gregoire said the International Speedway Corporation should consider moving the whole proposal to Lewis County. She said she met with leaders from the Kitsap Peninsula and concluded, "They don't object to NASCAR; they just don't want it in its location in Kitsap County."

She said she personally pitched Lewis County to ISC but was told it didn't meet ISC's criteria. Operators of a just-closed coal mine had offered to donate land, and the county would welcome the project with open arms, the governor said.

"So at this point in time, I don't see the political support to make NASCAR happen at the location that is currently proposed in Kitsap County," she said in late February 2007.

But just as Washington State appeared to be faltering, ISC announced that it was in talks to build a new track in Denver near the airport. ISC said it was evaluating 1,300-acre parcels of land in the area for a track that would seat about 75,000.

"Denver's a great sports market," NASCAR Chairman Brian France said. "It depends on the interest of the local community, and they wouldn't announce it if they didn't think there was pretty strong interest. I don't know the timeline, but it'll be a good market for NASCAR if it should come online."

EPILOGUE

The Car of Tomorrow, NASCAR's new generic race car, was another unknown as we entered the 2007 season. During SpeedWeeks in Daytona, it was hard to find a driver or car owner who had good things to say about it. While many applauded the NASCAR-designed car's new safety features, they were still working the performance kinks out in testing. Many wondered how the spoiler would affect the handling on super speedways and whether the car, set to debut at the March Bristol race, would be a step forward or a step back. Many believed the Car of Tomorrow had the potential to be NASCAR's New Coke.

I have my own theory about the Car of Tomorrow. I think it is the first step toward NASCAR actually building and selling cars to race teams. Think about it. What was the number one story out of the 2007 Daytona 500? Cheating. If the cars are built by NASCAR, that greatly reduces the likelihood that teams could cheat.

Not that they haven't tried already. A story making the rounds of the Daytona garage had one NASCAR team going back to NASCAR because one of the radio-frequency chips on the chassis of their Car of Tomorrow had "fallen off." Those things don't just fall off. Many believed that the team—which I won't name—pried it off to see if they could get away with it. If they could, they could substitute their own chassis parts for the originals, reaffix the radio-frequency chip, and no one would know.

That aside, I think NASCAR would very much like to be building these cars—and collecting all the revenue. If there's one constant—and legitimate—knock on NASCAR, it's that it likes to control *everything*. In 1999, NASCAR consolidated the television rights, which used to be negotiated by the individual tracks. While it made business sense, it also consolidated power in NASCAR's hands. NASCAR also created NASCAR Images to control photography and film and one day become the NFL Films of NASCAR. NASCAR also owns all the merchandising rights for NASCAR-related collectibles. The only thing it doesn't own is the teams and the cars. I think the Car of Tomorrow is a step toward doing just that.

The Car of Tomorrow has another significant potential. Former driver Brett Bodine, who drives the pace car and heads up the NASCAR Technology Center in Concord, North Carolina, has said that there's no reason that a single Car of Tomorrow couldn't be used at Daytona one week and Martinsville the next. In other words, it's an all-purpose car. If it could do that, it would significantly change the economics of NASCAR. That's because big-buck teams like Roush, Childress, and Hendrick have twenty different cars for each team. Some teams have three cars just for Charlotte—one they run in the All-Star Race, one they run in the Coca-Cola 600, and another they run in the fall race. That gives those teams a significant advantage over less-experienced, less well-funded teams. NASCAR could change that with the Car of Tomorrow. It could mandate that teams use just three Cars of Tomorrow—a short-track car, an intermediate track car, and a super speedway car. It would not only significantly reduce the number of cars needed, but slash the cost of entry to the Nextel Cup Series. A first-year team could have a serious chance of winning. For this reason and the others I've listed, I think the Car of Tomorrow could significantly change the face of NASCAR.

EPILOGUE

Finally, it will be interesting to see how NASCAR manages international growth. The Busch Series race in Mexico City has been a phenomenal success. The fledgling NASCAR Corona Series in Mexico is growing in size and prestige. In addition to the growth potential in Mexico, NASCAR is hoping the race—and the addition of Colombian driver Juan Pablo Montoyo—will help it woo the burgeoning Hispanic market, both in the United States and abroad.

NASCAR is also expanding north, into Canada. In June 2004, NASCAR opened a corporate office in Toronto in a joint partnership with Canadian media company TSN.

"This partnership, which goes far beyond televising NASCAR in Canada, will help grow the NASCAR brand in Canada, attract new fans to our sport, and bring new marketing opportunities to NASCAR sponsors and licensing partners," said then-NASCAR COO George Pyne. "It will be an important vehicle for NASCAR's continuing support of stock car racing in the Canadian market."

In January 2007, NASCAR and TSN signed a multiyear agreement to air the NASCAR Canadian Tire Series, which began in May 2007. TSN also acquired broadcast rights to all thirty-five NASCAR Busch Series races, including the inaugural Montreal race. During Daytona SpeedWeeks, NASCAR announced that TSN had extended its Nextel Cup broadcast contract another three years and its partnership pact on NASCAR Canada to 2015. The two also agreed that NASCAR Canada will serve as the sales and marketing agent for the newly formed NASCAR Canadian Tire Series through 2015.

Whether all of this is too much, we have yet to see. Pundits have long speculated that NASCAR was sowing the seeds of its own demise. Only time will tell. But as this book went to print in early 2007, it was clear that NASCAR had seen some hiccups over the past few years. But my guess is that they are just growing pains for a sport and a business that continues to confound its critics and please its acolytes.

INDEX